THE STATE
HERMITAGE

GUIDE

D0494437

THIS PUBLICATION HAS BEEN FINANCIALLY SUPPORTED BY THE INTERNATIONAL BANK
FOR RECONSTRUCTION AND DEVELOPMENT

TEXTS BY:

Veronika Afanasyeva, Andrei Alexeyev, Sergei Androsov, Irina Artemyeva,
Alexander Babin, Nina Biriukova, Andrei Bolshakov, Yekaterina Deriabina,
Viacheslav Fiodorov, Maria Garlova, Natalia Gritsai, Natalia Guseva, Anatoly Ivanov,
Liudmila Kagané, Ninel Kaliazina , Yelena Karcheva, Galina Komelova,
Tamara Korshunova, Maria Kosareva, Albert Kostenevich, Irina Kotelnikova,
Mark Kramarovsky, Marta Kryzhanovskaya, Tamara Kudriavtseva, Tatyana Kustodiyeva,
Marina Lopato, Valery Lukin, Tamara Malinina, Andrei Mazurkevich, Maria Menshikova,
Oleg Neverov, Alexander Nikitin, Nikolai Nikulin, Sergei Nilov, Karina Orlova,
Yuri Piotrovsky, Tatyana Rappe, Yelizaveta Renné, Kira Samosiuk, Evelina Tarasova,
Sergei Tomsinsky, Irina Ukhanova, Natalia Venevtseva, Svetlana Vsevolozhskaya,
Yuri Yefimov, Vera Zalesskaya, Larisa Zavadskaya, Yuna Zek

Compiled by Tatyana Mamayenko
Edited by Yelena Dianova and Olga Fedoseyenko
Designed by Alexander Lobanov
Translated from the Russian by Yuri Pamfilov and Igor Yegorov,
Yelena Kharkova, Zemfira Tsalagova
English text edited by Yuri Pamfilov
Photographs by Leonid Heifets, Yuri Molodkovets, Vladimir Terebenin,
Beatrice Durey (pp. 17, 28, 58), Yevgeny Siniaver (pp. 1, 27, 308)

ISBN 5-88654-130-6

On the cover: Thomas Gainsborough.
Portrait of a Lady in Blue

CONTENTS

The year 1764 is traditionally regarded as the date of the Hermitage's foundation. In that year 225 pictures from the collection of the Berlin merchant Johann Ernst Gotzkowsky were delivered to St Petersburg for Catherine II in payment of his debt to the Russian treasury. These canvases formed the nucleus of one of the largest and best-known museums in the world. This significant acquisition was followed by others, which Catherine II made through the assistance of acknowledged connoisseurs of art to build a picture gallery of her own. It was constantly enlarged with both individual canvases and famous European collections. In 1769, through the mediation of Prince A. Beloselsky-Belozersky, the collection of Count Heinrich von Brühl (1700–1764), Prime Minister of August III of Poland and Elector of Saxony, was purchased. It brought to the Hermitage 600 paintings by Dutch, Flemish, French and Italian artists. In 1772, through the mediation of Prince Dmitry Golitsyn and Denis Diderot, the Hermitage acquired the collection of Pierre Crozat (1665–1740), which was unequalled by any art gallery in Paris except that of the Dukes of Orleans. Sold by the collector's heir Louis-Antoine Crozat, Baron de Thiers, it included 400 first-rate canvases. A sensational purchase of the collection of Sir Robert Walpole (1676–1745), Prime Minister of Great Britain, was made in London in 1779 at the height of the Russo-Turkish War. Walpole's collection totalled 198 pictures of the Flemish and Italian schools, mostly of the 17th century. In 1781, the collection of Count Baudouin comprising 119 canvases, with nine Rembrandts and six portraits by Anthony van Dyck among them was bought in Paris. The first printed catalogue of the Hermitage collection issued in 1774 included 2,080 canvases, and when a special committee made up a new inventory of the imperial collection after Catherine II's death (1796), it already numbered 3,996 pictures. Thus, in Russia which had not any significant collection of paintings before Catherine II, a unique picture gallery was created during her reign only. Later, in the reign of her son, Paul I, and then of her grandson, Alexander I, Catherine's collection gradually acquired the status of a palace collection rather than a private imperial one. The major highlights in the first quarter of the 19th century were the acquisitions of the Malmaison collection of Empress Joséfine de Beauharnais (the first wife of Napoleon I Bonaparte) and the collection of the Amsterdam banker Coesvelt.

The reign of Nicholas I left its mark in the history of the Hermitage mainly by adding another building of the 'public museum', adjacent to those of the picture gallery of Catherine's times, the Small and Big Hermitages. This building was named the New Hermitage. The walls of it's fifty-six rooms were hung with masterpieces of the Italian, Flemish and Russian Schools of art and the exhibits were arranged according to a well-thought-out system. Besides the rooms housing painting, some premises of the new museum were specially furnished for displaying the enormous imperial numismatic collection, a collection of antique sculpture, works of the decorative and applied arts, archaeological artefacts, pieces of ancient jewellery, priceless books, manuscripts, drawings and engravings. There was a separate display of objects transferred from the Kunstkammer of Peter the Great. The picture gallery continued to grow: a collection of pictures was bought from the Barbarigo Palace in Venice, which enriched the Hermitage with canvases by Titian, while a number of pictures were acquired at the sale of the collection of King Willem II in The Hague. In the 20th century, the Hermitage received an immense collection of Dutch and Flemish paintings gathered by the well-known geographer and traveller Piotr Semionov-Tian-Shansky and the famous *Madonna with a Flower* by Leonardo da Vinci, formerly in the possession of a member of the Benois family.

After the October Revolution of 1917, when the entire palace ensemble, including the Winter Palace, was given the status of a state museum, the Hermitage had to part with a large number of outstanding works as a result of the redistribution of art treasures. On the other hand, in the same years the Hermitage was replenished with nationalised private art collections coming from the former royal palaces and the Petersburg mansions of the nobility: the Stroganovs, Shuvalovs and Yusupovs. The Hermitage collections were also considerably enriched in the 1930s–40s with works of contemporary French painting transferred from the Moscow State Museum of Modern Western Art, which was dissolved.

At present the State Hermitage collection includes about 3,000,000 exhibits displayed in more than three hundred rooms. In addition to the permanent exhibitions, the museum also mounts temporary ones, demonstrating works of art from its enormous reserves. The *Great Fabergé in the Hermitage*, *French Drawings of the 17th Century*, and *Under the Sign of the Eagle. The Empire Style* exhibitions are just tines among those that took place in 1999. *The Arbiter of European Fashion. The Works of Charles Wort and His Firms* and *The Petersburg Jewellers* are the most remarkable exhibitions from the museum reserves that were held in 2000. The Hermitage is daily visited by a great number of people wishing to feel the atmosphere of different epochs, to see with their own eyes the great works created in the course of the millennia-long history of our civilization.

THE MUSEUM'S ADDRESS:	34, Palace Embankment
INFORMATION DESK:	tel. (+7-812) 110-96-25

Open daily, except Monday, from 10.30 a.m. to 6 p.m.;
Sundays: from 10.30 a.m. to 5 p.m.; booking offices close an hour earlier

Booking offices are in the main entrance hall

TRANSPORT: Metro stations *Nevsky Prospekt, Gostiny Dvor*
Nos. 1, 7, 10 trolleybuses
No. 7 bus
Nos. 7, 128 express taxi-buses and taxi-minibuses

GUIDED-TOURS SERVICE: tel. (+7-812) 311-84-46;
specialized tours: tel. (+7-812) 110-96-88;
lectures: tel. (+7-812) 110-97-31;
School Centre: tel. (+7-812) 110-96-73
The Jewellery Gallery is admitted for guided tours only

Audio-guides can be hired on the upper landing of the Main (Jordan) Staircase

There are also the Museum's shop, cafeteria, currency exchange bureau
and the post-office open in the same hours as the Museum

THE WINTER PALACE OF PETER I: 32, Palace Embankment (booking offices are
in the main entrance hall)

**EXHIBIITIONS IN THE
GENERAL STAFF BUILDING:** 6–8, Palace Square

MENSHIKOV PALACE: Vasilievsky Island, 15, University Embankment

TRANSPORT: Metro station *Nevsky Prospekt*
No. 10 trolleybus
No. 7 bus

GROUND FLOOR

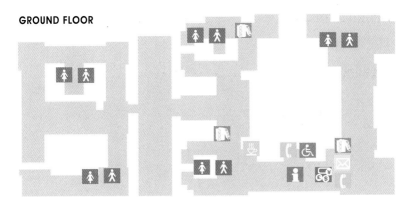

▲ ENTRANCE

FIRST FLOOR

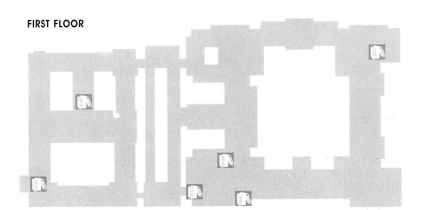

SECOND FLOOR

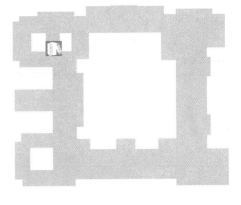

	INFORMATION SERVICE
	WC
	BOOKS, SOUVENIRS
	CAFETERIA
	POST OFFICE
	TELEPHONES
	CURRENCY EXCHANGE
	WHEELCHAIRS FOR INVALIDS

ART
OF ANTIQUITY

ART
OF ANCIENT
EGYPT

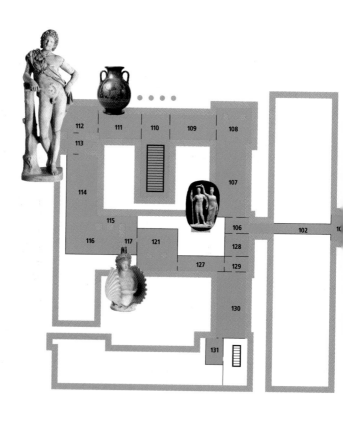

GROUND FLOOR

ART
OF WESTERN ASIA

JEWELLERY
GALLERY

ANCIENT CULTURES
OF EASTERN EUROPE,
SIBERIA, CENTRAL ASIA,
THE CAUCASUS AND
TRANSCAUCASIA

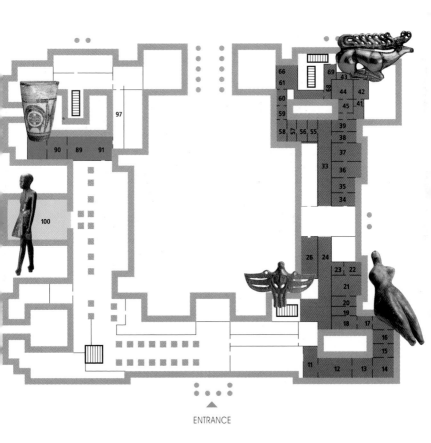

97

90 89 91

100

66 69
61
60
59
58 57 56 55
33
68

44 42
43
45 41
39
38
37
36
35
34

26 24
23 22
21
20
19
18 17
16
15
11 12 13 14

ENTRANCE

FLEMISH PAINTING.
17th CENTURY

SPANISH PAINTING.
15th–19th
CENTURIES

WESTERN EUROPEAN
SCULPTURE
OF THE 18th–19th
CENTURIES
IN THE GALLERY
OF THE HISTORY
OF ANCIENT PAINTING
AND THE GALLERY
OF THE NICHOLAS
STAIRCASE

WESTERN EUROPEAN
ARMS AND ARMOUR.
15th–17th
CENTURIES

DUTCH PAINTING.
17th CENTURY

NETHERLANDISH
PAINTING.
15th–17th
CENTURIES

DECORATIVE
AND APPLIED ARTS
OF MEDIEVAL EUROPE

ITALIAN ART.
13th–18th
CENTURIES

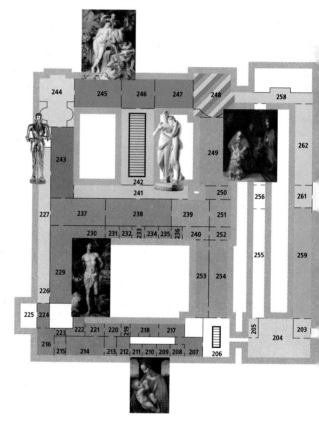

Room **192**

THE NEVA SUITE
OF THE WINTER PALACE:
ANTECHAMBER

Room **198**

THE EASTERN SUITE
OF THE WINTER PALACE:
ST GEORGE ROOM

Room **189**

THE NORTH-WESTERN PART
OF THE WINTER PALACE:
THE MALACHITE DRAWING-ROOM

FIRST FLOOR

GERMAN AND AUSTRIAN ART. 15th–18th CENTURIES

FRENCH ART. 15th–18th CENTURIES

ENGLISH ART. 16th–19th CENTURIES

RUSSIAN CULTURE. 9th–19th CENTURIES

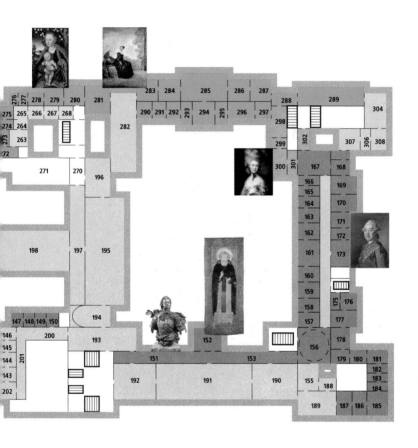

Room **204**

Room **304**

Rooms **226–227**

THE SMALL HERMITAGE: THE PAVILION HALL

THE SOUTH-WESTERN PART OF THE WINTER PALACE: THE GOLDEN DRAWING-ROOM

THE OLD HERMITAGE: THE RAPHAEL LOGGIAS

FRENCH PAINTING
AND SCULPTURE.
19th–20th CENTURIES

PAINTING
OF WESTERN EUROPE
AND AMERICA.
19th–20th CENTURIES

ART OF CHINA
AND CENTRAL ASIA

ART OF BYZANTIUM

ART OF IRAN
AND THE NEAR EAST

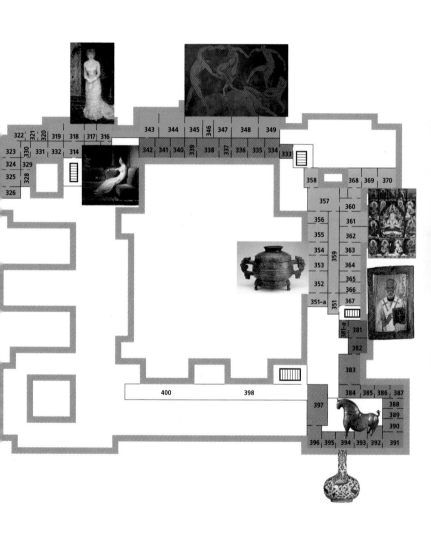

322 | 321 | 320 | 319 | 318 | 317 | 316 | | 343 | 344 | 345 | 346 | 347 | 348 | 349 |
323 | 330 | 331 | 332 | 314 | | 342 | 341 | 340 | 339 | 338 | 337 | 336 | 335 | 334 | 333
324 | 329
325 | 328
326

358 | | 368 | 369 | 370
357 | 360
356 | 361
355 | 362
354 | 359 | 363
353 | 364
352 | 365
351-a | 366
| 351 | 367
351-a | 381
382
383
397 | 384 | 385 | 386 | 387
388
389
390
400 | 398 | 396 | 395 | 394 | 393 | 392 | 391

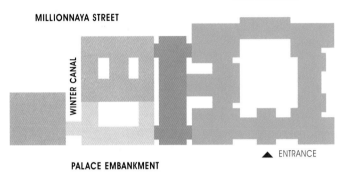

PALACE SQUARE

MILLIONNAYA STREET

WINTER CANAL

ADMIRALTY

▲ ENTRANCE

PALACE EMBANKMENT

| HERMITAGE THEATRE | BIG (OLD) HERMITAGE | NEW HERMITAGE | SMALL HERMITAGE | WINTER PALACE |

BUILDINGS AND ROOMS OF THE HERMITAGE

THE WINTER PALACE
THE SMALL HERMITAGE
THE BIG (OLD) HERMITAGE
THE NEW HERMITAGE
THE HERMITAGE THEATRE

The main Hermitage ensemble runs along the left bank of the Neva and comprises five buildings: the Winter Palace, the Small Hermitage, the Big, or Old, Hermitage, the New Hermitage and the Hermitage Theatre. Created by the outstanding architects Francesco Bartolomeo Rastrelli, Jean-Baptiste-Michel Vallin de la Mothe, Yuri Velten, Giacomo Quarenghi, Leo von Klenze in the 18th and 19th centuries, these buildings, although varying in style, make up a single architectural complex.

THE WINTER PALACE
1754–62. Designed by F.B. Rastrelli

16 June 1754 is a momentous date in the history of the Winter Palace. It was the day when Empress Elizabeth Petrovna gave her final approval to the drafts of the new imperial winter residence, which the architectural genius Francesco Bartolomeo Rastrelli (1700–1771) had been working on for three years. Having found an original composition for each of the four façades of the Winter Palace, which never repeats one another, he designed a building of unique distinction and beauty. It is interesting to note that initially the Palace was covered with a "sandy colour". The palace buildings make up an enclosed square with a large, cross-shaped court, *cour d'honneur*, opening into Palace Square. In the centre of all buildings there were large entrance halls. The service rooms were situated on the ground floor. The arrangement of the rooms on the first, state floor was carefully elaborated. The main premises – the Main Staircase, the Throne Room, the Chapel and the Theatre – were located in the four corner projections of the palace (*risalita*). They all were connected with four suites of rooms which made it possible to go round the whole palace. The most pompous of them was the Neva suite situated between the Main Staircase and the Throne Room, with the windows overlooking the Neva embankment. The rooms on the second floor were intended for ladies-in-waiting and other courtiers.

Elizabeth Petrovna died in late 1761, having not lived to her move to the new residence. The decoration of the palace state rooms went on after her death for twenty years. Giacomo Quarenghi, Auguste Montferrand and Carlo Rossi were responsible for the interior decor of the Winter Palace erected "to the glory of all Russia". And indeed, the palace became a personification of the might of the Russian Empire. In December 1837, a formidable fire ruined the huge palace, having left its charred frame. Fortunately, the palace property and works of art were carried out onto Palace Square and Admiralty Lane and thus saved. Just after the fire, a special commission was set up to supervise the reconstruction work. The architect Vasily Stasov was in charge of the reconstruction project for the façades and the state rooms of the Palace, while Alexander Briullov was responsible for the reconstruction of the living rooms. To prevent another fire, wherever possible, the wooden floors were replaced by metal structures made at the St Petersburg iron foundry works. To make vaulting and partition constructions lighter, in some cases hollow ceramic pots, totalling about five million, were used. Instead of stoves, a hot-air heating system developed by the engineer N. Amosov was installed. Subsequently the Palace underwent only minor alterations related, mainly, to interior decoration which was to be always in tune with the spirit of the time.

The Great Patriotic War of 1941–45 has left its mark in the history of the Palace. A number of the Hermitage researchers, with its director, Iosif Orbeli, stayed in the besieged city, among them the scholars of world repute, such as Vladimir Loewinson-Lessing, Boris Piotrovsky, and Professor Mikhail Dobroklonsky, who displayed infinite fortitude and devotion in serving their cause. Under hard condition of starvation and winter cold they managed to save the museum and the pieces of art that had not been evacuated in the summer of 1941.

As soon as the blockade was lifted, Orbeli made for the government a detailed plan of the reconstruction of all buildings of the museum ensemble. The restoration work began in 1944 and was partly completed as early as November 1945. Due to the efforts of the architects and restorers of the State Hermitage, the Winter Palace appears to us in all its magnificence, as it has been conceived by the great Rastrelli.

The Main, or Jordan, Staircase

The Jordan Staircase leading up to the state rooms of the first floor was originally, in the 18th century, called the Ambassadors Staircase, for ambassadors of foreign countries were shown in into the state rooms for the highest audiences along this staircase. Later it was renamed Jordan Staircase, because at Christmas the imperial family and the courtiers went down it to the Neva, where an ice-hole, known as Jordan, was cut through to hold the rite of the consecration of water. In Rastrelli's time the staircase was of wood, and the columns were faced with pink artificial marble. While reconstructing it after the fire of 1837, the architect Vasily Stasov, trying to preserve Rastrelli's Baroque character of decor, replaced the columns of artificial marble with granite ones. Standing at the foot of the stairs the visitor is already aware of its grandeur emphasized by the abundance of gilded stucco mouldings and painted ceilings.

The Field Marshals Hall (room 193)

The first room of the so-called East Suite of the Winter Palace was designed by Auguste Montferrand (1786–1858) in 1833, and was conceived as a gallery for portraits of the most outstanding Russian field marshals: Grigory Potiomkin-Tavrichesky, Piotr Rumiantsev-Zadunaisky, Alexander Suvorov-Rymniksky, Mikhail Kutuzov-Smolensky, Ivan Dibich-Zabalkansky, and Ivan Paskevich-Erivansky. The Field Marshals Hall was one of the first to be restored after the fire of 1837. At present this hall is a starting-point of the tour introducing visitors to the Western European art displayed on the first floor of the four buildings of the museum ensemble, i.e. the Winter Palace, the Small, the Old and the New Hermitages, which are interconnected by galleries and passages. The Hall is adorned with period specimens of Russian decorative porcelain, one of which, the Russia vase, may well be considered one of the most gigantic of its kind in Europe. The imperial carriage is on view too (see p. 217).

Vase *Russia*
1828. The Imperial Porcelain Factory.
St Petersburg. *Porcelain, painting.*
Height 222 cm. Inv. No. РФ 7429
From the Main Collection of the Winter Palace.

Petrovsky (Peter I's), or the Small Throne, Room (room 194)

It was created in 1833 by the architect Auguste Montferrand and dedicated to the memory of Peter the Great. The upper parts of the walls are decorated with pictures of Russia's victorious battles won by Peter the Great: *The Poltava Battle* and *The Battle at Lesnaya* executed by B. Medici and P. Scotti. The decor abounds in imperial emblems: two-headed eagles, crowns and Latin monograms *PP* (Peter Primus) of Peter I. In the depth of the big niche topped with a conch, between two jasper columns, there is a portrait of Peter I with an allegorical figure of Minerva, painted by the Venetian Jacopo Amiconi between 1732 and 1734. The throne, standing on a dais below the picture, was commissioned for Empress Anna Ioannovna and made in England in 1731 by Nicholas Clausen.

The Armorial Hall (room 195)

This grand hall, with its total area of 1,000 square metres, was designed in 1839 by Vasily Stasov (1769–1848) and was intended for formal receptions and balls. Its solid gilded columns of the Corinthian Order impart to the hall a festive look. The end walls feature sculptural groups of Russian warriors holding standards with staffs decorated with the coats of arms of Russian provinces, hence the name of the hall. The immense bronze chandeliers are also decorated with plaques with relief depictions of the coats of arms of Russian provinces. At present a collection of Western European silverware is displayed here.

Georghiyevsky (St George), or the Large Throne, Room (room 198)

This enormous room, with two tiers of windows, designed by Giacomo Quarenghi (1744–1817) in 1795 and restored by Vasily Stasov in 1837–42, is shining with white Carrara marble set off by gilded bronze. The ornament of the ceiling repeats the pattern of a unique parquet floor, composed of sixteen rare species of wood. The hanging copper ceiling is supported with iron structures. The marble bas-relief depicting St George slaying the dragon, executed by the Italian sculptor Francesco del Nero after the drawing by Vasily Stasov, was mounted into the wall above the throne place just after the restoration. As the room was intended for grand ceremonial occasions no furniture stood there except the emperor's throne.

The 1812 War Gallery (room 197)

The Gallery was designed by the architect Carlo Rossi (1775–1849) in 1826 as a memorial to the triumph of the Russian arms in the Patriotic War of 1812. The walls of the Gallery bear the names of the places where the Russian army fought the French: Borodino, Tarutino, Krasnoye, Paris. But the most important feature of the Gallery is a succession of portraits – over 300 – of the heroes of the war against Napoleon, people whose feats brought fame to Russia. Among them are the portraits of Rayevsky, Volkonsky, Davydov and Kulnev. The list of the portrayed was approved by the emperor. The portraits were painted by the English artist George Dawe (1781–1829) assisted by the Russian artists A. Poliakov and V. Golike. This painstaking work took more than ten years. The generals sat for their portraits in the studio arranged in the building adjoining the palace. Those who were unable to come were to send their depictions. The large equestrian portraits of Alexander I and of Frederick-William III were made by Franz Krüger.

FRANZ KRÜGER
1797–1857
Portrait of Emperor Alexander I on Horseback
1837. Oil on canvas. 484 x 344 cm. Inv. No. 7894

Alexander I (1777–1825), the favourite grandson of Catherine II, Russian Emperor (from 1801) went down in history as a controversial person. His initial efforts to liberalize Russia gave way, after the victory over Napoleon, to a reactionary home policy. As a result of victorious wars against Turkey and Sweden, during the reign of Alexander I new territories were annexed to Russia: Finland, part of Poland, Georgia, Azerbaijan, and Bessarabia. Krüger painted the equestrian portrait of the Emperor specially for the War Gallery, having depicted him with Paris in the background. The name of the stallion mounted by the emperor is Eclipse. It was presented to him by Napoleon in Erfurt in 1808, and in 1814 Alexander I entered Paris as the conqueror riding just the same horse.
From the Main Collection of the Winter Palace.

The Antechamber with the Malachite Rotunda (room 192)

The Neva Suite consists of three state rooms – the Antechamber, the Large (Nicholas) Hall, and the Concert Hall, with an adjacent gallery running along them, where portraits of Russian emperors and empresses are on display. From the architectural point of view, these state rooms are an example of later Russian Classicism characterized primarily by grandeur and harmony. In the centre of the Antechamber, stands the Rotunda with malachite columns made on the commission of A. Demidov in 1827–34. This true masterpiece of the monumental and decorative arts in the Empire style is lavishly decorated with the ornament of gilded bronze executed at the workshop of Pierre Philippe Thomire (1751–1843) in Paris.

The Great Hall (room 191)

The Great Hall, used now for temporary exhibitions, is the most spacious in the Winter Palace, with an area of 1,103 square metres. After the death of Nicholas I in 1855, his portrait painted by Franz Krüger was installed here, and since that time the Hall acquired a memorial character and the new name – the Nicholas Hall. While restoring the interior after the fire, Vasily Stasov used the device of the juxta-position of simple classical architectural forms: of the massive Corinthian colonnade, wide-bayed arches and clearly articulated walls. The flat ceiling is divided into three parts decorated round their perimeters with a border of caissons painted in grisaille technique.

The Concert Hall (room 190)

With the growth of musical culture at the turn of the 18th and the 19th centuries, rooms specially accommodated for concerts became a usual feature of the palaces of Europe. The architecture of the Concert Hall, like that of the other halls of the Neva Suite, impresses one with the exuberant plastic quality of classical forms. Nowadays the main treasure in this hall is the silver sepulchre of Holy Prince Alexander Nevsky, transferred here from the Alexander Nevsky Lavra (monastery) in 1922. It was made in 1747–52 at the St Petersburg Mint by order of Empress Elizabeth Petrovna. Nearly 1.5 tons of silver firstly obtained from the Kolyvan-Voskresensky mines in the Altai Mountains were used to produce it.

The Portrait Gallery of the Romanovs (rooms 151, 153)

BELLI
Portrait of Peter I
*Mid-19th century. Copy from the original
by G. Kneller. Oil on canvas. 239.3 x 147 cm.
Inv. No. 4521*

Peter I Alexeyevich (1672–1725), son of
the tsar Alexei Mikhailovich and his second
wife Natalya Kirillovna Naryshkina. From
1689, after his brother's, Ioann Alexeyevich,
death, he ruled Russia as a sovereign.
In 1721 he became the first emperor
of Russia. His portrait by the English artist
Godfrey Kneller (1646–1723) was commissioned by William III and painted in London
in 1697 when Peter I was on his first journey
abroad (the portrait is now in the Kensington
Palace in London). Next year the picture
was seen by the well-known Dutch traveller
and artist K. de Brein. When he met Peter I
in 1702 in Moscow, he remarked on the
likeness of the portrait to the artist's sitter.
The copy of the portrait was made by
Belli specially for the Romanovs Gallery
arranged by order of Nicholas I in the Small
Hermitage closed in 1918.
*Until 1918 in the Romanovs Gallery of the
Small Hermitage.*

LOUIS TOCQUE
1696–1772
Portrait of Empress Elizabeth Petrovna
*1758. Oil on canvas. 262 x 204 cm.
Inv. No РЖ 1280*

Elizabeth Petrovna (1709–1761), Russian
Empress (from 1741), daughter of Peter I
by his second wife Yekaterina Alexeyevna,
Catherine I. According to the records
of Jacob von Stählin, professor of the
St Petersburg Imperial Academy of
Sciences, the portrait was produced by
the Easter of 1758.
*Purchased from the artist, 1758; until 1918
in the Romanovs Gallery of the Small Hermitage.*

FIODOR ROKOTOV
1736–1808
Portrait of Empress Catherine II
1780s. Oil on canvas. 263 x 188 cm.
Inv. No. РЖ 11678

Catherine II (1729–1796), born Sophie Frederike Auguste of Anhalt-Zerbst, was the spouse of the Russian Emperor Peter III, dethroned by her, and the Empress of Russia (from 1762). This formal portrait of Catherine II was executed after the portrait by the Swedish artist Alexander Roslin painted in 1777–78. The Empress is depicted wearing a state robe, with the ermine mantle, the star and chain of the Order of St Andrew the First-Called and the badges of St George Order of the First Class.
The right hand of the empress is stretched out towards the bust of Peter I with the motto above it: *Completes what was begun.* This was to suggest Catherine's aspiration to strictly follow Peter I's will.
Until 1918 in the Romanovs Gallery of the Small Hermitage.

STEPAN SHCHUKIN
1762–1828
Portrait of Emperor Paul I
1796–97. Oil on canvas. 154 x 116 cm.
Inv. No. EP3X 1733

Paul I (1754–1801) is a son of Peter III and Catherine II, Russian Emperor (from 1796). He is presented wearing a full uniform of a colonel of the Preobrazhensky Regiment, with the ribbon and Order of St Andrew the First-Called, the star of the Holy Alexander Nevsky Order and the Order of St Anna. Paul liked this portrait very much, and the artist produced a few versions of it. This canvas comes from the collection of the Yusupov Palace in St Petersburg.
From the State Ethnographical Museum, Leningrad, 1941.

The Malachite Drawing-Room
(room 189)

It is one of the most lavishly decorated rooms of the Winter Palace. Over two tons of first-grade malachite from the Demidovs Mines were used for its decoration finished under the architect Alexander Briullov (1798–1877) in 1839. The green stone is in striking contrast to the gilded ceiling mouldings. The malachite decor, as well as all pieces of furniture, were made in the technique of the so-called Russian mosaic: malachite plates, a few millimetres thick, were stuck to a form made of stone, copper or other material covered with hot mastic. Having been meticulously adjusted to each other, the plates imitate the natural pattern of the stone. There were different kinds of such patterns called 'crumpled velvet', 'ribbon', and others. After final grinding and polishing the object looked as if it were made out of a solid block of malachite.

The Small Dining-Room (room 188)

In 1894, in view of the marriage of Crown Prince Nikolai Alexandrovich (1868–1918), the future Emperor Nicholas II (from 1894), a number of rooms in the north-western part of the Winter Palace, including the Small Dining-Room adjacent to the Malachite Drawing-Room, were reconstructed under the architect Alexander Krasovsky (1848–1923). The new interior decor combined the features of Classicism, Baroque and Rococo. The elegant furniture reveals the influence of the Rococo style. The walls are adorned with four Baroque tapestries woven at the St Petersburg Imperial Tapestry Factory. The crystal chandelier of 18th-century English make is provided with a musical mechanism. The bronze clock on the mantelpiece always shows 2.10 p.m., the time of the night of November 7–8 (New Style), 1917, when the Provisional Government was arrested in this dining-room.

The Golden Drawing-Room (room 304)

The room was created in 1838 to the design of the architect Alexander Briullov who made use of some elements of the 17th-century Moscow architectural style which was in fashion at the time. The state chambers of the Moscow Kremlin with their vaulted ceilings and highly ornate walls served as the model for the architect. The Golden Drawing-Room houses a unique collection of carved stones, among them intaglios and cameos from the collection of Catherine the Great.

Boudoir in the 'second Rococo' style (room 306)

It was in fashion in the second half of the 19th century to decorate boudoirs and drawing-rooms in the so-called 'women's half' of St Petersburg palaces in the 'second Rococo' style. It is to the French Emperor Napoleon III (1808–1873), that Europe was indebted for the revival of Rococo, for his famous chambers in the Louvre in the 1850s were decorated just in this style. This boudoir was created in 1853 by the architect Gerald Bosset for Maria Alexandrovna, wife of Grand Duke Alexander Nikolayevich (the future Alexander II). Its decor includes seven mirrors adorning the walls, fireplace and ceiling.

Library of Nicholas II (room 178)

This library situated in the north-western wing of the Winter Palace is yet another room designed after the Emperor's marriage in 1894. The fashion for the Gothic style, or its variant, the style of the English Queen Elizabeth (1533–1603), came to the Continent from England. All wooden elements of the interior and the furniture made at the court factories of N. Svirsky and F. Melzer in Petersburg are richly decorated with carving in stylized Gothic. The finishing touch is the fireplace of carved white marble.

THE SMALL HERMITAGE

1764–75. Designed by Yu. Velten
and J.-B.-M. Vallin de la Mothe

The erection of the Small Hermitage was the first step in the forming of a Hermitage suite of buildings which, together with the Winter Palace, constitutes a single architectural ensemble. Its general layout – a garden with a hothouse and two pavilions connected by galleries – was traditional for most palaces in the St Petersburg of the 18th century. There was no single initial project for the building. Several architects contributed to the planning of the Small Hermitage. First Vallin de la Mothe (1729–1800) built the Hanging Garden, next to which Velten (1730/32–1801) added the South Pavilion facing Millionnaya Street. Then, on the Neva embankment, Vallin de la Mothe erected the North Pavilion, and, finally, the pavilions were connected by galleries intended for the housing of pictures from the Catherine II collection. In Catherine II's times the North Pavilion was used for entertainment, the merry parties known as 'small hermitages'. Dinners and suppers were given in the room called 'hermitage' (from the French *ermitage* – a place of seclusion) on the first floor, and the meals were delivered from the ground floor by two tables lifted by a special device. Subsequently the building itself became known as the Small Hermitage, and later on the whole museum ensemble received the name of the Hermitage. In the 1840s, simultaneously with the Winter Palace, the Small Hermitage underwent a reconstruction with the main purpose to replace wooden structures by metal ones. According to Vasily Stasov's project, the whole interior of the South Pavilion was altered, and a second floor was added. The walls and constructions of the Hanging Garden were taken off, and the new-built terrace was supplied with efficient waterproof and ventilation systems. On both sides of the Garden, Stasov erected long galleries, similar to those which had been here earlier, but with lighter vaulted ceilings. In the 1850s, Andrei Stackenschneider (1802–1865) reconstructed the inner premises of the North Pavilion without altering its façade.

The Pavilion Hall (room 204)

The Pavilion Hall is justly regarded as the most gorgeous in the Small Hermitage. It was created by Andrei Stackenschneider in the 1850s in place of five rooms on the state floor of the North Pavilion. A sophisticated spatial solution of the hall with two tiers of windows, an upper gallery, a light two-tiered arcade of white marble, an ingenious combination of the Renaissance architectural forms with elements of the Moorish style, an abundance of gilding, the cut-crystal of the chandeliers, and four fountains resembling the Weeping Fountain of Bakhchisarai – all conspire to form the most original and festive interior, recognized as one of the best works of the architect. The floor of the hall is decorated with mosaic panels picturing Medusa Gorgon and some scenes from antique mythology. It is a reduced copy of the floor mosaic in the termœ of Ochriculum, near Rome.

The Peacock Clock

Late 1760s. The J. Coxe workshop. England.
Bronze, gilding; silver (the owl), glass.
Height 3 m. Inv. No. ЭИ 3425

A notable exhibit of the Pavilion Hall, the Peacock Clock was made in the workshop of the outstanding English jeweller James Coxe (1723–ca. 1791). Curiosities of this kind were fashionable in the 18th century. The clock was bought in 1788 by Grigory Potiomkin out of the estate of the late Duchess of Kingston and arrived in Russia disassembled. It was put together again by the famous master Ivan Kulibin in 1797. Up to now the Hermitage restorers have managed to keep this sophisticated mechanism in working order.
From the Main Collection of the Hermitage.

The Hanging Garden

A hanging garden is a feature characteristic of 18th-century palaces. Laid out in the 1760s, it came to us as it was reconstructed in the late 1830s by Vasily Stasov. Over the vaults of the ground floor, above the leaden planking, a layer of soil was put for planting trees and laying out flowerbeds.

The central avenue is lined with marble sculptures of the 18th century, and along the gallery walls there are wooden dovecotes. On the terrace, next to the North Pavilion, a parterre is laid out with a marble fountain surrounded by small marble statues made specially for the Hanging Garden.

THE BIG, OR OLD, HERMITAGE
1771–87. Designed by Yu. Velten

The building of the Old Hermitage was intended for the housing of the palace art collections and the library. Its façade is simple, austere and somewhat monotonous but this is only a manifestation of the architect's discretion, which enabled him to organically inscribe a new structure into those already existing without violating the harmony of the whole. The rooms of the ground and first floors run in two suites along the Neva embankment. In the 1850s the State Suite with the windows looking on to the Neva was reconstructed by Andrei Stackenschneider, who replaced all wooden structures by metal ones. The interior decoration abounds in gilding, coloured stones, precious species of wood, painting and stucco moulding. In place of the former Oval Hall the Sovetskaya (Council) Staircase was erected taking its name from the State Council (Sovet) accommodated in the rooms of the ground floor.

The Hall with Two Tiers of Windows
(room 214)

This originally austere interior acquired its sumptuous appearance after the main hall of the Old Hermitage was reconstructed in the 1850s. Andrei Stackenschneider took as the model the architecture of the time of Louis XIV combining the magnificence of Classicism and the polychromy of Baroque. The walls of the Hall (also known as the Leonardo Room and the Room of the Italian Renaissance) are faced with artificial marble, and along them stand columns of red-veined green marble on porphyry bases. The fireplaces inlaid with lazurite are topped with mirrors, framed by columns of Koshkuldin jasper. The unique doors made in the Boulle style (after Boulle, an outstanding cabinet-maker at the court of Louis XIV) are embellished in marquetry technique with an elaborate ornament of gilded bronze and inlaid tortoiseshells. The painted panels running along the frieze of the walls, the caryatids supporting the ceiling beams and massive chandeliers, as well as the whole decor, make a splendid setting for the world-famous masterpieces by Leonardo da Vinci (see pp. 38, 39).

The Raphael Loggias (rooms 226, 227)

It happened that, in 1778, Catherine II expressed her wish to have copies of the frescoes made by the great Raphael for the loggias of the Vatican Palace. She ordered J.-F. Reifenstein, a commissioner at the Russian Court to commission them. The frescoes were copied by Ch. Unterberger who was famous for his painting of the walls of the Vatican Library. On Reiffenstein's recommendation, the architect Giacomo Quarenghi was invited to Russia, and it was his idea to construct a new building adjacent to the east façade of the Big Hermitage in order to accommodate the copies. The Raphael Loggias are a fine example of grotesque style in wall-painting, demonstrating an infinite imagination of the artist in combining decorative motifs of the Roman masters of the 1st century A.D. with the aesthetics of the High Renaissance.

THE NEW HERMITAGE

1839–51. Designed by V. Stasov and N. Yefimov to the plans of F. K. L. von Klenze

In the middle of the 19th century, due to the rapid growth of the imperial collections, it became necessary to erect a new building to accommodate them, which was to be given the status, first ever in Russia, of a public museum. Emperor Nicholas I commissioned a design to the court architect of Louis I of Bavaria, Leo von Klenze (1784–1864) who had been already known by his buildings of the Pinacotheca and Glyptotheca in Munich, which the Emperor saw during his visit to Germany in 1838. The museum, named later the New Hermitage, was open on 7 February 1852. On display in its fifty-six rooms were masterpieces of world art – painting, sculpture, monuments of ancient writing, jewellery, numismatics, as well as many other things. The main façade of the New Hermitage in Millionnaya Street is decorated with a spectacular portico with ten Atlantes cut out of grey granite after the models by the sculptor Alexander Terebenev. The interior decoration of the New Hermitage has survived intact. While planning the museum, Klenze made over 800 drawings and sketches of imposing rooms and studies of this enormous building. The most important contribution to the realization of Klenze's interior designs was made by Nikolai Yefimov (1799–1851), who supervised the project after Vasily Stasov's death in 1848.

The Kolyvan Vase

1829–43. After A. Melnikov's design.
The Kolyvan Lapidary Works. Altai, Russia.
*Revnev jasper. Height 2.5 m, maximum
diameter 4.5 m. Inv. No. Э 2519*

The famous Russian geochemist and mineralogist, Academician Alexander Fersman (1883–1945) used to call the Hermitage "the repository of highly artistic objects made of coloured stones". Splendid decorative vases, candelabra and tabletops of semiprecious stones of Russian make decorate the museum rooms.
From the Main Collection of the Hermitage.

The Twenty-Column Hall (room 130)

The rooms on the ground floor of the New Hermitage are all occupied by the exhibition of antique art. The interiors display solemn monumentality and austere decoration. Their walls are faced with artificial marble of a superb quality, which makes it impossible to distinguish it with the naked eye from the natural stone. The capitals of the columns, walls and ceilings are painted with motifs inspired by the decor of antique vases, for displaying of which the Twenty-Column Hall was expressly intended. It is still serving that purpose today: the vases stand in glass showcases made of birch with a very rare kind of amaranth inlays; also displayed here are objects of Etruscan culture (see p. 236).

The Large Skylighted Hall (room 238)

Museum rooms with glass ceilings as the only source of light became widespread in the 19th century. The suite of the three largest rooms of the New Hermitage has just this type of lighting, hence their name. Their interior decor is made in the same style. The halls dazzle one with the brightness of gilding and the luxury of the furnishing. The ceiling around the skylights is covered with gilded ornamentation where the Renaissance motifs predominate. On display here is the Italian painting of the 17th and 18th centuries (see pp. 50–57) and Spanish painting (see pp. 107–115).

THE HERMITAGE THEATRE
1783–89. Designed by G. Quarenghi

The Hermitage Theatre is one of the few surviving theatre buildings from the 18th century. It harmoniously ends up the Hermitage ensemble to which it is connected with a gallery arranged over the arch across the Winter Canal. The Italian architect Giacomo Quarenghi was commissioned with the construction work. Originally the theatre auditorium with a stage was built into the premises of the Life-Campana Corps, located on the site of the former Winter Palace of Peter I, and it was not until 1786 that they started a new building specially for that purpose. The auditorium takes the form of an amphitheatre, with its walls and columns faced with artificial marble. In the album of Quarenghi's drawings, published in 1787, the architect wrote: "I sought to impart a noble and strict character to the architecture of the theatre."

FIRST FLOOR

● BEGINNING
OF THE FIRST-FLOOR
EXHIBITION

KNIGHTS HALL
(WESTERN EUROPEAN ARMS
AND ARMOUR. 15th–17th CENTURIES)

GALLERY OF THE HISTORY
OF ANCIENT PAINTING
(WESTERN EUROPEAN SCULPTURE.
18th–19th CENTURIES)

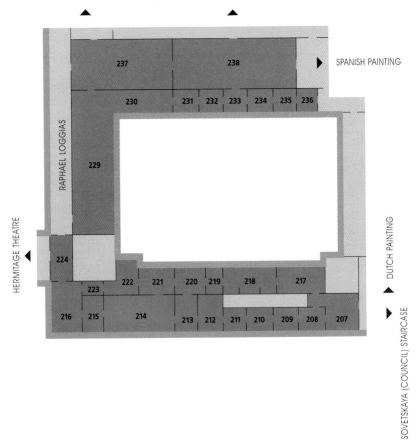

SPANISH PAINTING

RAPHAEL LOGGIAS

HERMITAGE THEATRE

DUTCH PAINTING

SOVETSKAYA (COUNCIL) STAIRCASE

237
238
230 231 232 233 234 235 236
229
224
222 221 220 219 218 217
223
216 215 214 213 212 211 210 209 208 207

ITALIAN PAINTING AND SCULPTURE.
13th–18th CENTURIES

Italian art, distinguished by its deeply-rooted links with the great legacy of antiquity, enriched world culture with the magnificent examples of the creative genius of man endowed with talent and fortitude, and committed to art. The exhibition of Italian art is one of the most significant in the Hermitage. It is housed in twenty-nine rooms and amply illustrates the course of Italian art from the Middle Ages to the 18th century. The major artistic schools, whose manifold variety was determined by the political division of the country, – the Venetian, Roman, Bolognese and others – are represented by works of their leading painters.

PAINTING. 13th–18th CENTURIES

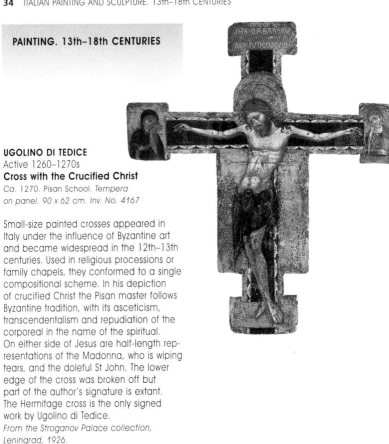

UGOLINO DI TEDICE
Active 1260–1270s
Cross with the Crucified Christ
*Ca. 1270. Pisan School. Tempera
on panel. 90 x 62 cm. Inv. No. 4167*

Small-size painted crosses appeared in
Italy under the influence of Byzantine art
and became widespread in the 12th–13th
centuries. Used in religious processions or
family chapels, they conformed to a single
compositional scheme. In his depiction
of crucified Christ the Pisan master follows
Byzantine tradition, with its asceticism,
transcendentalism and repudiation of the
corporeal in the name of the spiritual.
On either side of Jesus are half-length representations of the Madonna, who is wiping
tears, and the doleful St John. The lower
edge of the cross was broken off but
part of the author's signature is extant.
The Hermitage cross is the only signed
work by Ugolino di Tedice.
*From the Stroganov Palace collection,
Leningrad, 1926.*

SIMONE MARTINI
Ca. 1284–1344
The Madonna of the Annunciation
*1340–44. Sienese School. Wing of a diptych.
Tempera on panel. 30.5 x 21.5 cm.
Inv. No. 284*

The *Madonna of the Annunciation* is the
right wing of a diptych; the left wing with
the Archangel Gabriel is in the National
Gallery of Art, Washington. This refined picture is executed with the accuracy of a
miniature. The Madonna, an embodiment
of graceful femininity and spirituality, is
depicted on a conventional golden background. The flowing refined outlines of Her
silhouette impart to the image a special
lyricism. The work comes from the collection of Count Grigory Stroganov, Rome.
It was he who attributed the miniature
representation of the Madonna from his
collection to Simone Martini.
*From the G. Stroganov collection, Rome;
presented by his heirs in 1911.*

LORENZO DI NICCOLO GERINI (?)
Active 1392–1411
Madonna and Child
1400. Florentine School. *Oil on panel.*
82 x 47 cm (without frame); 130.5 x 69.5 cm
(with frame). Inv. No. 4045

Lorenzo di Niccolo Gerini painted pictures
and frescoes on religious subjects, borrow-
ing some characters from Giotto.
The frame of the panel, apparently executed by the artist himself, is designed in the
form of a Gothic arch, bearing representations of angels. Beneath the arch we see
the Madonna with the infant Christ on her
lap. In the lower part of the frame are the
half-length figures of Christ, St Catherine
and St Barbara.
From the Yuriev Monastery near Novgorod
(donated by Countess A. Orlova-Chesmenskaya),
1924.

VINCENZO FOPPA
Ca. 1430–after 1515
The Archangel Michael
Milanese School. *Tempera on panel.*
91 x 34 cm. Inv. No. 7773

Vincenzo Foppa was the leading painter
of the Milanese School before it was trans-
formed by the influence of Leonardo da
Vinci. It is not by accident that he was
placed on a par with this great master in
Lomazzo's *Treatise* (1584). In his handling
of colours and plastic problems the artist
still follows Gothic tradition, which is manifest in the golden background of this
painting, the S-curve of the Archangel
Michael's body and bright patches of
colour. Yet, the three-dimensionality of the
figure is already achieved by means of
highlights, a new technique borrowed by
the Italians from Netherlandish painting.
From the State Museum Reserve, Petrograd,
1921; formerly in the N. Roerich collection,
St Petersburg.

FRA BEATO ANGELICO (FRA GIOVANNI DA FIESOLE, GUIDO DI PIETRO)
Ca. 1400–1455
Madonna and Child with St Dominique and St Thomas Aquinas
Ca. 1430s. Florentine School. Fresco, tempera. 196 x 187 cm. Inv. No. 253

The fresco was painted by Fra Beato for the monastery of San Domenico in Fiesole near Florence. In the 1870s, after the monastery ceased to function, the fresco was purchased by the Florentine artists A. Mazzanti and C. Conti. Angelico, who often filled his compositions with beautiful minor details, is unexpectedly reserved and laconic in this work. This can be explained by his striving to create a monumental piece. The symmetrical composition with the Madonna in the centre flanked by two saints, known as *Sacra Conversazione*, was preserved throughout the Middle Ages and the Renaissance.
Bought from A. Mazzanti and C. Conti, Florence, 1883.

SCHOOL OF ANDREA VERROCCHIO
Madonna and Child
1469–70. Florentine School. Tempera and oil on canvas. 75 x 57 cm. Inv. No. 5520

The Madonna is depicted sitting on a throne in a magnificent architectural setting against the background of a beautiful landscape. The picture was long considered a work by Pietro Pollaiolo.
From the A. Rudanovsky collection, Petrograd, 1919.

FRA FILIPPO LIPPI
Ca. 1406–1469
The Vision of St Augustine
Late 1450s–early 1560s. Florentine School.
Tempera on panel. 28 x 51.5 cm.
Inv. No. 5511

The biography of this painter arouses great
interest up to now. The son of a butcher,
Lippi had to take monastic vows at the age
of fifteen as his family insisted on it, but he
preferred to work beyond the monastery
walls. Then in defiance of all regulations he
settled down in married life: when he was
fifty he abducted a nun named Lucrezia
Butti. Quite soon a son was born to them,
who later became known as the artist
Filippino Lippi. *The Vision of St Augustine*
was presumably made for a predella, the
strip of small paintings which form the lower
edge of a large Catholic altarpiece. The
main character is a real person, St Aurelius
Augustine (354–430), the bishop of the city
of Hippo in northwestern Africa. Legend has
it that when St Augustine was meditating
upon the dogma of the Holy Trinity he had a
vision: an angel in the guise of a child seated on the seashore was trying to pour the
water from the sea into a small pit. It was in
this way that God demonstrated to Augustine
the futility of all attempts of the human mind
to cognize the mysteries of the divine.
From the collection of Princess Eugenia
of Oldenburg, Petrograd, 1917; formerly
in the collection of Grand Duchess
Maria Nikolayevna, Florence.

FILIPPINO LIPPI
1457–1504
The Adoration of the Infant Christ
Mid-1480s. Florentine School. *Tempera*
on copper (transferred from panel).
Diameter 53 cm. Inv. No. 287

The kneeling Madonna is surrounded by
angels with transparent wings. The landscape, painted delicately and accurately,
is notable for its sense of aerial perspective,
which clearly demonstrates the achievements of the artists active in the second half
of the 15th century. There is an appreciable
difference between the works by Filippino
Lippi and those by his father. The landscape
painted by Filippino is not only part of the
pictorial space, it also creates a kind of
emotional atmosphere which imparts to the
picture its lyrical intonation.
From the Stroganov collection,
Petrograd, 1922.

LEONARDO DA VINCI
1452–1519
Madonna and Child
(The Benois Madonna)
1478–80. Florentine School. *Oil on canvas*
(transferred from panel). 49.5 x 33 cm.
Inv. No. 2273

This is one of the few indisputable originals by Leonardo, which can be dated on the grounds of a note made by the master on one of his drawings. The painter used here a symbol that was common enough: the Madonna is amusing the infant Christ with a four-petal flower, an allusion to His destiny. However, this symbol receives a new interpretation in the context of the present work: a human being coming into contact with the outer world for the first time is trying to satisfy his thirst for knowledge. The connection between the mother and her child is natural and very convincing.

Leonardo's Madonna has the features of an open-hearted Florentine girl. Her face still retains childlike chubbiness and is far from being the ideal of classical beauty. The serene smile of this 'mother girl' is an expression of both joy and pride she takes in her child. The preparatory pen drawings that most nearly approach the Hermitage painting are in the British Museum, London, and the Uffizi Gallery, Florence. In the *Benois Madonna* the master used the technique of oil painting brought to the south of Europe from the Netherlands. If compared to traditional tempera painting, it offered greater opportunities in rendering subtle light-and-shade gradations and helped to enhance the tangibility of objects. The picture won the admiration of Leonardo's contemporaries and was often copied during his lifetime.
From the M. Benois collection, Petrograd, 1914.

LEONARDO DA VINCI
1452–1519
Madonna and Child
(The Litta Madonna)
1490–91. Florentine School. Tempera on canvas (transferred from panel). 42 x 33 cm. Inv. No. 249

The *Litta Madonna* was painted by Leonardo during the Milan period of his career, when he worked at the court of Lodovico II Moro, Duke of Milan. The picture is a precursor of a new stage of development in Italian painting. The image of the Madonna is so elevated that we do not find here any elements of a genre scene, which makes this work so unlike the *Benois Madonna*. Due to the subtle chiaroscuro modelling, the body of the infant Christ appears to be three-dimensional, nearly tangible. He is gazing at something beyond the pictorial space, which creates an illusion of direct communication between the observer and the characters depicted. The *Litta Madonna* is the first example of so broad a generalization and typification for the sake of creating the sublime and ideal image. These artistic principles will underlie the period of High Renaissance ushered in by the works of Leonardo da Vinci in Central Italy. The preparatory drawing for the Madonna's head is in the Louvre, Paris.
From the collection of Duke A. Litta, Milan, 1865.

FRANCESCO MELZI
1493–1570
Flora
Ca. 1520. Milanese School. Oil on canvas (transferred from panel). 76 x 63 cm. Inv. No. 107

Francesco Melzi, one of the favourite pupils of Leonardo da Vinci, painstakingly studied and adopted the techniques of his teacher. The subject of the painting remains a vexed question up to now. A conjecture was put forward that the artist depicted here one of the noble ladies at the court of Francisc I. However, the ideal regular features of the character contradict to the conclusion that it is a portrait. It would rather seem that Melzi depicted Flora, the goddess of fertility and plants, an image eagerly borrowed by Renaissance artists from classical antiquity. Whatever was essential to his picture – the pose of the character, type of her face, style of her hairdo, dress, and even flowers – Melzi borrowed from various works by Leonardo. This work is also known as *Columbine* deriving its name from the flower called columbine (aquilegia), which the lady holds in her hand.
From the collection of King Willem II of the Netherlands, The Hague, 1850.

PERUGINO (PIETRO VANNUCCI)
Ca. 1450–1523
St Sebastian
Ca. 1495. Umbrian School. Tempera and oil on panel. 53.8 x 39.5 cm. Inv. No. 281

Perugino's art was devoid of dramatic tension as he was temperamentally unfit for depicting tragic subjects. Still he frequently reverted to the legend about St Sebastian, a Roman officer who was executed for his commitment to Christianity and died as a martyr. 15th-century painters most often depict him full length, tied to the pillar, his body pierced with nine arrows. Perugino showed only the upper part of the saint's figure, focusing on his face with agreeable regular features. The observer's attention is drawn to the suffering eyes of St Sebastian and the only mortal arrow that pierced his neck. The arrow bears the calligraphic signature of the painter.
Purchased from Marchesa Campanari, Rome, 1910; formerly in the collection of Princess Z. Volkonskaya.

LORENZO COSTA
Ca. 1460–1535
Portrait of a Woman
Early 1500s. Ferrarese School. Oil on canvas (transferred from panel). 57 x 44 cm. Inv. No. 5525

This is the earliest of the Renaissance painted portraits in the Hermitage collection. Like the majority of the Ferrara portraits, it is characterized by a strictly reserved composition and a somewhat dry painterly manner.
From the Princes Kochubei family collection, Petrograd, 1921; formerly in the collection of Grand Duchess Maria Nikolayevna, Florence.

RAPHAEL (RAFFAELLO SANTI)
1483–1520
Madonna and Child
(The Conestabile Madonna)
Late 1502–early 1503. Roman School. *Tempera on canvas (transferred from panel). 17.5 x 18 cm. Inv. No. 252*

Legend has it that the twenty-year-old artist had been commissioned the work by Duke Alfano di Diamante, who subsequently bequeathed it to his heirs. Early in the 18th century the family adopted the name of the Counts Conestabile della Staffa.
The master treats the traditional subject with the utmost simplicity: the young mother is represented with the Child in her arms, both of them are focusing their looks at the book, which would seem to be a purely formal element of the compositional scheme. During the transfer of the painting from panel to canvas it was discovered that the Child had originally had a pomegranate in his hand, not a book: the pomegranate was a symbol of the blood shed by Christ the martyr. Raphael has placed the main characters in the extreme foreground of the picture, while the background scene is presented as a spacious panorama, with carefully painted details, such as people, buildings and a boat floating on the lake.
From the Count Scipione Conestabile della Staffa collection, Perugia, 1870.

RAPHAEL (RAFFAELLO SANTI)
1483–1520
The Holy Family (Madonna
with the Beardless Joseph)
1506. Roman School. *Tempera and oil on canvas (transferred from panel). 72.5 x 56.5 cm. Inv. No. 91*

The picture could have been painted for Guidobaldo de Montefeltro, the captain of the Florentines, during Raphael's sojourn in Florence. It was there that the artist first acquainted himself with Leonardo da Vinci's art, which strongly influenced his later work. The painting had changed several owners before it found its way to the famous Crozat collection, which was purchased for the Hermitage Museum in 1772. The Madonna is shown here in the way typical of the master: she is an idealized and sublime representation of a real prototype; the Gospel characters seem to be devoid of all mundane and prosaic, epitomizing the best human qualities.
From the collection of L.-A. Crozat, Baron de Thiers, Paris, 1772.

**GIOVANNI BATTISTA CIMA
DA CONEGLIANO**
1459–1517
The Annunciation
1495. Venetian School. *Central panel
of the triptych. Oil on canvas (transferred
from panel). 136 x 107 cm. Inv. No. 256*

The *Annunciation* is the central panel
of the triptych that once graced the Church
of Santa Maria de' Crocicchieri in Venice.
According to contemporaries, the side wings
carried representations of St Sebastian
and St Mark (now in the National Gallery,
London). The master treats the Gospel subject as a genre scene and transferres it
into the setting of a palazzo in Venice:
a tall bed, which occupies almost half of
the room, stands under the canopy. The
huge window with wooden shutters and a
doubled marble column is a typical detail
of Venetian architecture. The Virgin is
engaged in reading a sacred book and has
not yet noticed the Archangel Gabriel, who
is quickly entering the room, with a white lily
in his hand (a symbol of the immaculacy of
the Virgin). The representation of the three-
dimensional space is so convincing that
the observer is ready to divert attention from
what is going on to believe in the optical
illusion created by the artist. The minor
details painted with the utmost accuracy,
as, for instance, a big fly on the leg of the
table, a bee seated on the sheet of paper
which bears the painter's signature, a book-
mark and a landscape seen from the window, are a feast to the eye.
From the Golitsyn Museum, Moscow, 1886.

**GIORGIONE
(GIORGIO DA CASTELFRANCO)**
Ca. 1478–1510
Judith
*Venetian School. Oil on canvas (transferred
from panel). 144 x 66.5 cm. Inv. No. 95*

Judith is one of the few original works by
Giorgione, who was the most mysterious
and romantic painter of the Venetian
School. According to the Bible, the fair
Judith rescued her native town from the
invasion of the Assyrians. Beautiful and
intelligent, she came to the enemy camp
and immediately won the heart of the
Assyrian general Olofernes. The general
made a splendid feast and invited Judith.
When she stayed alone with Olofernes, the
fearless woman beheaded the general
with his own sword and, having hidden his
head into a basket for provisions, returned
to her town. In the morning, when the
Assyrian camp was thrown into confusion,
the irregulars from the town could easily
put the enemy to flight.
*From the collection of L.-A. Crozat,
Baron de Thiers, Paris, 1772.*

**JACOPO PALMA VECCHIO
(JACOPO DI ANTONIO NIGRETTI)**
1480–1528
Portrait of a Young Man
1510s. Venetian School. *Oil on canvas.*
93.5 x 72 cm. Inv. No. 258

Portrait of a Young Man, painted by Palma
Vecchio in the spirit of Giorgione, is one of
the best achievements of Renaissance art.
The young man is represented in a three-
quarter turn. His right hand in a glove, which
is only half pulled on, is grasping the other
glove taken off his left hand. Gloves as well
as swords pointed to the high social standing of a person and played a significant
role in the 16th-century fashion. The colour
scheme of the painting matches well the
noble features of the character represented: it seems almost monochromatic, but
on closer examination reveals a greater
variety of greys and browns.
From the Golitsyn Museum, Moscow, 1886.

**DOMENICO CAPRIOLO
(DOMENICO DI BERNARDO)**
1494–1528
Portrait of a Man
1512. Venetian School. *Oil on canvas.*
117 x 85 cm. Inv. No. 21

There is no authentic information
concerning both the young man who
sat for the portrait and its author. The pre-
sumed author of the picture is Domenico
Capriolo. This attribution is supported
by the medallion placed in the bottom
right corner of the canvas which bears
a representation of a wild goat (*capriolo* in
Italian). The painter created a noble spiritual image, which is an epitome of the
best features of the Renaissance man and
which inspired 16th- and 17th-century
artists to repeat the picture many times.
*From the collection of L.-A. Crozat,
Baron de Thiers, Paris, 1772.*

LORENZO LOTTO
1480–1556
Portrait of a Married Couple
*Ca. 1523. Venetian School. Oil on canvas.
96 x 116 cm. Inv. No. 1447*

The Rijksprentenkabinet in Amsterdam
owns a preliminary drawing for the portrait.
As is typical of the artist, the numerous
minor details in this composition have an
allegorical meaning: the dog in the arms
of the lady symbolizes fidelity and the
squirrel, which curled up in a ball on the
table, is allusive of a popular legend about
the cruelty of the male squirrel chasing its
female companion out of the nest in lean
winters. The man, pointing to the squirrel,
holds a piece of paper with the Latin
inscription *Homo manqvam* ('Man never').

The married couple is sitting at the table,
covered with a Turkish carpet with a distinctive ornamentation, known as 'Lotto's
design', for such carpets often occur as a
decorative element in his works.
*Acquired between 1773 and 1785; formerly
in the G. and J. van Buren collection,
Antwerp.*

CORREGIO (ANTONIO ALLEGRI)
1489/94–1534
Portrait of a Woman
Ca. 1519. Parmesan School. Oil on canvas.
103 x 87.5 cm. Inv. No. 5555

A master of multifigured compositions on religious subjects, Correggio occasionally turned to the portrait genre as well. The enigmatic and intriguing image of a woman wearing a dark dress gave rise to a number of hypotheses as to who sat for the artist. The woman holds a cup bearing a Greek inscription, possibly a passage from Homer's *Odyssey* telling about a drink that grants oblivion of all calamities.
From the Yusupov Palace, Leningrad, 1925.

CESARE DA SESTO
1477–1523
The Holy Family with St Catherine
1515–20. Milanese School. *Oil on canvas (transferred from panel). 89 x 71 cm. Inv. No. 80*

By virtue of its lifelike and convincing images the picture was for a long time attributed to Leonardo da Vinci (Stendhal considered it the best piece ever created by the great master).
Acquired between 1753 and 1774.

ANDREA DEL SARTO (ANDREA D'AGNOLO)
1486–1531
Madonna and Child with St Catherine, St Elizabeth and St John the Baptist
1519. Florentine School. *Oil on canvas (transferred from panel). 102 x 80 cm. Inv. No. 62*

This top-class work that stands out for its artistic quality is signed by the author. He placed his name on the wheel, an attribute of St Catherine, in the right-hand part of the picture. The artist treats the well-known subject of *Sacra Conversazione* as a lively conversation between the three ladies holding their children on their lap, who have just sat down to take a rest. The infant Christ is laughing merrily on the lap of the Virgin Mary and St Elizabeth, carried away by the conversation, is absent-mindedly supporting little St John the Baptist. Beside her is St Catherine wearing a low decollete dress (the master represented as St Catherine his wife Lucrezia).
From the Empress Joséphine collection, Malmaison, 1814.

FRANCESCO PRIMATICCIO
1505–1570
The Holy Family with St Elizabeth
Between 1541 and 1543. Bolognese School. *Oil on blackboard. 43.5 x 31 cm. Inv. No. 128*

In 1531 Primaticcio and several other artists were summoned to France by François I (1494–1547) to work on the decoration of the Royal residence at Fontainebleau. The style evolved by these masters soon became widely known as the First School of Fontainebleau with Primaticcio as its most prominent representative. It is worthy of note that the artist has chosen the ruins of a Roman amphitheatre in Nimes in the South of France as a background for his painting.
From the collection of L.-A. Crozat, Baron de Thiers, Paris, 1772.

TITIAN (TIZIANO VECELLIO)
Ca. 1488–1576
Portrait of a Young Woman
Ca. 1536. Venetian School. Oil on canvas.
96 x 75 cm. Inv. No. 71

In the 1800s the picture was known as *Portrait of Titian's Beloved*, but later was tactfully renamed *Portrait of a Young Woman*. There is no trustworthy information about the name of the model, yet she attracted the painter's attention more than once. The same model sat for *Venus of Urbino* (Uffizi Gallery, Florence) and *A Fair* (Palazzo Pitti, Florence); she is also depicted in the *Portrait of a Woman in a Fur Coat* (Kunsthistorisches Museum, Vienna). Titian never endowed his female images with personal characteristics, he would rather focus on details and their texture. The softly iridescing velvet, the fluffy ostrich feathers, golden jewels and mat pearls set off beautifully the plump supple arms and tender face of the fair.

From the collection of L.-A. Crozat, Baron de Thiers, Paris, 1772.

TITIAN (TIZIANO VECELLIO)
Ca. 1488–1576
Mary Magdalene in Penitence
1560s. Venetian School. Oil on canvas (transferred from panel). 119 x 97 cm. Inv. No. 117

The theme of Mary Magdalene was one of the most favourite with Western European painters. According to the New Testament the fornicatrix Mary Magdalene was cured by Jesus of seven evil spirits, repented and became his follower. Titian represented Mary Magdalene as a young Venetian fair, who have brought a vessel of scented body ointment even to her hermitage (the vessel is one of the attributes of Mary Magdalene). Placed in front of her is the skull, symbolizing the frailty of the earthly existence. The inflamed reddened eyelids, the face slightly swollen with weeping, the eyes, turned to the skies – all combine to expresses a deep and sincere grief of the penitent sinner.

From the Barbarigo collection, Venice, 1850.

TITIAN (TIZIANO VECELLIO)
Ca. 1488–1576
St Sebastian
1570s. Venetian School. *Oil on canvas.*
210 x 115.5 cm. Inv. No. 191

St Sebastian is one of the last works by
the great master. The canvas is sewn
of three pieces, which were successively
added as the painter worked on the composition. At a closer look, the painting may
seem to be a confusion of scattered spots
and strokes, but if examined from a distance the illusion of chaos disappears.
The master would seem to tell us that
though one can destroy the body
the human spirit is indomitable.
From the Barbarigo collection, Venice, 1850.

TINTORETTO (JACOPO ROBUSTI)
1518–1594
Birth of St John the Baptist
1554–55. *Venetian School. Oil on canvas.*
181 x 266 cm. Inv. No. 17

The objects in the foreground of the picture are symbolical. An empty font signifies the purity of John's birth and his future role as the Baptist, a young rooster is the forerunner of the sun, just like John – the forerunner of Christ, a sneaking cat personifies the night or death, a copper basin on its right contains the burnt animal bones which served, as legend has it, to purify waters. This detail is allusive of the future second 'martyrdom' of John whose bones were publicly burnt after his death and the ashes scattered.
From the collection of L.-A. Crozat,
Baron de Thiers, Paris, 1772.

PAOLO VERONESE (PAOLO CALIARI)
1528–1588
The Adoration of the Magi
Early 1570s. *Venetian School. Oil on copper.*
45 x 34.5 cm. Inv. No. 159

The Adoration of the Magi might have been a preliminary version of the large composition painted for the Church of San Niccolo dei Frari, Venice. The Gospel scene is set among the ruins of a formerly magnificent palace, all the characters are dressed in 16th-century costumes, their shot silks, iridescent velvets and glimmering jewels enhance the decorative effect of the canvas.
From the collection of L.-A. Crozat,
Baron de Thiers, Paris, 1772.

PAOLO VERONESE (PAOLO CALIARI)
1528–1588
Pietà
Between 1576 and 1582. Venetian School.
Oil on canvas. 147 x 111.5 cm. Inv. No. 49

The Hermitage's Pietà ranks among the best works by the artist. Painted for the Venetian church of SS Giovanni e Paolo, the Hermitage canvas stands out from other works on the same subject thanks to its expressive and laconic composition. Second to none as a colourist, Veronese uses the contrasting warm and cold tones to heighten the dramatic effect of the scene. The Pietà was repeatedly engraved, among others, by Agostino Carracci in 1582.
From the collection of L.-A. Crozat, Baron de Thiers, Paris, 1772.

CARAVAGGIO (MICHELANGELO MERISI DA CARAVAGGIO)
1573–1610
The Lute-Player
Ca. 1595. Roman School. Oil on canvas.
94 x 119 cm. Inv. No. 45

Caravaggio left an indelible mark on the subsequent development of art; he was the father of a realistic trend in 17th-century painting known as Caravaggism. In his early canvases he used to arrange half-length figures closer to the viewer against a neutral background. His strong chiaroscuro was also to become the main painting technique of his followers. During his short life the artist painted a large number of magnificent canvases on religious themes and subjects from classical mythology as well as genre scenes. The *Lute-Player* was painted for Cardinal Francesco del Monte, the artist's patron. Striving to create a mirror image of nature, Caravaggio has reproduced the notation of a popular madrigal with a documentary precision.
From the Giustiniani collection, Paris, 1808.

ANNIBALE CARRACCI
1560–1609
Rest on the Flight into Egypt
Ca. 1604. Bolognese School.
Oil on canvas. Diameter 82.5 cm.
Inv. No. 138

Together with his brothers Lodovico and Agostino, Annibale Carracci founded in the 1580s an Academy in Bologna to teach painting and to revive the canons of classical art and the High Renaissance, based on the idealistic concept of the beautiful. In the opinion of contemporaries Annibale was by far the greatest of the three. He had a large studio in Rome with many pupils and followers.
From the collection of L.-A. Crozat, Baron de Thiers, Paris, 1772.

ANNIBALE CARRACCI
1560–1609
The Three Maries at the Sepulcre
1597–98. Bolognese School. *Oil on canvas.*
121 x 145.5 cm. Inv. No. 92

The canvas was painted for the Bolognese antiquarian Pasqualini. Carracci has depicted the moment when the three Maries came to Christ's tomb to anoint His body with myrrh, but to their great surprise discovered that the tomb was empty. An angel sitting on the tomb announced to the women standing in awe before him that Christ had arisen.

From the Coesvelt collection, London, 1836.

BERNARDO STROZZI (IL PRETE GENOVESE)
1581–1644
The Healing of Tobit
Ca. 1635. Genoese School. Oil on canvas.
158 x 223.5 cm. Inv. No. 16

The subject is based on the scriptural story of Tobit and his son Tobias. Having become blind and sunk into poverty, Tobit sent his son to the city of Ragi in Media to collect certain money due to him. Tobias was accompanied by the Archangel Raphael, who introduced himself to the young man as Asariah. On his way to Media Tobias caught a fish and, following the Archangel's advice, took its heart, liver and gall. When they returned home, Tobias healed his father of his blindness by smearing the gall on his eyes. The archangel would not accept the lavish gifts offered to him by the old man in reward for his help and, having urged them to thank God, he disappeared. Strozzi turned to this subject on more than one occasion. This canvas shows the moment of the miraculous healing of Tobit.

From the collection of L.-A. Crozat, Baron de Thiers, Paris, 1772.

SALVATOR ROSA
1615–1673
The Prodigal Son
Neapolitan School. *Oil on canvas
(transferred from panel). 253 x 201 cm.*
Inv. No. 34

Salvator Rosa, painter, engraver, poet,
actor and musician, was one of the most
prominent artists of the 17th century.
He painted religious and mythological
subjects, portraits, landscape and battle
scenes. His works were so popular that at
one time they caused the appearance
of numerous imitations and even fakes.
The Prodigal Son was executed for Agostino
Corregio, evidently during the artist's stay
in Florence in 1639–49. It is one of the few
surviving works by Salvator Rosa with the
life-size figures. *The Prodigal Son* was
greatly admired in the 18th century and
many engravings were made from it.
*From the R. Walpole collection,
Houghton Hall, England, 1779.*

DOMENICHINO (DOMENICO ZAMPIERI)
1581–1641
The Assumption of the Magdalene
Ca. 1620. Bolognese School. Oil on canvas.
129 x 110 cm. Inv. No. 113

Domenichino experienced a strong
influence of Raphael, but he was as well
much influenced by the Carracci brothers,
the founders of the Academy in Bologna.

Exemplifying the so-called Classicist Baroque,
the artist's work had an immense impact on
Poussin. Incredibly popular in the heyday of
his career, from which the *Assumption of
the Magdalene* dates, Domenichino then
sank into oblivion to be rediscovered only
in the 20th century.
From the collection of L.-A. Crozat,
Baron de Thiers, Paris, 1772.

**GUERCINO (GIOVANNI FRANCESCO
BARBIERI)**
1591–1666
The Assumption of the Madonna
1623. Bolognese School. Oil on canvas.
307 x 332 cm. Inv. No. 64

Guercino was influenced by Caravaggio
and Guido Reni, hence the pathetics of his
characters and accentuated
monumentality of his compositions. *The
Assumption of the Madonna* was executed
for Marquis Alessandro Tanari in Bologna.
From the Tanari collection, Bologna, 1843.

GIOVANNI BATTISTA TIEPOLO
1696–1770
**Maecenas Presenting the Liberal
Arts to the Roman Emperor Augustus**
*Ca. 1745. Venetian School. Oil on canvas.
69.5 x 89 cm. Inv. No. 4*

The picture was painted for Count Francesco
Algarotti in Venice in 1743. The artist extols
here the Polish King Augustus III as a
patron of the arts. The main characters
represented by Tiepolo are real historical
persons. Gaius Julius Caesar Octavianus
(from 27 B.C. the Roman Emperor Augustus)
was a grandnephew of Gaius Julius Caesar
and his successor to the throne. He put an
end to the civil wars which began after
Caesar's death. Maecenas (Gaius Cilnius),
whose name has become a common noun
to denote patrons of the arts, was a person
in attendance to Emperor Augustus and was
often entrusted diplomatic and political
missions. He patronized a group of authors,
among them the famous Latin poets Horace
and Virgil. In Tiepolo's picture Augustus sits
upon the throne flanked by the statues of
Apollo and Minerva. Maecenas, standing
left of him, presents the arts to the Emperor.
The three kneeling female figures at the
base of the throne embody Painting,
Sculpture and Architecture, and the blind
Homer personifies Poetry.
*From the collection of Count H. Brühl,
Dresden, 1769.*

FRANCESCO GUARDI
1712–1793
View of a Square with a Palace
*1775–80. Venetian School. Oil on canvas
(transferred from panel). 27 x 23 cm.
Inv. No. 262*

In his small-size townscapes, or *vedutas*,
Guardi managed to create an inimitable
romantic image of Venice. Not infrequently
the artist solved purely pictorial tasks at
the cost of topographical precision. In all
probability, the *View of a Square with a
Palace* is a *capriccio*, a free fantasy on
the Venetian theme, rather than a concrete location in the city. Frequently
repeated by Guardi, the motif of a street
or a square viewed from under an arch
makes it possible to achieve the most picturesque effect: compared to the foreground immersed in darkness, the colours
of a sunny day appear especially tender
and translucent.
*From the Kostromitinova collection,
St Petersburg, 1895.*

ALESSANDRO MAGNASCO
1667–1749
The Bandits' Bivouac
1710s. Genoese School. *Oil on canvas.*
112 x 162 cm. Inv. No. 4036

An exponent of Mannerism, Magnasco turned to life of various strata of society in search of new subjects. However, the figures of his characters set in strained or distorted poses would often seem to be incorporeal phantoms. *The Bandits'*

Bivouac is one of a series of four pictures painted by Magnasco in the 1710s. The architectural backgrounds for the series were executed by Clemente Spera, with whom Magnasco collaborated for many years. All the four paintings were acquired by the painter Georg Christoph Grooth in 1745 in Prague or Bohemia for the Russian Empress Yelizaveta Petrovna.
From the Museum of the Academy of Arts, Petrograd, 1922; formerly in the Count I. Shuvalov collection.

FRANCESCO GUARDI
1712–1793
Landscape
Ca. 1780. Venetian School. Oil on canvas.
120 x 156 cm. Inv. No. 4305

Full of a tempestuous movement and evidently owing its creation to the artist's imagination rather than a real impression,

this landscape may be regarded as a *capriccio*, the Guardi's favourite genre. The contrasting play of deep brownish shadows and silvery glimmering light, together with the bizarrely bent trees, impart a fantastic tinge to the depiction which is reminiscent of the landscapes of Marco Ricci.
From the Gatchina Palace, 1928.

GIOVANNI BATTISTA TIEPOLO
1696–1770
Triumph of the Commander
Ca. 1725. Venetian School. Oil on canvas.
550 x 322 cm. Inv. No. 7475

The picture is one of Tiepolo's works on subjects from Roman history, which were commissioned to the artist by the brothers
Dolfino for their palace in Venice. Tiepolo
might have depicted here the triumph of
the commander Manius Curius Dentatus.

In 275 B.C., he inflicted a crushing defeat
to Pyrrhus's army mounted on white battle
elephants. This version is supported by an
extant fragment of the inscription which
reads "...*set out with Pyrrhus's elephants...
grateful Rome*". The huge canvas is notable
for its decorative effects and is painted with
great freedom typical of Tiepolo.
*From the Museum of the Baron A. Stieglitz
School of Technical Design, Leningrad,
1934; acquired by A. Polovtsov; formerly
in the Dolfino collection, Venice.*

BERNARDO BELLOTTO
1720–1780
The New Market Place in Dresden
1747. Venetian School. *Oil on canvas.*
134.5 x 236.5 cm. Inv. No. 204

The picture belongs to a large series
of canvases featuring views in Dresden
and Pirna which was executed by Bellotto
between 1747 and 1755 for Count Heinrich
Brühl, minister of the Elector of Saxony and
King of Poland Augustus III. The picture
was purchased in 1769, with the collection
of Count Brühl in Dresden. Bernardo Bellotto,
the nephew and pupil of Antonio Canale,
worked in Venice, Munich and Dresden.
From 1768 to the end of his life he lived in
Warsaw where he was Court Painter to
Stanislas August Poniatowski.
From the collection of Count H. Brühl,
Dresden, 1769.

CANALETTO (ANTONIO CANALE)
1697–1768
**The Reception of the French
Ambassador in Venice**
1720s. Venetian School. *Oil on canvas.*
181 x 259.5 cm. Inv. No. 175

The scene is depicted against the back-
ground of the famous Doge's Palace in
Venice. The ceremonial welcome of the
French Ambassador Jacques Vincent
Languet took place on November 4, 1726.
Antonio Canale used this occasion to
portray the splendid centre of Venice,
with the Doge's Palace looking onto
Canale Grande. The Hermitage picture
is a companion piece to the canvas
*The Departure of the Doge for the Festival
of the Bethrothal of Venice and the Adriatic*
which is kept in the Pushkin Museum of Fine
Arts, Moscow.
Acquired between 1766 and 1768.

SCULPTURE. 15th–18th CENTURIES

ANTONIO ROSSELINO
1427–1479
Madonna and Child
1460s. Florentine School. *Marble. 67 x 54 cm.*
Inv. No. H.ск. 517

Various versions of this composition were
unusually popular in Florence in the second
half of the 15th century. Skilfully using the
planes and the play of light and shade, the
sculptor has managed to achieve an illusion
of depth. A special picturesque softness
inherent in this image of Madonna and Child
is also characteristic of other reliefs by
Rosselino.
*Gift of A. Zhuravlev, Petrograd, 1915; formerly
in the Bibikovs collection, St Petersburg.*

MICHELANGELO
(MICHELANGELO BUONARROTI)
1475–1564
The Crouching Boy
*Ca. 1530–34. Florentine School. Marble.
Height 54 cm. Inv. No. H.ск. 154*

The sculpture, which is the only work by
Michelangelo in Russia, was created as
part of the decor of the Medici family
mausoleum in the sacristy of St Lorenzo,
Florence. One of the preparatory sketches
for the chapel show two figures similar to
the *Crouching Boy* which should have

been placed in the bays in profile to the
spectator. The Hermitage sculpture might
have been integrated into the overall
compositional scheme of the chapel.
The symbolism of the statue has not been
clarified yet: some scholars would regard
it as an image of the soul in its prenatal
state, others would rather interpret it as an
embodiment of the genius of death.
The figure created by Michelangelo is
a tragic image of man overcome by
some hostile force.
*From the collection of G. Lyde Browne,
Wimbledon, 1785.*

GIUSEPPE MAZZUOLA
1644–1725
The Death of Adonis
1709. Marble. Height 193 cm.
Inv. No. H.ск. 1113

Giuseppe Mazzuola, one of the talented
followers of Lorenzo Bernini, has chosen as
the subject for his composition the most
dramatic scene from the antique myth of
Adonis. The sculptor captures the moment
when the youth, admired by the goddess
Venus for his striking beauty, is attacked
by a ferocious wild boar during the hunt.
Doing justice to the masterful compositional scheme and the superb finishing of the
details, one, nevertheless, has to admit
that the image of Adonis is treated rather
superficially. His head, thrown back, looks
somewhat theatrical, and the mask of suffering on his face is too conventional.
From the State Museum Reserve, 1923;
formerly in the Musin-Pushkins collection,
Petrograd.

FIRST FLOOR

● BEGINNING
OF THE FIRST-FLOOR
EXHIBITION

TWELVE-COLUMN HALL
▲

RAPHAEL LOGGIAS

243

▼
ITALIAN ART

WESTERN EUROPEAN ARMS AND ARMOUR.
15th–17th CENTURIES

The Knights Hall (room 243) has an extensive display of Western European arms and armour from the 15th to 17th century, including cold steel and fire-arms, tournament arms and sporting guns. The exhibition features items from the enormously rich and significant imperial collection which began to take shape as early as 1810. In 1885 it was transferred from the Arsenal in Tsarskoye Selo to the Hermitage. Today the Hermitage collection, boasting some 15,000 items is one of the largest in Russia. It is reputed for the high artistic merit of the works crafted by renowned European gunsmiths, armourers, carvers, chasers and jewellers.

Full Gothic armour

1490s. By L. Helmschmidt. Germany, Augsburg.
Steel. Inv. No. 3.O. 3002

Augsburg was one of the leading German centres of armour and cold steel production. This armour belongs to the Gothic type which was widespread in the second half of the 15th century. It consists of a sallet (a visored helmet, but without a chinpiece that was attached separately to the breast-piece), a breast-cum-belly piece and pieces protecting hips, back, arms and legs; the legs have peaked toes preventing the feet from slipping out of stirrups during the battle. The armour covered almost the whole body of a knight with movable plates (from 60 to 160 pieces).
From the Arsenal in Tsarskoye Selo, 1885.

Dagger

Second half, 16th century. Italy, Venice (?).
Steel, gold and silver notching, agate.
Length 46 cm. Inv. No. 3.O. 2752

The dagger is a work by an unknown Italian master of the 16th century. At one time it was housed in the Kunstkammer. The dagger is notable for its superb decor and was for a long time ascribed to the great Benvenuto Cellini (1500–1571). Its handle is made of agate; depicted in high relief on its knob is the *Judgement of Paris*; on the sheath is the *Rape of Helen* and a battle scene. The blade, in its upper part, is decorated with an arabesque ornament of gold and silver against a dark blued background. Some art historians believe that the dagger was acquired by Peter I during his journey to Western Europe.
From the Arsenal in Tsarskoye Selo, 1885; formerly in the Kunstkammer.

Ceremonial shield (buckler)

Mid-16th century. By L. Piccinino. Italy, Milan. *Steel, gold and silver notching. Diameter 57.2 cm. Inv. No. 3.O. 94*

This round shield (buckler) comes from the Milanese workshop where the renowned Italian gunsmith Lucio Piccinino worked in the mid-16th century. Ceremonial arms made by Milanese masters are characterized by a virtuoso combination of chasing, blueing and gold notching.
From the Arsenal in Tsarskoye Selo, 1885.

Tournament half-armour

1590. By A. Peffenhauser. Germany, Augsburg. *Steel, blued and gilt. Inv. No. 3.O. 3932*

This half-armour is one of the twelve identical armours made by the renowned gunsmith Anton Peffenhauser (ca. 1525–1603) for Christian I, Elector of Saxony. It is made of violet-blued steel and decorated with a large vegetable ornament executed by means of acid etching and gilding.
From the Arsenal in Tsarskoye Selo, 1885.

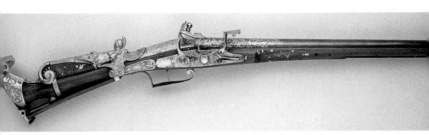

Sporting gun

Ca. 1605–10. By M. Le Bourguais. France, Normandy. *Steel, gold and silver notching, brass, gilt. Length 141 cm. Inv. No. 3.O. 94*

With the appearance of hand fire-arms the gun hunt became a favourite pastime of European sovereigns, in which they indulged on their hunting grounds. According to a well-substantiated opinion, this richly decorated sporting gun was presented to Henri IV, the first Bourbon King of France, by the citizens of Lizieux, and then, for a long time, it was kept in the famous collection of Louis XIII (1610–1643).
From the Arsenal in Tsarskoye Selo, 1885.

FIRST FLOOR

BEGINNING
OF THE FIRST-FLOOR
EXHIBITION

NETHERLANDISH, FLEMISH AND DUTCH PAINTING

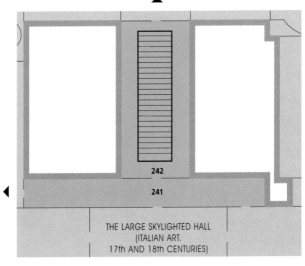

242

241

KNIGHTS HALL
(WESTERN EUROPEAN ARMS AND ARMOUR.
15th–17th CENTURIES)

THE LARGE SKYLIGHTED HALL
(ITALIAN ART.
17th AND 18th CENTURIES)

WESTERN EUROPEAN SCULPTURE. 18th–19th CENTURIES
In the Gallery of the History of Ancient Painting and the Gallery of the Nicholas Staircase

The Hermitage collection of Western European sculpture is for the most part scattered around various rooms of the museum. Exception has been made for the sculpture of the second half of the 18th and the first half of the 19th century, which is on display in the upper gallery of the Nicholas Staircase (the Main Staircase leading to the rooms of the New Hermitage from the entrance in Millionnaya Street), as well as in the Gallery of the History of Ancient Painting which was conceived as an ante-room to the Picture Gallery of the New Hermitage. The walls of the room are adorned with pictures by Georg Hiltensperger (Munich, Germany) which illustrate the legendary history of the rise and development of painting (hence the name of the room). The interior made to the design of Leo von Klenze, serve as an imposing setting for works by Antonio Canova, Bertel Thorvaldsen, Rudolph Schadow, Lorenzo Bartolini and other Neo-classical sculptors.

ANTONIO CANOVA
1757–1822
Cupid and Psyche
1796. Italy. *Marble. Height 137 cm,
length 172 cm. Inv. No. H.ск. 1252*

The Hermitage collection includes
fifteen works by Canova. Like the
Dane Bertel Thorvaldsen, Canova
was the most renowned representative
of the so-called Roman School which
came into being in the early 19th century. This sculptural group of Cupid and
Psyche is one of his most fascinating works.
It depicts the happy ending of a story
told by Apuleus in his *Metamorphoses,
or Golden Ass,* when Cupid with
his kiss awakens his beloved.
The movement of the figures,
the harmony of the
silhouettes, the ele-
gance and mastery
of execution
all bear an
affinity
with 18th-
century
works.
*From the
Yusupov Palace,
Leningrad, 1926.*

ANTONIO CANOVA
1757–1822
The Three Graces
1813. Italy. *Marble. Height 182 cm.
Inv. No. H.ск. 506*

The sculptural group *The Three Graces*
was commissioned by the French Empress
Joséphine, the first wife of Napoleon Bonaparte, but was not finished by the time
of her death. It was Eugène Beauharnais,
Joséphine's son, who later bought the
work from the sculptor.
*From the collection of Duke Nicholas
of Leuchtenberg, St Petersburg, 1901.*

ANTONIO CANOVA
1757–1822
Cupid and Psyche
1802. Italy. Height 148 cm. Inv. No. Н.ск. 17

Canova used the *Cupid and Psyche* theme several times, creating horizontal and vertical compositions on this subject. In 1789 he carved a standing Psyche, and then, after years of work, produced a two-figure vertical composition. The first vertical marble version of *Cupid and Psyche* was made after a plaster-of-Paris in 1797. In 1802 he made another copy with slight variations in the drapery and pedestal. This work found its way to Empress Joséphine's collection and, later, as part of the Malmaison collection, was bought by Alexander I to adorn the Winter Palace.

From the Empress Joséphine collection, Malmaison, 1814.

BERTEL (ALBERT) THORVALDSEN
1768/70–1844
Shepherd
After 1817. Denmark. Marble. Height 142 cm.
Inv. No. Н.ск. 508

Thorvaldsen, the first Danish sculptor of international stature, is one of the best representatives of the Neo-classical school of sculpture on a par with Canova. A graduate of the Royal Academy in Copenhagen, he won a scholarship to Italy, where he spent most of his life. Thorvaldsen's studio in Rome became a centre of attraction for sculptors from all over the world. His oeuvre was dominated by mythological and religious subjects. The *Shepherd* is one of his best creations and also one of his few genre works. The sculpture is marked by an elegant silhouette and fine finish of marble.
Donated by A. Polovtsov, St Petersburg, 1910.

LORENZO BARTOLINI
1770–1850
Nymph Stung by a Scorpio
1846. Italy. *Marble. Height 90 cm,
length 130 cm. Inv. No. Н.ск. 115*

Bartolini first carved the *Nymph Stung by
a Scorpio* in 1833–44 for Count Charles
de Beauvaux. The next year, by the sculptor's permission, it was exhibited at the
Paris Salon and was a great success.
In December, 1845, Emperor Nicholas I.
while in Florence, visited Bartolini's studio
and commissioned him to make a copy
of this statue in marble. By the time of
the sculptor's death, however, the statue
remained unfinished, so Giovanni Dupré
(1817–1882), a Florentine master, was
asked to complete it. The *Nymph Stung
by a Scorpio* is one of Bartolini's best
works. Instead of the superficial imitation
of antique prototypes, Bartolini was seeking
inspiration in life. It's worth noting how
skillfully the master has conveyed the
girl's spontaneous gesture and the slight
grimace of pain on her face.
From G. Dupré, before 1852.

**The exhibition of Western European
sculpture in the upper gallery
of the Nicholas Staircase
of the New Hermitage**

The Neo-classical style in its academic
forms was widely spread in the 19th century,
especially in sculpture intended to adorn
public buildings. This style seems to be
dry due to the purely formal imitation
of antique models and lack of emotion.
Examples of academic sculpture, exhibited in the upper gallery of the Nicholas
Staircase, are set off by the grey granite
predominant in the staircase interior
decoration.

FIRST FLOOR

● BEGINNING
OF THE FIRST-FLOOR
EXHIBITION

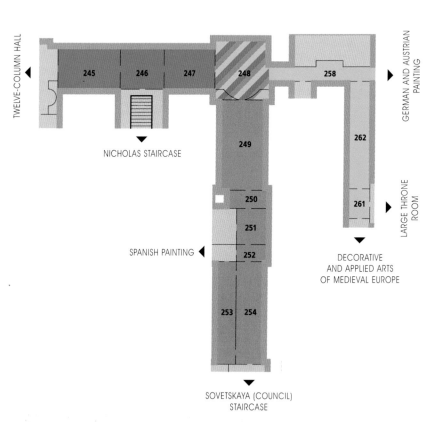

TWELVE-COLUMN HALL ◄

245 246 247 248 258

GERMAN AND AUSTRIAN PAINTING ►

NICHOLAS STAIRCASE ▼

249

262

250
251
252
253 254

261

SPANISH PAINTING ◄

LARGE THRONE ROOM ►

DECORATIVE
AND APPLIED ARTS
OF MEDIEVAL EUROPE ▼

SOVETSKAYA (COUNCIL)
STAIRCASE ▼

NETHERLANDISH PAINTING

FLEMISH PAINTING

DUTCH PAINTING

NETHERLANDISH, FLEMISH AND DUTCH PAINTING.
15th–17th CENTURIES

The Netherlandish, Flemish and Dutch Schools of painting, formed within one state, gave the world such names as Robert Campin, Roger van der Weyden, Lucas van Leyden, Peter Paul Rubens, Anthony van Dyck and Rembrandt. The revolution of 1566–1609 resulted in the division of the Netherlands and formation of the United Provinces of the Netherlands, or the Dutch Republic (after the name of one of the provinces), which freed itself from Spanish rule. As a result of the political split, on the basis of Netherlandish artistic traditions two independent schools of painting took shape in the 17th century. The Hermitage collection of Dutch and Flemish painting, comprising more than 1,000 canvases, is considered one of the best in the world and is unique in its artistic significance.

NETHERLANDISH PAINTING.
15th–17th CENTURIES
(rooms 248, 258, 261, 262)

ROBERT CAMPIN (MASTER OF FLÉMALLE)
Ca. 1380–1444
The Trinity
Madonna and Child
by the Fireplace
1430s. Diptych. Oil on panel. 34.3 x 24.5 cm
(each wing). Inv Nos. 442, 443

These two works by Robert Campin now
mounted in one frame once made a diptych (hinged icon of two parts). The left
wing of the diptych, *The Trinity*, depicts the
dead body of Christ supported by
God the Father, while the right wing,
Madonna and Child by the Fireplace,
is devoted to the childhood of Christ.
The treatment of the figures represented
on the left wing attest to the strong influence of Gothic sculpture on the artist.
Religious thought of the 15th century
engendered attraction towards symbolism,
that is why all the details of the composition are imbued with a symbolic meaning.
The pelican figure on the right elbow-rest
of the armchair embodied the Christian
sacrament of the Holy Communion
(Eucharist). The carved sculpture of a
lioness on the left elbow-rest was reminiscent of the legend telling that the still-born

lion cubs are brought back to life by the
lion's roar on the third day, which symbolized the Resurrection of Christ by God the
Father. The *Madonna and Child* is less traditional and conventional. Campin transferred the Gospel scene into the setting
of a typical 15th-century Netherlandish
house. The Madonna is about to swaddle
Her baby and is warming her palm by the
fire not to disturb the Child with the touch
of her cold hand. The interior is reproduced with an astonishing care for detail.
Many of the objects depicted have hidden
meaning in keeping with the tradition, e.g.
the wash-basin, jug, and white towel symbolize the immaculacy of the Madonna.
Robert Campin successfully used the new
oil painting technique that had been first
introduced by the Netherlandish artist
Jan van Eyck. This allowed him to achieve
an amazing vibrancy and light saturation
of the colours. The tempera technique
mostly used at that time made practically
impossible the rendering of the play of
light in the folds of the garments or the
shine of metal objects as was masterfully
done by Robert Campin.
*Acquired in 1845 by will of D. Tatishchev,
St Petersburg.*

ROGER VAN DER WEYDEN (ROGIER DE LA PASTURE)
Ca. 1400–1464
St Luke Drawing a Portrait of the Virgin
Oil on canvas (transferred from panel).
102.5 x 108.5 cm. Inv. No. 419

Roger van der Weyden was the most talented student of Campin. The subject of the painting is inspired by the Christian legend of Greek derivation, whose origins may be traced to the 6th century. The legend narrates about Christ's disciple, the Evangelist Luke, who was the first to create a portrait of the Virgin. St Luke was considered to be the patron of painters; in the 15th–17th centuries, artists' guilds were often named in his honour. That is why compositions on the same subject were as a rule intended for professional associations of artists.
We know several versions of the composition that are now housed in the Museum of Fine Arts, Boston, Alte Pinakothek, Munich, and the Municipal Fine Arts Museum, Brugge. The figures of St Luke and the Virgin, elongated and angular, are reminiscent of Gothic sculpture. The attire worn by St Luke was typical of the 14th-century doctors: tradition has it that among other sciences he was studying medicine. Behind his back there is a cell where the bull is to be found. The bull's representation always accompanies the image of St Luke. The realistically depicted facial features of St Luke would suggest that it is a self-portrait of Roger

van der Weyden. The painter succeeded in rendering the mood of the saint, who is overwhelmed with the feeling of reverence, and, at the same time, concentrated. Emotional depth of the painting was strikingly new for the Netherlandish painting of that period. Placed in the middle ground are the figures of the Virgin Mary's parents – Joachim and Anna. In the central background the painter depicted a landscape with a river meandering toward the distant horizon. Upon the banks of the river we see town quarters painted with such accuracy that subsequent researchers could identify them as the buildings of old Brussels. Netherlandish artists mastered the skills of rendering perspective much later than the Italians. They tried to achieve spatial depth by means of abrupt foreshortening of the human figures. Until 1813, the picture had been housed in a Spanish monastery. It was subsequently sawn into two parts. In 1850, the right part with a representation of St Luke was purchased at the sale of the collection of King Willem II of the Netherlands in The Hague as an independent work. The left part with the Virgin was for a long time kept in the collection of Baron de Beurnonville in Paris and only in 1884 was purchased from the art dealer A. Baer in St Petersburg. Already in the Hermitage both parts of the picture were transferred onto canvas and joined together.
Right part – from the collection of King Willem II of the Netherlands, The Hague, 1850; left part – acquired in 1884.

JAN PROVOST
Ca. 1465–1529
The Virgin Mary in Glory
1524. Oil on canvas (transferred from panel).
203 x 151 cm. Inv. No. 417

One of the best pictures by Provost, *The Virgin Mary in Glory* is a typical altarpiece. It was executed for the Church of St Donatian in Brugge. The depth of religious feeling is conveyed by depicting the Virgin solemn and austere, her figure devoid of any movement. Surrounded by the radiant halo, She is standing on the crescent moon amidst the clouds with the Child in Her arms. On either side of Her, angels are hovering, playing the viola and the mandoline. The composition is crowned with the image of God the Father and the Holy Ghost depicted in the form of a dove. While the upper part of the com-

position is conceived in the medieval tradition the lower part is treated in keeping with new trends of the period. The characters here represented – King David, playing the harp, the Roman Emperor Augustus holding a crown in one hand and a sceptre in the other, the two nice-looking sibyls, who placed the hands upon their shoulders, the Persian Sibyl and two prophets – all of them are wearing 16th-century costumes. Representations of sibyls, characters of Greek mythology, in the works by Netherlandish artists was a new feature which revealed their growing interest in classical antiquity. In the 1560s, the painting was bricked up in the wall of the church to protect it from iconoclasts. It was discovered in 1795, during the demolishion of the church by the French. *From the collection of King Willem II of the Netherlands, The Hague, 1850.*

JEAN BELLEGAMBE
Ca. 1470–ca. 1534
The Annunciation
Triptych. Oil on canvas (transferred from
panel). 109.5 x 80 cm (central part),
103 x 33 cm (each wing). Inv. No. 5574

The donor Guillaume of Brussels (d. 1532),
who is depicted in the centre of the triptych
reverently kneeling at the feet of the Virgin
Mary, was a prominent clergyman and
a patron of the arts. He was also Abbot of
two monasteries – the Monastery of St Amand
near Valenciennes and the Monastery of
St Trudo not far from Douai. This explains why
we find these particular saints depicted on
the wings of the triptych (St Amand on the

right wing and St Trudo on the left one).
Shown in the middle ground of the right wing
are St Guillaume, Archbishop of Bourges,
and St Benedict, on the left wing we see
St Bernard and St Guillaume of Aquitaine.
When the paint film was transferred onto
canvas the pictures on the reverse of the
wings were transferred onto separate canvases. That is why the triptych is accompanied with two more paintings – *The Miracle
of Lactation* and *St Bernard*. It is known that
the paint film was transferred onto canvas
by the Hermitage restorers in 1871, hence
the work had found its way to Russia earlier.
*From the Museum of the Society
for the Encouragement of the Arts,
Petrograd, 1919.*

JAN GOSSAERT (MABUSE)
Ca. 1478–1532
The Descent from the Cross
*Central part of a triptych. Oil on canvas
(transferred from panel). 141 x 106.5 cm.
Inv. No. 413*

The painter called Mabuse after the name
of his native town acted as one of the
founders of Romanism after his trip to Italy.
In his *Descent from the Cross* he made
an attempt to build up a monumental composition with numerous figures based on
the principles of Renaissance art. The well-
balanced composition, with the cross
placed in its centre, is borrowed by the artist
from the engravings of the school of Andrea
Mantegna, while the group depicting the
three Maries in the left foreground repeats
the engraving by Marcantonio Raimondi.
The Descent from the Cross was the central
part of a triptych which was painted for the
capella of the Church of St Augustin in
Brugge. From 1837 to 1850 it was to be
found in the collection of King Willem II of
the Netherlands. The triptych had been
divided into parts during the sale of the
King's collection. The central part found its
way to the Hermitage and the wings were
brought to America. It is generally recognized that the representation of St John is
a portrait of Don Pedro de Salamanca,
who commissioned the altarpiece to Jan
Gossaert, while St Peter is believed to be
the self-portrait of the artist.
*From the collection of King Willem II
of the Netherlands, The Hague, 1850.*

LUCAS VAN LEYDEN
1489/94–1533
The Healing of the Blind Man of Jericho
*1531. Triptych. Oil on canvas (transferred
from panel). 115.7 x 150.3 cm (central part),
89 x 35.5 cm (each wing). Inv. No. 407*

Lucas van Leyden is one of the most
important Netherlandish artists of the first
half of the 16th century. The triptych
The Healing of the Blind Man of Jericho is
one of the best works by Lucas van Leyden
and the only painting by the master in the
Hermitage. This work, finished not long
before the master's death, epitomizes the
achievements of his artistic career. The
subject of the painting is borrowed from
the Gospels and is based on the legend
about the healing of the blind man by
Jesus near the city of Jericho. The triptych
was not conceived as an altarpiece, it
might have been executed for the Leyden
hospital. The painter has introduced into
the picture on religious subject some elements of the genre scene. He used here
the compositional principles of Italian
painting, placing two groups of people,
witnesses of the miracle, on either side
of the compositional focus – the figures of
Jesus and the blind man guided by the boy.
Depicted on the wings are the warrior and
the young woman proudly demonstrating
the coats of arms of the clients – Jacob
Floriszon van Monfort and his wife, Dirkgen
van Lindenburch, the daughter of the
Amsterdam burgher Dirck Boelens. The heralds
represented on the reverse of the wings were
added to the main composition later.
*From the collection of L.-A. Crozat,
Baron de Thiers, Paris, 1772.*

MASTER OF THE FEMALE HALF-LENGTHS
Active in the first half of the 16th century
Virgin and Child
Oil on panel. 53 x 42.4 cm. Inv. No. 4090

The identity of this remarkable master has
not been established yet. The artist possibly
lived in Antwerp, where he must have
headed a large workshop. His style shares
some common features with the output
of the Bruges School, especially with the
works by Ambrosius Benson and Adriaen
Isenbrandt. The *Virgin and Child*, notable
for its superb workmanship, must have
been produced without any aid of the
artist's apprentices, which is supported
by photographs in infrared light.
From the Stroganov Palace, Petrograd, 1922.

JAN SANDERS VAN HEMESSEN
Ca. 1504–after 1574
St Jerome in Penitence
1543. Oil on panel. 102 x 83.5 cm.
Inv. No. 451

Jan Sanders van Hemessen was admired
as a master of compositions with large-
scale figures as well as of the portrait.
St Jerome, one of the Fathers of the Church,
was venerated as a patron of scholars.
This saint was frequently depicted by 16th-
century Netherlandish artists, who mostly
favoured two subjects with him. They would
represent St Jerome contemplating death

in his cell or St Jerome atoning for his sins
with prayer in the wilderness. Hemessen
depicted the penitent St Jerome in the
wilderness. The saint's large nude figure
of monumental proportions is placed in
the foreground and stands sharply out on
the background of the rock. The unnatural-
ly exaggerated muscles are well modelled
with chiaroscuro. Choosing such a complicated foreshortening for the figure the
master revealed his good knowledge of
anatomy. The achievements of the painter
in the field of realism had a great significance for the subsequent evolution of
Netherlandish painting. The present work
is not the only one painted by Hemessen
on the subject. A variant very close to
the Hermitage picture dated 1545 is kept
in Hampton Court Palace, England.
*Purchased from Counsellor
D. Predtechensky, St Petersburg, 1895.*

MARINUS VAN REYMERSWAELE
Ca. 1490–after 1567
Tax-collectors (?)
*Oil on canvas (transferred from panel).
84.3 x 59.6 cm. Inv. No. 423*

The title *Tax-collectors* (in the 1958
Hermitage catalogue, *Money-changers*) is
only correct if the entries in the book really
relate to taxes. The costumes are reminiscent of the period of King Philip the Kind
(15th century). They may have been a sort
of uniform worn by tax-collectors at the
time when the picture was painted. There
are more than thirty versions of this picture,
and the Hermitage canvas is one of them.
It is possible that the original is in the
National Gallery in London.
*From the R. Walpole collection,
Houghton Hall, England, 1779.*

MAERTEN VAN HEEMSKERK
1498–1574
Calvary
Triptych. Central part: oil on canvas (trans-ferred from panel), 100.7 x 58.3 cm; wings: oil on panel, 100 x 28 cm (the top once was figured and is now supplemented with additions). Inv. No. 415

The works of Italian masters had undoubt-edly made a great impression on the artist. Particularly strong was the influence of Michelangelo which may be traced not only in the conception of the donors' fig-ures but mainly in the treatment of the nude human bodies in the central part of the triptych. The triptych was supposedly created in 1543, i.e. quite soon after the author's return from Italy.
Acquired in 1811.

DIRCK JACOBSZ
Ca. 1497–1567
Group Portrait of the Shooting Corporation of Amsterdam
1532. Oil on canvas (transferred from panel). 115 x 160 cm. Inv. No. 414

Netherlandish portrait painting which got its start already in the works by Jan van Eyck and Roger van Der Weyden, was enriched by a new genre in the 16th century. This genre of the group portrait subsequently became widespread in the north of the Netherlands. Dirck Jacobsz was one of the founders of the genre. This picture is an early example of the genre. The composition of

the portrait is conventional, the characters are positioned in three rows, their figures are brought together shoulder to shoulder, as if compressed by the picture's frame. The impression of monotony that may arise at first glance is explained first of all by the fact that all the members of the shooting corpo-ration are depicted in the uniform of their guild, all the faces are given a three-quarter turn and are placed in one line. But if the picture is examined more scrupulously the spectator cannot overlook the master's skill in representing individual features and pecu-liarities of disposition of each person.
From the collection of Count H. Brühl, Dresden, 1769.

FRANS POURBUS THE ELDER
1545–1581
Portrait of a Man
Portrait of a Woman
Oil on panel. 87 x 78 cm. Inv. Nos. 399, 400

The pair portraits were characteristic of the painter who lived in Antwerp and produced his pictures mostly to order.
From the J.-E. Gotzkowsky collection, Berlin, 1764.

ABEL GRIMMER
Ca. 1570–before 1619
Winter Landscape
Oil on panel. Diameter 27.8 cm. Inv. No. 5219

The tondo *Winter Landscape* by Abel Grimmer, a painter and an architect from Antwerp, would seem to be one from the four-piece series devoted to the seasons of the year. This landscape is painted in a delicate manner and full of lyricism.
From the Yusupov Palace, Leningrad, 1925.

PIETER BRUEGEL THE YOUNGER
Ca. 1564–1638
The Adoration of the Magi
Oil on canvas (transferred from panel).
36 x 56 cm. Inv. No. 3737

The painting is a replica of the work by Pieter Bruegel the Elder (1525/30–1569), the father of the artist. The original is kept in the collection of Oskar Reinhart, Winterthur. The Gospel scene of the Adoration of the Magi is placed in the left-hand corner of the painting. The artist has transferred it into the setting of a small Netherlandish town in winter and it hardly stands out among numerous genre scenes. In the picture Bruegel reveals his talent of a great landscape painter, who has a keen feeling for the beauty of northern nature and a skilful hand to depict it.
From the Museum of the Academy of Arts, Petrograd, 1922.

PIETER BRUEGEL THE YOUNGER
Ca. 1564–1638
The Sermon of John the Baptist
1604. Oil on canvas (transferred from panel).
107.5 x 167 cm. Inv. No. 3519

This is a copy of the picture by Pieter Bruegel the Elder. John the Baptist is shown amidst the crowd of people listening to his sermon, among them peasants, monks, luxuriously dressed burghers, soldiers, children and foreigners wearing exotic Oriental garments. To represent large numbers of people the artist uses a device traditional for Netherlandish painting: he sharply reduces the scale of figures receding into the distance. There is an opinion that the canvas depicts a real event, one of the numerous secret meetings held by Netherlandish Protestants on the eve of the Revolution of 1566–1609. Protestants, the adherents of Calvin and Luther, accused the Roman Catholic Church of distorting Christ's Teaching, and were the main driving force of the movement for the independence of the Netherlands from the power of Spanish Hapsburgs.
From the Baron Pritwitz collection, St Petersburg, 1889.

KERSTIAEN DE KEYNINCK
Ca. 1560–ca. 1635
Landscape with Tobias and the Angel
Oil on panel. 40 x 63 cm. Inv. No. 6188

Kerstiaen de Keyninck painted almost exclusively mythological and religious subjects.

The *Landscape with Tobias* belongs to the mature period of his creative career. It is not so much an illustration for the Old Testament Book of Tobit as an idealized mountain landscape which serves as a magnificent setting for the biblical drama.
From the N. Roerich collection, Petrograd, 1921.

GIJSBRECHT LIJTENS
(MASTER OF WINTER LANDSCAPES)
1586–after 1643
Winter Landscape
Oil on panel. 71.5 x 89 cm. Inv. No. 4678

The work of the Antwerp landscape painters anticipates the flowering of Dutch and Flemish realism in the 17th century. Many experts in art history identify the Master of Winter Landscapes with the Antwerp artist Gijsbrecht Lijtens. It is

known that Lijtens headed a large workshop in Antwerp, and his apprentices often painted staffage for his landscape scenes. Lijtens's landscapes manifest his keen feeling for harmonizing shades of colour within the overall colour scheme, which was generally typical of the Antwerp landscape painters of the first half of the 17th century.
From the V. Argutinsky-Dolgoruky collection, Petrograd, 1921.

FLEMISH PAINTING. 17th CENTURY
(rooms 245–248)

JAN BRUEGEL THE ELDER (VELVET BRUEGEL)
1568–1625
The Adoration of the Magi
Between 1598 and 1600. *Oil on copperplate.*
26.5 x 35.2 cm. Inv. No. 3090

Jan Bruegel was the younger son of Pieter Bruegel the Elder. Because of his predilection for wearing luxurious clothes he was called 'Velvet Bruegel' but this cognomen can also be regarded as an appraisal of the artist's skills. The works by Jan Bruegel are distinguished by a tender 'velvety' quality of their pictorial surface, which was achieved by virtuoso combinations of var-

ied, carefully counterpoised sonorous colours. All the Hermitage pictures by Bruegel can be assigned to the landscape genre, including the *Adoration of the Magi*, although the primary role here belongs to human figures, which are over one hundred in the canvas. The landscape imparts a realistic touch to the narrative scene, which on the whole is treated in the spirit of a fairy tale. The imaginary buildings incorporated into the composition alternate with real motifs of the urban architecture.
From the P. Semionov-Tian-Shansky collection, Petrograd, 1915.

PETER PAUL RUBENS (PIETRO PAULO)
1577–1640
Statue of Ceres
Ca. 1615. Oil on panel. 90.3 x 65.5 cm.
Inv. No. 504

This decorative composition is imbued with a symbolic meaning. The frolicking putti, evocative of 'happy times', offer garlands of fruits and other gifts of nature to Ceres, the Roman goddess of fertility. Rubens saw the Hellenistic statue of Ceres, depicted in this painting, in the Borghese collection in Rome. These offerings to the antique goddess are symbolic of the artist's tribute to the great art of Antiquity.
From the Cobentzl collection, Brussels, 1768.

PETER PAUL RUBENS (PIETRO PAULO)
1577–1640
The Descent from the Cross
Ca. 1618. Oil on canvas. 297 x 200 cm.
Inv. No. 471

This altarpiece was painted by Rubens
with some of his pupils for the church at
the Capuchin monastery in Lier, Belgium.
Before us is a lofty image of Christ's heroic
death. The pathetic scene is full of solem-
nity and calm. There is no 'rage of the
brush' typical of Rubens.
From the Empress Joséphine collection,
Malmaison, 1814.

PETER PAUL RUBENS (PIETRO PAULO)
1577–1640
**Feast at the House of Simon
the Pharisee**
Between 1618 and 1620. *Oil on canvas*
(transferred from panel). 189 x 254.5 cm.
Inv. No. 479

The *Feast at the House of Simon the
Pharisee* was executed to Rubens's design
by his pupils. The master has only put the
finishing touches to the most important
sections of the canvas. In the late 1610s
this was a common practice with artists'
workshops. In this painting, the figures sitting on the right of Christ have been close-

ly worked out by Anthony van Dyck, the
master's best pupil and chief assistant. The
subject, based on the Gospel story, served
as a background on which the artist has
skillfully depicted the collision of different
human characters and a broad range of
emotions from elevated trust and compas-
sion in the group of Christ and his disciples
to undisguised animosity in the group of
pharisees. The insoluble conflict is stressed
by various artistic devices, such as the dramatic contrasts of light and shade and
of calm and movement, expressed in the
drawing, composition and colour scheme.
*From the R. Walpole collection, Houghton
Hall, England, 1779.*

PETER PAUL RUBENS (PIETRO PAULO)
1577–1640
The Union of Earth and Water
Ca. 1618. Oil on canvas. 222.5 x 180.5 cm.
Inv. No. 464

The Union of Earth and Water was conceived by Rubens as a decorative panel. The artist celebrates here the beneficial union of the two elements – Earth and Water. Earth is personified by Cybele, the Mother of Gods, and Water, by Neptune, the god of the sea. The engraving made after the picture by Peter de Jode shows Cybele as the goddess of Antwerp and Neptune as Scaldis, the god of the Scheldt,

the river on which Antwerp lies. The subject of the picture is connected with the most painful geopolitical problems of the artist's day. After the partition of the Netherlands into Northern and Southern provinces in 1581, the Dutch blockaded the mouth of the Scheldt and Flanders lost its access to the sea and its trading routes. In his work Rubens has embodied the innermost dreams of the Flemish about lifting the Dutch blockade from the mouth of the Scheldt, their hopes for regaining access to the sea as well as their wish to see the country powerful and flourishing again.
From the Chigi collection, Rome,
between 1798 and 1800.

PETER PAUL RUBENS (PIETRO PAULO)
1577–1640
Hagar Leaves the House of Abraham
Between 1615 and 1617. *Oil on panel.*
62.8 x 76 cm. Inv. No. 475

Peter Paul Rubens, one of the greatest Western European artists, played the crucial role in the formation of the Flemish School of painting. The Hermitage collection boasts over forty Rubens's pictures dating from various periods of his artistic career. A replica of this early work by the master is in the collection of the Duke of Westminster.
From the collection of L.-A. Crozat,
Baron de Thiers, Paris, 1772.

PETER PAUL RUBENS (PIETRO PAULO)
1577–1640
Perseus and Andromeda
Ca. 1622. Oil on canvas (transferred from panel). 99.5 x 139 cm. Inv. No. 461

Perseus and Andromeda is one of the indisputable summits of Rubens's oeuvre. The artist drew the subject from Ovid's *Metamorphoses* that served as a kind of reference source for Netherlandish painters. Flying over the sea, the celebrated Greek hero Perseus saw the rock to which the fair Andromeda, daughter of the Ethiopian king Cepheus, was chained. Her mother, Cassiopeia, boastfully saying that her daughter's beauty outshone the beauty of all the sea nymphs, had insulted the god of the sea Poseidon. Taking vengeance for this Poseidon sent down a terrible sea monster on Cepheus' kingdom. To save his country the king had to sacrifice Andromeda to the monster. In a severe fight Perseus slew the monster and released Andromeda. Rubens treats the antique myth with utmost freedom, endowing the daughter of the Ethiopian king with the features of a blond and white-faced Flemish girl.
From the collection of Count H. Brühl, Dresden, 1769.

PETER PAUL RUBENS (PIETRO PAULO)
1577–1644
Bachus
Between 1638 and 1640. *Oil on canvas (transferred from panel). 191 x 161.3 cm. Inv. No. 467*

The artist apparently attached great importance to this canvas as he kept it in his studio till the last days of his life. The painting was mentioned as one of the artist's last works in a letter written by his nephew, Philip, to the French historian Roger de Piles. It appears in the inventory of Rubens's possessions made immediately after his death (Inv. No. 91). A marble bust, of which six copies have survived, of the Roman Emperor Vitellius, who was branded by posterity as a drinkard and glutton, served as the prototype for Bacchus' head. The perfection of the master's brushwork elicits admiration from the spectator. Rubens turned to this subject on more than one occasion.

From the collection of L.-A. Crozat, Baron de Thiers, Paris, 1772; formerly in the collection of Duc de Richelieu, Paris.

PETER PAUL RUBENS (PIETRO PAULO)
1577–1640
**Portrait of a Lady-In-Waiting
to the Infanta Isabella**
Mid-1620s. *Oil on panel. 64 x 48 cm.*
Inv. No. 478

The painting's traditional title comes from the inscription, possibly made in the 17th century, on a preliminary drawing. An attempt has been made to identify the person depicted as the artist's eldest daughter Clara Serena, who died at the age of twelve and a half. This assumption is based on a resemblance between the model and other painted representations of Clara Serena. Evidently, the artist painted the portrait after his daughter's death, depicting her as he imagined she might looked as an adult.
From the collection of L.-A. Crozat,
Baron de Thiers, Paris, 1772.

ANTHONY VAN DYCK
1599–1641
Self-Portrait
1622–23. *Oil on canvas. 116.5 x 93.5 cm.*
Inv. No. 548

Anthony van Dyck, a master of bright talent, made a great career as a portraitist. The Hermitage possesses both official portraits commissioned from the painter and less formal smaller portraits of his near relations. In all, there are more than twenty portraits by the master in the Museum's collection, including one of his best self-portraits. Van Dyck is depicted here as a slim youth, with a carefully tended, attractive and somewhat feminine face and delicate supple hands. The artist, beyond a doubt, idealizes himself. Still his appearance is full of true elegance and aristocratism enhanced by the graceful carelessness of posture, negligence of costume and a dreamy, somewhat mysterious expression of his eyes. The portrait epitomizes the concept of an ideal artist typical of the epoch: we see here a virtuoso of brush, the one who belongs to the sphere of beauty and harmony. Variants of the self-portrait are kept in the Alte Pinakothek, Munich, and the Metropolitan Museum of Art, New York.
From the collection of L.-A. Crozat,
Baron de Thiers, Paris, 1772.

ANTHONY VAN DYCK
1599–1641
Portrait of Elizabeth and Philadelphia Wharton

1640. Oil on canvas. 162 x 130 cm.
Inv. No. 533

Depicting children was Van Dyck's forte. The artist took delight in portraying children, skilfully conveying the freshness and naivete of their attitude. Never sugary or doll-like, his images of children are charmingly tender and vivid. In his *Portrait of Elizabeth and Philadelphia Wharton* one's attention is arrested by lack of unity of the figures and the background. This imperfection as well as the dry and inexpressive landscape in the background led art critics to the conclusion that Van Dyck resorted here to the services of his assistants, which was a common practice with famous workshops to fulfil multitudes of commissions. Nonetheless, the figures of the girls that have been executed by the master himself belong to the best works he created in England.

From the R. Walpole collection, Houghton Hall, England, 1779.

ANTHONY VAN DYCK
1599–1641
Rest on the Flight into Egypt (Madonna of the Partridges)

Early 1630s. Oil on canvas. 215 x 285.5 cm.
Inv. No. 539

The right-hand part of the composition shows a round dance of carefree angel-like children entertaining the infant Christ.

The whole scene is treated very much in the spirit of Flemish tapestries: plants and fruits are placed in the foreground, and the trees, with a flock of partridges taking wing off the branches, are beautifully arranged in the background.

From the R. Walpole collection, Houghton Hall, England, 1779; formerly in the collection of the Prince of Orange, Holland.

ANTHONY VAN DYCK
1599–1641
Portrait of Court Ladies
*Late 1630s. Oil on canvas. 131.5 x 150.6 cm.
Inv. No. 540*

This portrait stands out among the artist's
works created in England for its sonority of
colour. Yet his taste and control help him to
avoid any unbalanced clashes of colour-
sand achieves an amazingly subtle harmony
of tones. The brilliancy and splendour of the
foreground is enhanced by the black drapery touched with gold, and the landscape
dimly seen in the middle ground. The unity
of all the three planes is achieved by the
harmonious combination of colours.
Acquired between 1763 and 1774.

JACOB JORDAENS
1593–1678
The Bean King
*Ca. 1638. Oil on canvas (relined).
157 x 211 cm. Inv. No. 3760*

Jacob Jordaens won the fame of the
'most Flemish' artist. The Hermitage possesses one of the best variants of his *Bean
King*. The picture features the merry ceremony of the January festival of the Three
Kings or the Three Magi who came to
Bethlehem to pay homage to the infant
Christ. According to the old Netherlandish
tradition, guests of the festival were offered
a cake with a bean baked inside. The one
who got the bean was proclaimed the
'bean king' and could choose a 'queen'
and a 'retinue'. Jordaens has represented
the merriment at its peak, when the participants of the carousal, warmed with wine,
drink another goblet to the health of their
king, a good-natured grey-haired old
man, with joyful cheers 'the King drinks!'
Jordaens's models were always real persons. More often than not he would have
his relatives sit for his pictures. For example, Jordaens's father-in-law, Adam van
Nort, sat for the bean king, and the artist's
daughter Elizabeth, for the queen.
The man behind them, with a jug in his
raised hand, who seems to be one of the
most boisterous participants of the revelry,
is endowed with the features of the artist
himself.
*From the Museum of the Academy
of Arts, Petrograd, 1922; formerly in
the A. Bezborodko collection.*

FRANS SNYDERS
1579–1657
The Fishmonger's Shop
1620s. Oil on canvas. 209.5 x 341 cm.
Inv. No. 606

Snyders's four large-scale canvases depicting various shops are a hymn of praise to the fertility of nature. Initially the four *Shops* constituted a single cycle adorning the dining-hall in the palace of Bishop Antonius Triest in Brugge. In the cycle the artist celebrates the exuberance of all nature realms – earth, water and air. A peculiar compositional scheme of the paintings gives grounds to believe that they have been designed to form a strict sequence. The still-life genre was used by the artist to create a vision of wealth and prosperity, to embody the dream of the golden age which imbued the Flemish art of Rubens's era.
From the collection of L.-A. Crozat,
Baron de Thiers, Paris, 1772.

JAN FYT
1611–1661
Hare, Fruit and Parrot
1647. Oil on canvas. 70.5 x 97 cm.
Inv. No. 616

Jan Fyt is one of the greatest painters of animals and decorative small-scale still lifes. His favourite subjects were hunting scenes, fruit and dead game. Fyt's oeuvre was mainly influenced by his work in Snyders's studio and his long-term trip abroad. In Flanders there were no equals to Fyt among still-life artists as regards the refined coloration and decorative qualities of painting.
From the Hermitage Pavilion in Peterhof, 1921.

DAVID TENIERS THE YOUNGER
1610–1690
Monkeys in a Kitchen
Mid-1640s. Oil on canvas (transferred from panel). 36 x 50 cm. Inv. No. 568

This picture, with its well-pronounced satirical overtones, was perceived as a political parody in the times of the French Revolution. There is a well-known print after the picture, bearing the inscription: *The majority and the minority in the Directory* (The Directory or Directoire was the government of the French Republic from 1795 to 1799.)
From the Empress Joséphine collection, Malmaison, 1814.

DAVID TENIERS THE YOUNGER
1610–1690
Group Portrait of Members of the Antwerp Town Council and Seniors of the Shooting Companies
1643. Oil on canvas. 135 x 183 cm. Inv. No. 572

Teniers the Younger painted almost every kind of picture but was especially famous for his genre scenes of peasant life, treated with a subtle sense of humour. The artist also won the reputation of a great portraitist. The Hermitage canvas, depicting members of the Antwerp Town Council and seniors of the shooting companies in the town square, is the most famous work by the artist in the genre of the group portrait.
From the Empress Joséphine collection, Malmaison, 1814.

DUTCH PAINTING. 17th CENTURY
(rooms 248–254)

FRANS HALS
1581–1666
**Portrait of a Young Man
with a Glove in His Hand**
Ca. 1650. Oil on canvas. 80 x 66.5 cm.
Inv. No. 982

Hals' activity coincides with the flourishing period of Dutch realistic art. In his pictures the artist strove to express the vigorousness, joie de vivre and self-assurance of his contemporaries. His portraits are painted in masterly bold brushstrokes, recording for posterity the fleeting gestures of the models depicted. The artist mastered the Renaissance devices which enabled him to reveal the dynamic aspect of portraiture: he brought the half-length figures of his models closer to the viewer or resorted to the visual 'break' of the canvas surface, laying the emphasis on the elbow or gaze of the sitter. He modelled the form with colour, making it 'breathe' in the specks of light, picking out of the dark depth of the canvas only what was necessary for the accurate and well-thought-out characterization. These qualities of Hals' painting, along with the rejection of fused brushstrokes and smooth surfaces peculiar to the works of most portraitists of his time, exerted an influence on Edouard Manet and Vincent van Gogh in the 19th century.
From the J.-E. Gotzkowsky collection, Berlin, 1764.

WILLEM CLAESZ HEDA
1594–1680/82
Breakfast with Lobster
1648. Oil on canvas. 118 x 118 cm.
Inv. No. 5606

This is a brilliant example of the still-life type known as Breakfast Pieces. The rendition of all objects shows the artist's deep understanding of their texture and form, his personal attitude to them. In such pictures one can always feel the invisible presence of man: he has laid the table, peeled the lemon and poured the wine. The crumpled tablecloth appears as a fleeting glimpse of real life. The artist achieves the unity of the colour scheme by subordinating all the hues to the greyish-pearl gamut which adds a sense of certain aloofness to the still life.
From the State Museum Reserve, 1920.

JAN DAVIDSZ DE HEEM
1606–1684
Fruit and a Vase of Flowers
1655. Oil on canvas. 95 x 124.5 cm.
Inv. No. 1407

Not only the Dutch burghers but also the European nobility used to decorate the interiors of their houses with still lifes by Dutch painters. The Russian aristocrats were no exception, adoring such pictures of wonderful fruit and flowers.
Acquired between 1763 and 1774.

PIETER CLAESZ
1597–1661
Breakfast with Ham
1647. Oil on panel. 40 x 61 cm. Inv. No. 1046

The artist sought to depict as convincingly as possible the world of objects surrounding man in his everyday life. One cannot but admire the almost tangible texture of the objects composing this still life: the juicy hem, the tender bloom of the peaches, the ruby gleam of the wine, all perceived as a hymn to the unpretentious joys of life.
Acquired from V. Kostromitinova, St Petersburg, 1895.

PAULUS POTTER
1625–1654
Watchdog
Oil on canvas. 96.5 x 132 cm. Inv. No. 817

Paulus Potter was one of the most famous Dutch animal painters who produced numerous pictures strikingly accurate in their rendition of animals. This 'portrait' of a dog shows the artist's remarkable ability to reveal the most essential features of the animal's character. The low horizon underscores the plain character of the Dutch scenery, while the fine gradation of pale hues conveys the humid air medium that softens the contours of the objects receding into the distance.

From the Empress Joséphine collection, Malmaison, 1814.

PAULUS POTTER
1625–1654
The Farm
1649. Oil on panel. 81 x 115.5 cm. Inv. No. 820

A keen observer, the artist vividly conveyed the habits of animals invariably depicted with great warmth and humour. A lady, who commissioned this landscape, was shocked with the excessively naturalistic depiction of a scene from life in the centre of the picture, as a result of which the canvas acquired a scandalous reputation. Nevertheless, the empress of France purchased it without a moment's hesitation. *From the Empress Joséphine collection, Malmaison, 1814.*

JACOB ISAAKSZ VAN RUISDAEL
1628/29–1682
The Marsh
1660s. Oil on canvas. 72.5 x 99 cm. Inv. No. 934

The Hermitage houses twelve canvases by Jacob van Ruisdael. Created at the different stages of his artistic career, they include his early landscapes executed in greens and browns by which the artist sought to attain the almost tangible rendition of nature, and his mature severe *Mountainous Landscape* lit by a disquieting light of the moon. In the *Marsh*, the mighty trees seem to be a personification of eternity. At the same time, they are part of nature subject to the inexorable course of time, as evidenced by the fallen trunk of a dead tree; but near this still mighty forest giant a slender young birch is rising towards the sun. The work of the outstanding Dutch landscape painter of the second half of the 17th century is remarkable for its profound philosophic attitude to nature and its well-thought-out and expressive compositions. *Acquired between 1763 and 1774.*

ADRIAEN VAN OSTADE
1610–1685
Scuffle
1637. Oil on panel. 25 x 33.5 cm. Inv. No. 799

The genre subject that was considered low in 17th-century monarchial countries was one of the most favourite in Holland. Small-size pictures, peopled with tiny figures, matched beautifully the interior of the burgher's home. This genre most vividly reflected the discoveries of realistic artists who often took interest in the most commonplace, even vulgar scenes. They painted numerous *Guard-houses* with merry-making soldiers or grotesquely treated *Scuffles* of poor townsfolk and villagers. Among these artists was Adriaen van Ostade who ridiculed the rough amusements of peasants, accentuating their primitive character and inability to control their animal instincts.
From the collection of Peter I in the Monplaisir Palace, Peterhof, 1882.

JAN STEEN
1625/26–1679
The Revellers
Ca. 1660. Oil on panel. 39 x 30 cm.
Inv. No. 875

The Hermitage works by Jan Steen confirm his reputation as a wonderful 'story-teller in painting'. His genre scenes are amusing and, sometimes, anecdotal. In this picture, the smoker is openly making fun of his unfortunate wife who took too much wine. To all appearances, the artist has depicted here his wife Margaretha and himself.
From the J. Gotzkowsky collection, Berlin, 1764.

JAN STEEN
1625/26–1679
Backgammon Players
Ca. 1667. Oil on panel. 45.5 x 39 cm.
Inv. No. 873

A very popular game in Europe, backgammon was played not only in the aristocratic salons, but also in the drawing-rooms of the ladies of the third estate. An invitation to take part in this game might serve as a plausible excuse for a rendezvous, as is implied in this picture by Steen.
From the F. Tronchin collection, Geneva, 1770.

PIETER DE HOOCH
1629–after 1684
Mistress and Her Maid
After 1660. *Oil on canvas. 53 x 42 cm.
Inv. No. 943*

Pieter de Hooch, like other painters active in Delft, preferred poeticized everyday scenes to amusing subjects. This ordinary scene, in which a mistress is instructing her maid on what should be done with the bought fish, has been turned by the artist into a hymn to the calmness and comfort of a small Dutch town. The Hermitage picture, generally regarded as one of Hooch's masterpiece, stands out for its harmony and thoroughness with which the artist has painted every detail. The calm, cold range of greys and whites is enlivened with colour accents. All details are skillfully correlated in space being fused together by the scattered rays of northern light. The artist's wife, whose image often recurs in his pictures, served as a model for the maiden.
Acquired from the antiquarian Lafontaine, Paris, 1810.

GERARD TERBORCH
1617–1681
A Glass of Lemonade
1660s. *Oil on canvas. 67 x 54 cm. Inv. No. 881*

The picture belongs to the later period of the artist's career when his works acquired a touch of aristocratism in line with the demands of his well-to-do bourgeois clients. Terborch used to depict one, two or three persons in an interior, engaged in such occupations as reading a letter, a music lesson, visit to the sick or courtship. Yet all these actions served merely as a pretext for the depiction of splendid interiors. The artist, as nobody else, was able to convey the beauty of an enclosed world, paying particular attention to the rendering of precious fur, gleaming satin, glistening glass and faience.
From the Empress Joséphine collection, Malmaison, 1814.

REMBRANDT HARMENSZ VAN RIJN
1606–1669
Flora

1634. Oil on canvas. 125 x 101 cm.
Inv. No. 732

Painted in the year of the artist's marriage, this picture is imbued with light and joyful feelings. Depicted as Flora is Rembrandt's first wife Saskia van Uylenborch (d. 1642). There is nothing in her appearance that recalls the antique goddess of spring and flowers. She is dressed in rich Oriental clothes glittering with silk and golden embroidery, and her face radiates happiness which makes this ordinary woman really beautiful.
Acquired between 1770 and 1774.

REMBRANDT HARMENSZ VAN RIJN
1606–1669
Danaë

1636. Oil on canvas. 185 x 202.5 cm.
Inv. No. 723

The artist's brush turns this mythological subject into a hymn to love, light and humaneness. For many years this work, one of the most famous Hermitage pictures, presented a lot of enigmas. There was much controversy about its subject-matter. Some researchers believed that the title *Danaë* did not correspond to the treatment of the woman's image in the picture. Thorough investigations have shown that the canvas of 1636 was later repainted by the artist and that some details of the original composition coincided with the work of Correggio. Such a bold depiction of a naked woman in close-up, as was done by Rembrandt, is an unusual phenomenon in 17th-century Dutch painting. Although the woman's figure is far from perfection, and her facial features are not very appealing, the image of a woman waiting for her beloved is strikingly truthful to life, making the subject-matter of the picture more profound than the myth it was based on.
From the collection of L.-A. Crozat,
Baron de Thiers, Paris, 1772.

REMBRANDT HARMENSZ VAN RIJN
1606–1669
The Sacrifice of Isaac
1635. Oil on canvas. 193 x 132 cm.
Inv. No. 727

This is one of the most dramatic stories of
the Bible. To test Abraham's faith, God
commanded him to sacrifice his beloved
son, Isaac. At the moment the father drew
the knife, an angel sent by God stayed his
hand. *The Sacrifice of Isaac* is an early
work by the great artist on a biblical subject. Influenced by Baroque art, Rembrandt
created a composition filled with movement and pathetics, in which Isaac's obe-
dient body, suffused with an inner light, is
reminiscent of a sacrificial lamb.
From the R. Walpole collection,
Houghton Hall, England, 1779.

REMBRANDT HARMENSZ VAN RIJN
1606–1669
David and Jonathan
1642. Oil on panel. 73 x 61.5 cm. Inv. No. 713

The subject is taken from the Bible. King
Saul decided to kill his commander David.
The king's son, Jonathan, warned his friend
David of Saul's murderous intentions. The
friends secretly met in a desert place
where they parted, and David fled to the
mountains. Rembrandt depicted the tragic
moment of their parting. The artist was
probably very fond of this subject, as there
are several extant drawings on this theme,
dating from the first half of the 1640s.
From the collection of Peter I
in the Monplaisir Palace, Peterhof, 1882.

REMBRANDT HARMENSZ VAN RIJN
1606–1669
Portrait of an Old Jew
1654. Oil on canvas. 109 x 85 cm. Inv. No. 737

Rembrandt's portraiture is one of the highest peaks in the 17th-century European painting. His depictions of old people are unprecedented in their psychological profundity. The artist seemed to stretch the notion of time, providing insights into the manyfaceted and complex inner world of his models and revealing their spiritual essence as the sum total of their life. These portraits are static, without details; light is merely used to enhance the emotional impact, and the virtuoso painterly technique is combined with the colour scheme built upon brownish-blacks and deep reds. Such works of Rembrandt are often called 'biographical portraits'.
From the Count Baudouin collection, Paris, 1783.

REMBRANDT HARMENSZ VAN RIJN
1606–1669
The Holy Family
1645. Oil on canvas. 117 x 91 cm. Inv. No. 741

Rembrandt's works of the 1640s are quite varied, including portraits of the artist's friends and pictures on biblical subjects, such as the *Holy Family*. The artist depicts a scene from everyday life: a poor room with a child's cradle in the foreground and Joseph at work in the middle distance. If it were not the angels descending from Heaven, the whole scene with a young mother who tore herself from the book to look at her child would seem to take place in any Dutch house. A pen sketch for this picture is in the Musée Bonnat in Bayonne.
From the collection of L.-A. Crozat, Baron de Thiers, Paris, 1772.

REMBRANDT HARMENSZ VAN RIJN
1606–1669
The Return of the Prodigal Son
*Ca. 1668/69. Oil on canvas. 262 x 205 cm.
Inv. No. 742*

This is one of the last paintings of the great artist, probably the most famous one in the Hermitage collection. At the end of his artistic career Rembrandt created static compositions, devoid of any entertaining elements and focusing on the emotional state of his characters. The subject of the painting is based on the biblical parable of a light-minded youth who left his father's house, indulged in riotous living, and after many hardships returned home penitently.

With purely painterly means the artist has revealed the emotional tension of the scene. The torn clothes of the knelt youth tell that the way of the wanderer was hard and long. The light and tender hands of the blind father are laid on his son's shoulders in a benedictory gesture. The viewer seems to be among the depicted people who, deep in thoughts, are watching the scene. This work is perceived as the sum total of the artist's creative activity. It was produced when Rembrandt, not recognized by society, sick and lonely, lost almost all his friends and relatives. But with his work he asserted the ideals of kindness, forgiveness and faith.
From the Duke d'Amezune collection, Paris, 1767.

FIRST FLOOR

● BEGINNING
OF THE FIRST-FLOOR
EXHIBITION

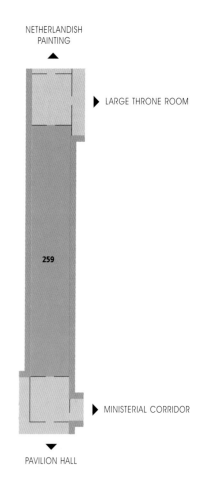

NETHERLANDISH
PAINTING
▲

▶ LARGE THRONE ROOM

259

▶ MINISTERIAL CORRIDOR

▼
PAVILION HALL

DECORATIVE AND APPLIED ARTS
OF MEDIEVAL EUROPE

By the high standards of its objects the Hermitage collection of Western European applied arts from the 9th to 16th centuries can be placed on a par with such world-famous museums as the Louvre, the Musée de Cluny in Paris and the Victoria and Albert Museum in London. The Department of Medieval Art was established in 1885 following the acquisition of the famous collection built up by the eminent Russian collector Anton Basilewsky in Paris. It contained a great variety of magnificent metalwork from the 11th to 16th centuries, including Limoges and Rheinland champlevé enamels, Limoges painted enamels from the 15th and 16th centuries, bone carvings from the 9th to 11th centuries, items of furniture and artistic wood-carving, tapestries, textiles and embroideries, Hispano-Moresque faiences, Italian majolicas and Venetian glassware.

Bowl

Mid-12th century. England. *Silver, gilding.*
Height 14.5 cm. Inv. No. Φ 810

In the 11th and first quarter of the 12th
century the Romanesque style flourished
in France, Italy, Britain and Germany,
combining elements of Roman and
Byzantine art with the artistic traditions of
the Carolingian and Ottonian periods.

The unique examples of metalwork owned
by the Hermitage include this splendid
bowl decorated with engraving, chasing
and niello. The motifs of the depictions –
the warriors and fabulous monsters
adorned with a stylized plant ornament –
are derived from Christian and folklore
mythology.
From the collection of the merchant
A. Zaitsevsky, Zaraisk, 1832.

**Reliquary-casket with scenes from the
life of St Valeria**

*Ca. 1170. France, Limoges. Wood, copper,
enamel, gilding. Height 23.8 cm.*
Inv. No. Φ 175

The reliquary-casket with a gable cover,
executed in the technique of champlevé
enamel, is a typical product of 12th-century

Limoges workshops. The master's choice
of a subject from the life of St Valeria is
not fortuitous: she was considered the
patron saint of Limoges. The decor consists
of separate scenes revealing the legend of
St Valeria. She is shown wearing a tight robe
with long sleeves characteristic of that period.
From the A. Basilewsky collection,
Paris, 1885.

Reliquary: *St Stephan*

Late 12th century. France. Wood, silver, gilding, coloured stones. Height 42.5 cm. Inv. No. Ф 105

In the 12th century the shortage of silver in Europe called into being a special manufacturing technique of silverware. The moulding and chasing were substituted for the application of thin silver plates onto a wooden base. The present reliquary is a unique work. The master has accurately rendered the details of a deacon's robe typical for 12th-century France. The saint is holding the Bible in a luxurious mount. The reliquary is adorned with intaglios of classical make and a big 12th-century cameo of green and red banded jasper.

From the A. Basilewsky collection, Paris, 1885.

Top of a bishop's crosier

14th century. Italy. *Ivory, painting.*
Height 32 cm. Inv. No. Φ 56

An indispensable attribute of a bishop's
ceremonial attire, the crosiers had the lavishly adorned spiral-like tops made of different materials including ivory. In the
scene decorating this top the infant Christ
is shown handing a shepherd's crook –
a symbol of the bishop's office over his
flock – to the bishop.
From the A. Basilewsky collection,
Paris, 1885.

The Fortuni vase

Mid-14th century. Spain, Málaga. *Faience,*
lustre painting. Height 117 cm. Inv. No. Φ 317

In the 14th century the pottery centre of
Western Europe was Spain, in particular,
the Málaga workshops which produced
clay vessels coated with a lustrous glaze.
Such products first appeared in the East.
The Spanish pottery, having borrowed from
the Middle East the opaque glaze con-
cealing the dark colour of clay and providing the necessary ground for the fireproof
paints, had, in turn, become a model for
Italian clay articles, called 'majolica'.
A masterpiece of Málaga ceramic art, the
famous Fortuni vase was named after
a Spanish artist who discovered it in the
19th century in the village of Salar outside
Granada. It belongs to a small group
of vases with a conventional name of
Alhambra – after the first one found as far
back as the 16th century in the basements
of the Alhambra Palace of the Granada
sovereign. The vase stands out for its beautiful forms. The tall handles bear the magic
signs (the hand of Fatima) intended to protect its contents. It is adorned with Eastern
ornament, mostly inscriptions in Arabic,
expressing good wishes and blessings. The
manufacturing techniques of such vases –
moulding, painting, lustre coating and firing at 800° C – were very complicated
and the results did not always meet the
client's wishes. In this regard, the Fortuni
vase, free of the defects so frequent with
the vessels of such dimensions, is a particularly rare example and justly enjoys
a worldwide fame.
From the A. Basilewsky collection,
Paris, 1885.

Cover of a mirror-box

First quarter, 14th century. France. *Ivory.*
Diameter 13.6 cm. Inv. No. Ф 54

The mirror-boxes consisting of two threaded ivory covers and a metal disc, an indispensable utility of the women of fashion, were in vogue not only in France but also far beyond its borders. The boxes' covers were usually adorned with episodes from chivalry novels. Their composition was repeated by a number of workshops without any alterations.
From the A. Basilewsky collection,
Paris, 1885.

Tapestry: *The Apostles St Thomas and St Matthew*

Late 15th–early 16th century. Germany.
Cotton, wool, flax. 85 x 75 cm. Inv. No. T 489

This tapestry depicting the Apostles St Thomas and St Matthew can be considered the earliest one in the Hermitage collection. Its composition, small size and ornamental motifs are typical for German monastery-made tapestries from the late 14th and early 15th centuries. It was presumably woven in Basel. The apostles are shown full-length in long robes, barefooted, holding travellers' staffs. Over their heads is an inscription in Latin: *St Thomas and St Matthew.* According to the hierarchic order, the nun's figure (a client or donor) is smaller in scale than those of the two Evangelists. The upper part of the tapestry depicts a convent with towers against a background of blue sky and large stars, typical for the German tapestries of that period.
From the Museum of the Baron
A. Stieglitz School of Technical Design,
Petrograd, 1923.

FIRST FLOOR

● BEGINNING
OF THE FIRST-FLOOR
EXHIBITION

GALLERY OF THE HISTORY OF ANCIENT PAINTING
▲

THE LARGE SKYLIGHTED HALL
(ITALIAN ART.
17th AND 18th CENTURIES) ◄

239

► DUTCH PAINTING

240

▼
DUTCH PAINTING

SPANISH PAINTING.
15th–EARLY 19th CENTURIES

The Hermitage collection of old Spanish masters is quite varied in composition and represented by such celebrities as Ribera, Zurbarán, Velázquez, Murillo and Goya. The origins of the collection go back to the 18th century when a few single works by Ribera, Velázquez and Murillo were acquired. At that time Spanish painters were known only in their own country. The invasion of Spain in 1808 by Napoleon's armies, the revolution and civil war that followed all created a situation favourable for the purchase and removal of paintings from the country. Among those who took advantage of the situation was the English banker Coesvelt who assembled a large number of Italian and Spanish canvases between 1808 and 1810. In 1814 he exhibited them in Amsterdam and the Russian Tsar Alexander I, who visited Holland at that time, purchased his entire Spanish collection. This marked the beginning of the first gallery of Spanish painting in Europe. At a later date the Hermitage collection was augmented with many remarkable works, particularly during the post-revolutionary period when a host of paintings entered the museum from the former palaces of the Imperial family and the nobility. Today it comprises almost two hundred Spanish canvases and is considered one of the best outside the Iberian peninsula.

UNKNOWN ARTIST OF THE 15th CENTURY
The Entombment

1490s. Castilian school. *Oil and tempera on panel. 94 x 182 cm (in the bottom centre, part of the panel lost). Inv. No. 7646*

This late-15th-century work is not only a tribute to International Gothic, a style dominant in Spain during that time, but also a reflection of the Weltanschauung of the Renaissance. The central scene, treated in traditional manner, is set against a landscape background incorporating architecture, exquisite flowers on top of the sarcophagus and a portrait of the donor. A similar picture is in the parish church of Manzanillo, Valladolid province. *From the Antiquariat, Leningrad, 1933.*

UNKNOWN ARTIST OF THE 15th CENTURY
St Sebastian and St Fabian

1475–1500. Aragon school. *Tempera and oil on panel. 141.4 x 89.5 cm. Inv. No. 4760*

Legend has it that St Fabian was the Pope of Rome and St Sebastian – the centurion of the first cohort. Both lived in the 3rd century and were put to death for their devotion to Christianity. As the day of their death and, accordingly, their feast-day coincide, the two saints were often represented together. The canvas is stylistically close to paintings produced by the Aragon workshop of Martin Bernat in the last quarter of the 15th century. *From the E. Shuvalova House Museum, Leningrad, 1926.*

LUIS DE MORALES
Ca. 1509–1586
**Virgin and Child
with a Cross-shaped Distaff**
1570s. *Oil on canvas (transferred from
panel). 71.5 x 52 cm. Inv. No. 364*

The oeuvre of Morales reflected the tragi-
cal and mystical moods characteristic of
the wide strata of the Spanish population,
especially its intellectual and religious
circles, in the second half of the 16th century. The subject of the Virgin and Child,
borrowed by the painter from Italian art,
is suffused with a dramatic tension. The
cross-shaped distaff, allusive of the Virgin's
domestic occupations, also serves as a
symbol of Christ's fate, His future sufferings
and death. The smooth, enamel-like surface of the canvas is set off by an expressive intensity of line and colour.
*Bequeathed by D. Tatishchev,
St Petersburg, 1845.*

JUAN PANTOJA DE LA CRUZ
1553–1608
Portrait of Diego de Villamayor
1605. *Oil on canvas. 88.5 x 70.5 cm.
Inv. No. 3518*

Juan Pantoja de la Cruz developed the style
of the formal court portrait which took shape
in Spain in the mid-16th century. The *Portrait
of Diego Villamayor* is signed and dated
(cipher 5, which can be easily mistaken for
9, is written in the old Arabic script). Judging

from the inscription, the youth portrayed
is seventeen years old. He is shown wearing
the badge of the Order of Alcantar. The
painter has faithfully conveyed the young
grandee's disproportionate and unattractive
features. At the same time his arrogant posture, beautiful and carefully-tended hands,
the rich ornamentation of his gilt armour
and a large round collar, all betray his aristocratic descent and high social status.
*From the Coesvelt collection,
Amsterdam, 1814.*

**EL GRECO
(DOMENIKOS THEOTOCOPOULOS)**
1541–1614
St Peter and St Paul
Between 1587 and 1592. *Oil on canvas.*
121 x 105 cm. Inv. No. 390

One of the greatest Western European
painters, El Greco left a legacy truly
unique in its artistic idiom. Born in Crete,
he studied icon-painting in his native
Greece, then lived in Venice and Rome,
imbibing the lessons of the great masters
of the Renaissance and classical art.
At the age of thirty-six he came to Spain,
where his work took its final form. In the
present picture, St Peter and St Paul, the
principal apostles of the Christian Church
are shown discussing the doctrine.
El Greco might have meant to record their
famous meeting in Antioch which was considered a crucial point in the history
of Christianity, when the two opinions on
this religion clashed. St Peter tended to
confine it to the limits of Judaism, while
St Paul would rather interpret it as a universal religion. St Paul, who had won the day,
is the main character of the painting, con-
fidently and ardently insisting on his view.
The artist has vividly represented the two
contrasting characters: the strong, fanati-
cal St Paul and the soft and forgiving
St Peter, ready for a compromise. The
images of both saints are endowed with
portrait features and there is some evidence attesting to the fact that St Paul
is a self-portrait of the master. The broad,
sweeping brushstrokes show a strong influence of the Venetian style, and the powerful, energetic treatment of volumes recalls
the works of Michelangelo.
Gift of P. Durnovo, St Petersburg, 1911.

JOSÉ DE RIBERA
1591–1652
St Sebastian and St Irene
Oil on canvas. 156 x 188 cm. Inv. No. 325

Ribera was born in Valencia where he received initial training in painting. In 1611 he moved to Italy, and in 1615 and 1616 he was mentioned in Roman records as a member of the Accademia di St Luca. In 1616 Ribera finally settled in Naples, the town under the patronage of the Spanish crown. According to legend, St Sebastian, a martyr shot by the archers for his devotion to Christianity, was healed by St Irene, who had extracted the arrows from his body. The dramatic night scene of the saint's salvation is permeated with subtle lyricism. The painter treats the nude body of the youth and the beautiful face of St Irene with a special care, which attests to the fact that he was not alien to the ideals of the Renaissance and Antiquity. The picture is typical of Ribera's early period, when he favoured the strong chiaroscuro of Caravaggio.
From the Duchess of Saint-Leu collection, Paris, 1829; formerly in the Malmaison Palace.

JOSÉ DE RIBERA
1591–1652
St Jerome Listening to the Sound of the Trumpet
1626. Oil on canvas. 185 x 133 cm. Inv. No. 311

St Jerome (347–420), one of the four doctors of the Roman Church, lived a few years in seclusion and made the first Latin translation of the Bible. In this canvas he is depicted listening to the sound of the Doomsday trumpet. The picture was produced at approximately the same time as *St Sebastian and St Irene* and is painted in a similar chiaroscuro manner, but here the painter seems to be particularly interested in rendering the sufferings of the old man. Merciless in his realism, Ribera conveys the expression of horror on the martyr's face and his wizened old body.
Acquired from M. Godoy, Paris, 1831.

FRANCISCO DE ZURBARÁN
1598–1664
St Lawrence
1636. Oil on canvas. 292 x 225 cm. Inv. No. 362

Francisco de Zurbarán received initial training in Seville and from 1626 to 1658 he worked regularly for monasteries and churches in this city. St Lawrence was painted for the church of the San José Monastery (La Merced Descalzas) in Seville. As story goes, St Lawrence was a Christian deacon, who, in 258, was put to death by being roasted on a grid in Rome. A native of Aragon, he was very popular in Spain. His attribute is a gridiron, the instrument of his execution. The famous Escorial, designed in the form of a grid, is consecrated to the saint. In the present picture the martyr is endowed with a portrait likeness and appears as a national hero. His monumental figure recalls a painted sculpture. Zurbarán favoured saturated colours and was especially famous for his masterful rendition of white, finely elaborated by means of light-and-shade contrasts. *St Lawrence* is one of the pictures marking a new stage in Zurbarán's artistic development when the tenebrous backgrounds of his earlier works gave way to landscape scenes.
Acquired at the auction sales of the Marshal Soult collection, Paris, 1852.

ALONSO CANO
1601–1667
The Crucifixion
Ca. 1640. Oil on canvas. 265 x 173.
Inv. No. 5572

Alonso Cano, an architect, sculptor and painter, stood out among the Spanish artists for his multifarious talent. He was born in Granada, and when still young moved to Seville. In 1638 Cano was invited to Madrid, where he lived, with some intervals, until 1652, and thereafter settled in Granada. The *Crucifixion* had been long considered a work by Zurbarán, and its austerity, pathos and painterly manner are indeed reminiscent of Zurbarán's works. However, Cano's treatment of the figure is more elegant and refined. The Hermitage picture is similar to a version in the Museum of the Academy of San Fernando, Madrid.
From the Marble Palace, Petrograd, 1919.

DIEGO VELÁZQUEZ DE SILVA
1599–1660
Luncheon
Ca. 1617. Oil on canvas. 108.5 x 102 cm.
Inv. No. 389

One of the greatest Spanish painters, Velázquez was born and began his career in Seville. Early in life he became attracted to genre painting which was rarely practised by Spanish artists at that time. Like Caravaggio he would paint scenes in dark taverns lit by the bright rays of light streaming from one source, thanks to which the volumes of bodies and objects in his pictures stand out in sharp relief. Such scenes came to be called *bodegón* (from the Spanish *bodega*, tavern). The *Luncheon*, one of the master's very early works, shows a merry feast. The facial expressions and gestures of the characters captured with the utmost precision, as well as the superbly rendered still life in the foreground, demonstrate the artist's limitless powers in the depiction of the real world. *Acquired between 1764 and 1774.*

DIEGO VELÁZQUEZ DE SILVA
1599–1660
Portrait of Count Olivares
Ca. 1640. Oil on canvas. 67 x 54.5 cm.
Inv. No. 300

Don Gaspar de Gusman (1587–1645), Count Olivares, Duke de San Lucar, from 1622 to 1643 was an omnipotent minister at the court of the Spanish King Philip IV. The owner of large estates in Andalucia, Olivares associated with Sevillian humanists, he knew and appreciated local painters and would often invite them to the Court. It is thanks to his patronage that Velázquez came to Madrid in 1623. The artist painted portraits of Olivares throughout his life. The Hermitage portrait belongs to the latest period of his career. By that time Olivares had already grown old, he was sick and felt frustrated because his hopes that Spain would restore its former might had not come true. The artist chose to represent Olivares half-length since it enabled him to bring out the spiritual qualities of his sitter. Without flattering the minister, Velázquez has conveyed his unattractive features – his grasping look and morbid swollen face – but behind this exterior one can sense a remarkable individuality, endowed with great will and powerful intellect. During this period the artist's painterly manner acquired a softness and a complex gradation of shades unlike the dense brushwork of his early Caravaggesque pictures. *From the Coesvelt collection, Amsterdam, 1814.*

BARTOLOMÉ ESTEBAN MURILLO
1617–1682
The Immaculate Conception
1670s. Oil on canvas. 195.6 x 145 cm. Inv. No. 387

Murillo was born and spent all his life in Seville. He became famous when still a young man and enjoyed immense popularity. The painter produced many pictures on the theme of the Immaculate Conception. The subject stems from the belief that, like Jesus himself, the Virgin was conceived in her mother's womb free from all stain of original sin. The image of the Virgin in art is often associated with the vision of St John the Evangelist: she was depicted soaring in the air, her figure lit by the sun and moon. Murillo treats the subject of the Immaculate Conception in his own original way. In his painting the Virgin appears as a twelve- or thirteen-year-old girl (*La Nica*), her image is full of spiritual beauty and grace. The skillfully rendered air medium and the refined combinations of light blues, whites and pinks exemplify the achievements of the master's later period.
From the R. Walpole collection, Houghton Hall, England, 1779.

BARTOLOMÉ ESTEBAN MURILLO
1617–1682
Boy with a Dog
1655–60. Oil on canvas. 74 x 60 cm. Inv. No. 386

Murillo was an unsurpassed master of children's portraits. His beggar-boy pictures of the early period, including the Hermitage canvas, reflect the artist's keen interest in street characters and are very spontaneous. The lively and expressive dialogue between the boy and the dog, captured by Murillo, caught the fancy of Edouard Manet, who used this subject in his analogous picture and engraving.
From the Duke de Choiseul collection, Paris, 1772.

ANTONIO PEREDA
1611–1678
Still Life with a Sideboard
1652. Oil on canvas. 80 x 94 cm. Inv. No. 327

Antonio Pereda, one of the leading Madrid artists of the mid-17th century, painted mainly religious canvases, but also produced excellent still lifes in which Spanish painters were past masters. The Hermitage *Still Life*, one of Pereda's best works, stands out for its well-balanced composition, masterly handling of various textures and surfaces, and the dense succulent brushwork. A companion piece, *Still Life with a Clock*, was transferred to the Pushkin Museum of Fine Arts, Moscow.
From the Coesvelt collection, Amsterdam, 1814.

FRANCISCO JOSÉ DE GOYA-Y-LUCIENTES
1746–1828
Portrait of the Actress Antonia Sarate
1810–11. Oil on canvas. 71 x 58 cm.
Inv. No. 10198

The oeuvre of Goya closes the 18th century and ushers in a new era in 19th-century European painting on which the Spanish master left an indelible mark. His numerous representations of writers, poets and actors include two portraits of Antonia Sarate (1775–1811), a hereditary actress, wife of the popular comedian Bernardo Jil and mother of the famous man of letters Antonio Jil-y-Sarate. One of the portraits (now in the National Gallery of Ireland, Dublin) shows her seated on a sofa. The Hermitage portrait is more intimate and romantic in character. The headgear of the actress is decorated with a half-moon, probably alluding to some of the parts she played. Her beautiful face has a touch of sadness: the portrait was painted not long before her death.
Gift of A. Hammer, USA, 1972.

FIRST FLOOR

BEGINNING
OF THE FIRST-FLOOR
EXHIBITION

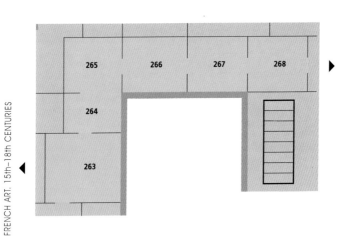

FRENCH ART. 15th–18th CENTURIES

FRENCH ART. 15th–18th CENTURIES

265

266

267

268

264

263

GERMAN AND AUSTRIAN PAINTING.
15th–18th CENTURIES

The Hermitage collection of German and Austrian painting comprises over 700 works, including a number by outstanding artists. Such a vast scope of the collection is largely due to the centuries-old Russo-German relations. Its nucleus was laid by the acquisition, in 1764, of the famous Berlin collection of Johann-Ernest Gotzkowsky, in which German works, however, occupied a rather insignificant place. Subsequently, the dynastic relations of the Russian court with Germany and Austria, as well as the execution of paintings by German artists active in Russia, contributed to an expansion of the German and Austrian sections in Russian collections. Following their nationalization in 1917, the Museum's holding of German and Austrian paintings was considerably enriched. The Hermitage collection does not give a full idea of the achievements of the German and Austrian schools because it has no works by the greatest masters of the German Renaissance such as Dürer and Holbein the Elder. Yet the Hermitage boasts five magnificent paintings by Cranach the Elder and a marvellous selection of German and Austrian works from the 17th, 18th and 19th centuries.

UNKNOWN MASTER
Christ on Judgement Day with
Interceding Mary and John the Baptist
Early 15th century. North German School.
Tempera on panel. 46.5 x 70 cm. Inv. No. 691

Pictures with representations of Christ
as the judge on the Day of the Last
Judgement were intended for court rooms
in town halls to remind councillors of
equity, honesty and fairness of justice.
Iconographically and stylistically the painting follows the Late Gothic tradition. Prior
to 1712, when the work was presented to
Peter I, it was in the Town Hall of Elbing.
From the Peter I collection.

UNKNOWN SWABIAN MASTER
The Adoration of the Infant Christ
(The Nativity)
16th century. *Oil on panel. 182 x 94.5 cm.*
Inv. No. 5586

The painting was originally a wing of a
polyptych, the other panels of which are
missing. The manner of execution shows an
obvious link with the Netherlandish School,
particularly Roger van der Weyden, whose
lessons were imbibed by German artists in
the late 15th century. Some researchers
believe that the work was painted by the
Swabian master Friedrich Herlin (d. ca. 1500)
as the architectural landscape here
depicted is similar to those that occur
in his altarpieces.
From the State Museum Reserve, 1923.

HANS WERTINGER, CALLED THE SWABIAN
Between 1465 and 1470–1533
Rural Festival (October)
Oil on panel. 22 x 40 cm. Inv. No. 5579

Hans Wertinger, a German painter,
engraver, draughtsman and miniaturist,

created a series of paintings illustrating the
twelve months of the year. Nine companion paintings are in Germany, two in Spain
and one, *October*, is owned by the
Hermitage.
From the Shuvalov Palace,
Leningrad, 1925.

**LUCAS CRANACH THE ELDER
(LUCAS MÜLLER ?)**
1472–1553
Venus and Cupid
*1509. Oil on canvas (transferred from
panel). 213 x 102 cm. Inv. No. 680*

The great artist, the early years of whose
work are not documented, came to call
himself "Cranach" (after his birthplace) during his stay in Vienna in 1502; under this
name he has gone down in the history of
world art. In 1505, at the invitation of the
Saxon court, Cranach went to Wittenberg
and lived until 1550 there. He made the
acquaintance of Martin Luther, who taught
in Wittenberg University, and absorbed the
ideas of German humanism. Responding
to the tastes of Electors of Saxony, Cranach
deliberately cultivated the refined and
elegant Gothic drawing in his paintings.
Venus and Cupid is the first painting
on a subject from classical mythology
in Cranach's work.
*From the H. Brühl collection,
Dresden, 1769.*

**LUCAS CRANACH THE ELDER
(LUCAS MÜLLER ?)**
1472–1553
**The Virgin and Child under
the Apple-tree**
*Ca. 1530. Oil on canvas (transferred from
panel). 87 x 59 cm. Inv. No. 684*

Cranach's masterpiece, The Virgin and
Child under the Apple-tree, was painted
when the artist was at the peak of his creative talent, and is treated in keeping with
the spirit of the German Renaissance.
The innermost meaning of the painting lies
in the Christian dogma of the Fall of Man
and the salvation of mankind. The depiction of apples is a direct hint at Original
Sin. The apple and bread, held by the
infant Christ, allude to his future redemp-
tive sacrifice at the price of his flesh.
The colour range of the painting is exquisite, pleasing to the eye. In accordance
with the general Renaissance tendency
to interpret the image of the Virgin in wider
terms then was practised in the Middle
Ages, Cranach has turned Mary into
a fairy-tale golden-haired queen of the
Garden of Eden, the ruler of Nature.
The landscape plays as important a role
as it does in his other works.
Acquired in 1851.

LUCAS CRANACH THE ELDER
(LUCAS MÜLLER ?)
1472–1553
Portrait of a Woman
1526. Oil on panel. 88.5 x 58.5 cm. Inv. No. 683

The portrait was painted at the peak of Cranach's creative powers, foreshadowing the characteristic features of his later period. The most intricate pattern of dress and ornaments acquires a self-sufficient importance and the representation of human values gives way to a virtuoso command of the line and a plethora of decorative details. In their attempt to identify the depicted lady, researchers point out her resemblance to Sybille of Cleves, the fiancée of John Frederick of Saxony. It is more probable, however, that the painting embodies Cranach's idea of female beauty. Not by chance, the same, Cranach's, type of face can be found in other works by the master.
Acquired before 1797.

BARTHEL (BARTHOLOMAEUS)
BRUYN THE ELDER
1493–1555
Portrait of a Woman and Her Daughter
Oil on canvas (transferred from panel).
75.5 x 46 cm. Inv. No. 679

An outstanding master of the Cologne school, Barthel Bruyn is represented by two portraits in the Hermitage. The *Portrait of a Woman and Her Daughter*, probably painted in the late 1530s–early 1540s, is marked by a static composition and a heightened interest in details.
From the Count C. Cobentzl collection, Brussels, 1768.

AMBROSIUS HOLBEIN
Ca. 1495–ca. 1520
Portrait of a Young Man
1518. Oil and tempera on panel.
44 x 32.5 cm. Inv. No. 685

This is one of a few extant portraits by
Ambrosius Holbein, the elder brother of
the celebrated painter Hans Holbein the
Younger. The Hermitage work demonstrates
an impeccable mastery of the artist who
was not indifferent to the achievements of
the Italian Renaissance. At one time the
interwoven letters *FG* on the beret of the
young man led researchers to assume that
the person depicted was an unknown
Basel engraver who signed his works with
the initials FG. On the left, by the column
in a cartouche, is an inscription: *At the
age of 20, 1518,* relating to the model.
Acquired ca. 1773.

ADAM ELSHEIMER
1578–1610
St Christopher
1598/99. Oil on copper plate. 22.5 x 17.5 cm.
Inv. No. 694

According to the *Golden Legend* by the
13th-century Italian theologian Jacobus
de Voragine, St Christopher was one of
the Christian martyrs who served God
and devoted himself to carrying travellers
across a river. Christophoros in Greek
means 'Christ-bearer'. His image was very
popular in Germany and he was venerated
as the patron saint of travellers and sailors,
who protected them from sudden death.
The painting illustrates the evolution of
North German art towards a new, Italian,
idiom.
Acquired between 1763 and 1774.

HANS VON AACHEN
1552–1615
Allegory of Peace, Art and Wealth
Oil on canvas. 197 x 142 cm. Inv. No. 695

Hans von Aachen painted most exclusively
allegorical and mythological subjects.
He studied in Venice (1574–77), worked
in Rome (1577–88), then returned to his
native Cologne and in 1598 became
Court Painter to Emperor Rudolph II in
Prague. This intricate allegorical composition was intended to glorify the emperor
as a patron of the sciences and arts.
The female figures personify Peace
(the one with an olive branch), Art
(holding a palette) and Wealth (holding
a cornucopia).
*From the J.-E. Gotzkowsky collection,
Berlin, 1764.*

JÜRGEN OVENS
1623–1679
Self-Portrait
Oil on canvas. 125 x 95 cm. Inv. No. 2782

The artist studied in Rembrandt's studio in Amsterdam, hence the subdued brownish colour scale favoured by Dutch realist painters. This is the latest self-portrait and one of the best works produced by Ovens. It differs from his commissioned works by a more realistic and intimate character.
From the P. Semenov-Tian-Shansky collection, Petrograd, 1915.

JOHANN HEINRICH SCHÖNFELD
1609–1682/83
The Marriage at Cana
Oil on canvas. 145.5 x 182.5 cm. Inv. No. 5357

The second half of the 17th century saw the emergence of many excellent German artists, who were mainly active abroad. The most talented of them, Johann Heinrich Schönfeld was one of the few German artists who adhered to the distinctive national idiom while working in Italy. He was very famous in his day, but then forgotten to be rediscovered only several decades ago. The fantastic architectural landscape against which the biblical subject of the Marriage at Cana is unfolded, creates a romantic atmosphere peculiar to the Baroque and Mannerism. Schönfeld's works also show a marked influence of the classicist Nicolas Poussin with whom he had met in Rome.
From the State Museum Reserve, 1924.

CHRISTOPH PAUDISS
Ca. 1625–1666
Still Life
Oil on canvas (transferred from panel).
62 x 46.5 cm. Inv. No. 1035

A talented German painter, Christoph
Paudiss studied in Holland in the 1640s
and was, probably, a pupil of Rembrandt.
The similarity of his works to the circle of
Rembrandt is obvious. This still life can
be classed among the best 17th-century
works in the Museum's section of German
painting. Carefully combining the objects,
the artist has achieved the impression
of their casual arrangement. The main
emphasis, however, is placed not so much
on the objects as their reaction to light.
The volumes constitute an inseparable
whole with the vibrating atmosphere and
the shadows appear not as the mute spots
of colour but as a transparent medium
gleaming with reflections. A bunch of
onions hanging on the wall is a motif
recurring in the artist's still lifes.
Acquired before 1859.

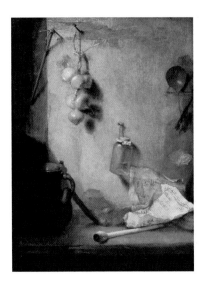

DANIEL SCHULTZ
Ca. 1615–1683
Family Portrait
1654 (?). Oil on canvas. 166 x 231 cm.
Inv. No. 8540

Daniel Schultz was born in Danzig
(Gdansk). In 1646–49 he lived in the
Netherlands and upon his return home until
1660 was Court Painter to the Polish king
Jan II Casimir in Warsaw. Art historians have
not reached a unanimous opinion as to
who is depicted in the portrait. Due to the
Mongoloid type of the faces, the portrait
was entitled *A Tatar Family, A Kalmyk and
His Family, Portrait of Dedesz Aga with His
Family and Servants*, and so on. Dated
1654 (or 1664) on the strength of a poorly
readable inscription on the base of the pillar detected in 1908.
From the Yekaterininsky Palace,
Pushkin, 1937.

ANTON RAFFAEL MENGS
1728–1779
Self-Portrait
Ca. 1775. Oil on panel. 102 x 77 cm.
Inv. No. 1330

The leading German painter of the middle and second half of the 18th century, Mengs enjoyed an immense popularity in Europe. He belonged to the Neo-classical circle of Winckelmann and despite the influence of the French school succeeded in demonstrating the vitality of German painting. Mengs' portraits are character- ized by a harmonious colour scale and an accurate rendition of the facial features of his models.
Acquired in 1794 (?).

ANTON RAFFAEL MENGS
1728–1779
Perseus and Andromeda
1774–77. Oil on canvas. 227 x 153.5 cm.
Inv. No. 1328

This is an illustrious example of the Neo-classicist Mengs' effort to revive the classical traditions. Its concept was prompted by an antique cameo owned by his wife. The antique relief from the Doria Pamphili Gallery in Rome served him as a model for Andromeda, and the statue of Apollo of Belvedere for the figure of Perseus.

After completing the painting Mengs exhibited it in the Palazzo Barberini in Rome where it caused an enormous furore. According to the memoirs of the English artist Jones, it was commissioned by Sir Watkin William Winn, who paid Mengs 300 livres. In 1778 the painting was sent to Britain by sea, but the ship was seized by French pirates, who sold it in the Spanish port of Cadiz to the French naval minister. There it was bought for Catherine II and transported via Málaga and Madrid to Versailles.
Acquired in 1780.

ANGELICA KAUFFMANN
1741–1807
**Virgil Reading His *Aeneid* to Octavia
and Augustus**
1788. *Oil on canvas. 123 x 159 cm.
Inv. No. 4177*

Like many Neo-classical artists, Kauffmann
was influenced by the ideas of Winckelmann,
that great researcher of Antiquity. But in
her paintings on mythological subjects
the well-balanced composition and the
abstract imagery are charged with an emotion signalling the advent of sentimentalism
in painting.
From the Lazienki Palace, Warsaw, 1902.

ANGELICA KAUFFMANN
1741–1807
Self-Portrait
Between 1780 and 1785. *Oil on canvas.
76.5 x 63 cm (oval). Inv. No. 7261*

This is the most fascinating work in Angelica
Kauffmann's legacy. Her spontaneous,
true-to-life portraits are vastly superior
to her rather anaemic and speculative
allegorical compositions.
*From the Yusupov Palace,
Leningrad, 1925.*

HEINRICH FÜGER
1751–1818
Portrait of Prince Nikolai Yusupov
Oil on canvas. 112 x 87 cm. Inv. No. 7261

Heinrich Füger was a representative
of the 18th-century Austrian school,
a Neo-classical artist, Director of the
Vienna Academy of Arts. Nikolai Borisovich
Yusupov, a Russian statesman, collector
and bibliophile, at one time headed the
Imperial Hermitage. He was sent to Italy on
a diplomatic mission and, besides his main
occupation, purchased paintings and
sculptures for Catherine II. This portrait was
presumably commissioned by Yusupov
in 1783, when he stayed in Rome.
From the Yusupov Palace, Leningrad, 1925.

FIRST FLOOR

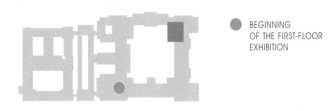

● BEGINNING
OF THE FIRST-FLOOR
EXHIBITION

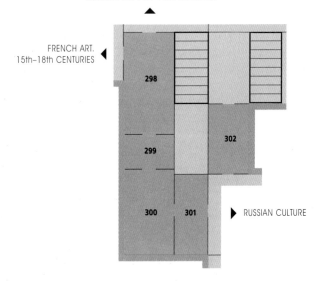

FRENCH ART. 15th–18th CENTURIES

FRENCH ART.
15th–18th CENTURIES ◄

298

299

300

301

302

► RUSSIAN CULTURE

ENGLISH PAINTING.
16th–19th CENTURIES

English art in the Hermitage is represented by paintings, graphic works and numerous items of the applied and decorative arts. The collection traces its origins back to the last quarter of the 18th century when, in 1774, it received its first English painting, *The Forge*, by Joseph Wright of Derby, bought from the artist. In 1779 the Museum acquired a superb collection of the English Prime Minister Robert Walpole (1676–1745), which brought in works by renowned European masters and English paintings from the late 16th to the early 18th centuries. This acquisition formed the nucleus of the future collection of English painting in the Hermitage. Between 1785 and 1786 the Museum obtained the *Landscape with Aeneas and Dido*, one of the finest works by Thomas Jones and in 1790 another three large canvases, *The Infant Heracles Strangling the Serpents Sent by Hera*, *The Continence of Scipio* and *Cupid Untying the Girdle of Venus*, commissioned by Catherine II from Joshua Reynolds. Thus, by the early 19th century St Petersburg had amassed a rather significant collection of English painting and applied art, which was second to none outside England at the time. Although many works were intended for the decoration of suburban royal residences, they eventually found their way to the Hermitage collection. Throughout the 19th century the Hermitage collection of English painting had practically no additions. It was only in 1912 that the Museum received a number of fine 18th-century portraits bequeathed by the renowned Petersburg collector Alexei Khitrovo. Among them were first-class works by Thomas Gainsborough, George Romney, John Hoppner and Henry Raeburn. After 1917 numerous works of art entered the Hermitage from the nationalized private collections or were acquired through the Expert-Purchasing Commission. Today the Hermitage collection totals nearly 120 English paintings.

**UNKNOWN ARTIST OF THE LATE
16th CENTURY (CIRCLE OF MARCUS
GHEERAERTS THE YOUNGER)
Portrait of a Man**
1595. *Oil on panel. 114.5 x 89 cm.*
Inv. No. 7333

The earliest English easel paintings in the
Hermitage date from the 16th century
when English painting developed under
the influence of foreign masters.
In the first half of the 16th century the
renowned German artist Hans Holbein
lived and worked in London. It was
through his work that England first came
into immediate contact with the art of the
High Renaissance with its emphasis on
humanistic ideals. The art of portraiture
not only glorified the monarch and his
environment but also extolled the so-
called cult of ancestors, which led to the
creation of portrait galleries in many mansions of the English nobility. In this formal
court portrait the artist pays particular
attention to details emphasizing the
social status of his model.
From the State Museum Reserve, 1921.

THOMAS GAINSBOROUGH
1727–1788
Portrait of a Lady in Blue
Late 1770s. Oil on canvas. 76 x 64 cm.
Inv. No. 3509

Essential changes in English painting and
especially in portraiture, which remained
the leading genre throughout the 17th and
18th centuries, took place under the influence of Anthony van Dyck. Active in
London for a long period of time, Van Dyck
created the genre of poetically elevated
portrait, and his work left a strong mark on
the following generation of artists. One of
the brilliant galaxy of 18th-century English
portraitists was Thomas Gainsborough.
All his life he regarded landscape as his
real bent, but he had to paint portraits
for a living. It was in this genre that he
reached unprecedented heights.
The *Portrait of a Lady in Blue* is among
his finest creations.
*From the A. Khitrovo collection, bequeathed
by the owner, St Petersburg, 1912.*

JOHN WOOTTON
Ca.1682–1764
Hounds and Magpie
1740s. Oil on canvas. 152 x 128 cm.
Inv. No. 9781

English artists were as earnest in representing the pedigree horses and hounds as in portraying their masters. Wootton painted hunting and racing scenes and depicted animals against a landscape background. According to the inscription on the engraving made by W. Birn from this painting, the Hermitage canvas shows "the Lord Orford's favourite hounds and a magpie, which followed them during the hunt". "Lord Orford" is Robert Walpole who was granted the title of Earl of Orford in 1742.
From the R. Walpole collection, Houghton Hall, England, 1779.

JOSEPH WRIGHT OF DERBY
1734–1797
The Forge
1773. Oil on canvas. 105 x 140 cm.
Inv. No. 3149

The romantic trends inherent in late 18th-century English art were most vividly reflected in the oeuvre of Joseph Wright of Derby. The master's keen interest in lighting effects and bold contrasts of light and shade found many admirers among his contemporaries. Catherine II acquired three canvases directly from the artist who was very proud of it. The light of the furnace in *The Forge* is meant to create a magic circle, warming and uniting the figures, while the dark frightening reign of night beyond it is full of mystery.
From the artist's studio, 1774.

JOSHUA REYNOLDS
1723–1792
**The Infant Heracles Strangling
the Serpents Sent by Hera**
*1786–88. Oil on canvas. 303 x 297 cm.
Inv. No. 1348*

Joshua Reynolds, the first president of
the Royal Academy in London, a gifted
painter and theorist, was one of the most
respected and influential artists of the
18th century. This painting was commissioned from Reynolds by Catherine II.
The artist was versed in history and literature well enough to find a proper subject
without much effort. It was in the image
of Heracles doing his first heroic deeds
that Reynolds has pictured – not without
a flattery – the power of the young Russian
Empire. The soothsayer Tiresius, an old
sage who foretold the great labours
of Heracles, was given the features of
Reynolds' late friend Samuel Johnson,
an eminent literary critic and lexicogra-
pher of the 18th century. Sarah Siddons,
a famous tragic actress, was probably a
prototype for Hera. To astound the spectator, to make him draw an analogy
between the history and the present –
that is what Reynolds aimed to achieve
in his historical paintings.
From the collection of Catherine II, 1789.

JOSHUA REYNOLDS
1723–1792
Cupid Untying the Girdle of Venus
*1788. Oil on canvas. 127.5 x 101 cm.
Inv. No. 1320*

The painting was acquired from the artist
for Grigory Potiomkin in 1788. This fascinating canvas on an erotic subject is the
author's replica of his own work done
in 1784 for Lord Carisfort (Tate Gallery,
London). The painting can only condition-
ally be referred to the historical genre so
revered by the artist as he breaks away
from the academic canons, using free
and easy brushstrokes. The work's main
appeal lies in its saturated colours and
virtuoso manner of execution. It is very
likely that Emma Hamilton was the artist's
model for Venus.
*From the G. Potiomkin collection,
St Petersburg, 1792.*

GEORGE ROMNEY
1734–1802
Portrait of Mrs. Harriet Greer
1781. *Oil on canvas. 76 x 64 cm. Inv. No. 3511*

A younger contemporary of Reynolds
and Gainsborough, George Romney experienced the influence of both yet managed to create an artistic idiom of his
own. His skill in bringing out the elegant
appearance of his models, their appeal
and bon monde refinement captivated
many a client. In the *Portrait of Mrs. Harriet
Greer* Romney strove to reveal the earthly
charm and the femininity of a young
pretty woman.
*From the A. Khitrovo collection bequeathed
by the owner, St Petersburg, 1912.*

HENRY RAEBURN
1756–1823
Portrait of Mrs. Elinor Bethune
1790s. *Oil on canvas. 76 x 64 cm.
Inv. No. 3512*

A Scotsman and a friend of Sir Walter
Scott, Raeburn spent most of his life in
Edinburgh and left us portraits of almost
all his famous contemporaries. One of the
gems of English painting in the Hermitage
collection, the romantically elevated
Portrait of Mrs. Elinor Bethune, was created
in the 1790s.
*From the A. Khitrovo collection bequeathed
by the owner, St Petersburg, 1912.*

THOMAS JONES
1742–1803
**Landscape with Aeneas and Dido
(Storm)**
1769. *Oil on canvas. 137.5 x 193.5 cm.
Inv. No. 1343*

The landscape genre held a prominent
place in English painting of the second
half of the 18th century. The presentation
of nature was among the most favourite
themes treated by English artists in the
epoch of industrialization. An eminent figure in this genre was Thomas Jones. One
of his most perfect paintings, as the artist
himself admitted, was the Hermitage
Landscape with Aeneas and Dido, planned
as a pendant to the large landscape
of 1767. The figures painted by John
Hamilton Mortimer, a friend of the artist,
represented an episode from Virgil's
Aeneid. However, the main 'hero' of the
canvas is nature – the mighty trees bending in the gusts of wind, the stormy sky and
the distant outlines of legendary Carthage.
At the end of the 18th century the developing romantic trends paved the way for
an enormous flourishing of the landscape
genre in the first half of the 19th century.
*From the G. Potemkin collection,
St Petersburg, 1792.*

JOHN HOPPNER
1758–1810
Portrait of Richard Brinsley Sheridan (?)
Late 1780s–early 1790s. *Oil on canvas.*
77 x 64 cm. Inv. No. 3510

This portrait provides an idea of English
portrait painting at the turn of the
19th century. Richard Brinsley Sheridan
(1751–1816) was an eminent playwright,
the author of *School for Scandal*, a politi-
cian and renowned orator of the period.

Researchers believe that the person
depicted, if compared with the most
authentic portrait of Sheridan painted by
Reynolds in 1788–89, does not allow to
admit an unquestionable portrait likeness.
A highly competent master, Hoppner was
in no way an innovative portraitist resorting
to the compositional and painting techniques of his senior contemporaries.
*From the A. Khitrovo collection bequeathed
by the owner, St Petersburg, 1912.*

THOMAS LAWRENCE
1769–1830
**Portrait of Emily Wellesley-Pole
(Portrait of Lady Raglan)**
*Ca. 1814. Oil on panel. 76 x 63 cm.
Inv. No. 3513*

The most renowned English portraitist of the
early 19th century was Thomas Lawrence.
His 1790 portrait of the famous actress Miss
Farren immediately raised him to the ranks
of the most popular portrait painters. On
the death of Reynolds in 1792, Lawrence
was granted the title of court painter and
in 1820 became President of the Royal
Academy. Almost all the European royalty,
military and diplomatic celebrities of the
period sat for the artist. His early works
include the *Portrait of Emily Wellesley-Pole*,
which may have been commissioned
on the occasion of her marriage to Lord
Fitzroy-Somerset (Baron Raglan from 1852).
The pictorial qualities of this portrait make
it one of the artist's best.
*From the A. Khitrovo collection bequeathed
by the owner, St Petersburg, 1912.*

THOMAS LAWRENCE
1769–1830
Portrait of Count Mikhail Vorontsov
1821. *Oil on canvas. 143 x 113 cm.*
Inv. No. 5846

Count Mikhail Semionovich Vorontsov, the son of the Russian Ambassador to England, was an eminent statesman and a combat general who took part in the military campaigns against Napoleon. The head proudly turned against the stormy sky and the coat effectively thrown on a shoulder to reveal the jacket full of decorations, impart a certain theatrical quality to this portrait.
Through the State Museum Reserve
from the Vorontsovs-Dashkovs collection,
Petrograd, 1923.

CHRISTINA ROBERTSON
1796–1854
Children with a Parrot
1850s. *Oil on canvas. 112 x 104 cm.*
Inv. No. 8330

The work of Christina Robertson is related to the so-called Victorian epoch in the history of English art. The portraiture of this period was marked by an exaggerated sentimentality, illusory accuracy in rendering the costumes, superficial characterization and fashion-plate beauty. Yet within the framework of salon painting Robertson managed to create images of children, very attractive and full of life.
Acquired from A. Zenger, Leningrad, 1938.

FIRST FLOOR

ROOM 2

ROOM **273**

ROOM 1

ROOM **229**

ROOM **223**

ROOM **229**

ROOM **200**

ROOM **210**

WESTERN EUROPEAN DECORATIVE AND APPLIED ARTS. 15th–18th CENTURIES

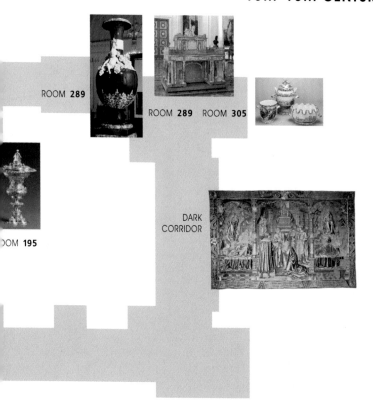

ROOM **289**

ROOM **289**   ROOM **305**

DARK CORRIDOR

OM **195**

The Hermitage collection of Western European decorative and applied arts, gathered in the course of three centuries, totals more than 60 thousand works. In the18th and 19th centuries numerous items of furniture, textiles, bone-carving, faience, porcelain, silverware and artistic bronze, produced by the best European workshops, found their way to the Winter Palace, the Hermitage and suburban royal residences. They included diplomatic gifts, objects commissioned from celebrated European manufactories and acquisitions made by members of the Imperial family through the mediation of renowned art experts. In 1918 the Department of Applied Art was established in the Hermitage, which incorporated the Imperial collections and the nationalized collections of the Russian nobility – the Yusupovs, Dolgorukys, Sheremetevs, Bobrinskys and others. In 1923 the famous collection of the former Museum of the Central School of Technical Design, founded by Baron Stieglitz, was transferred to the Hermitage. Today the Hermitage exhibition is divided into several sections, such as Western European silverware, Limoges enamels and French applied arts of the 17th and 18th centuries; other works form part of the interior decoration of the palace.

FURNITURE

Cabinet and support

Late 16th–early 17th century. Southern Germany. *Pine, ash, intarsia. 154 x 129 x 56 cm. Inv. No. M6 204*

The decorative technique of incrustation was known even to the ancient Egyptian furniture-makers. During the Renaissance, Italian masters widely used inlays of contrasting woods (intarsia) notable for their illusionistic effects, which were subsequently employed by cabinet-makers in other countries. The Hermitage cabinet may

have been made by Tyrolean masters. This is evidenced by a marble-like finish revealing the texture of the crosscut end of a log. Cabinets, or the cupboards with drawers and two doors, for the first time appeared in Italy during the Late Renaissance and became a popular type of office furniture in the17th and later centuries. Their name derives from the Italian *cabine* for keeping precious objects.
From the Museum of the Baron A. Stieglitz School of Technical Design, Leningrad, 1933.

Armchair

Early 18th century. Italy. *Wood, gilt, velvet, silver thread embroidery. 157 x 83 x 74 cm. Inv. No. M6 337*

This lavishly adorned armchair is a typical example of the Italian formal furniture of the early 18th century. A high back widening at the top is exuberantly decorated with Baroque carving. At the same time, the master's striving for the elegant contours, evident in the handling of the armchair's legs, made him use typical Rococo devices.
From the Museum of the Baron A. Stieglitz School of Technical Design, Petrograd, 1923.

Cupboard

Second half, 17th century. Workshop of
A.-Ch. Boule. France, Paris. *Ebony, tortoiseshell,
bronze mounts, marquetry, intarsia.*
255 x 170 x 64 cm. Inv. No. M6 420

The highest standard of craftsmanship
achieved by the French ébenistes in the
late 17th and early 18th centuries is
demonstrated by the Hermitage furniture
pieces from the workshop of André-
Charles Boule (1642–1732), Cabinet-
Maker to Louis XIV, who also worked for
Philippe V of Spain and other European
sovereigns. This highly gifted artist gave
his name to the style of furniture decoration (boulework) incredibly popular in
the 18th and 19th centuries. Boule used
the marquetry technique (a sort of ornamental mosaic with the application of
a wide variety of materials – wood,
mother-of-pearl, brass, silver) and his
works were a virtuoso combination of
ebony and semi-transparent, brown tortoiseshell contrasting with gilded bronze
and light-coloured ivory. An outstanding
designer, Boule evolved singular forms
of furniture combining features inherent
in the pompous Louis Quatorze style.
The doors and lateral walls of the unique

Hermitage cupboard are adorned with
inlaid decorative panels.
*From the Museum of the Baron A. Stieglitz
School of Technical Design, Petrograd,
1923.*

Corner cupboard

First third, 18th century. Master E. Doiarat.
France. *Wood, painting on lacquer, bronze.*
173 x 78 x 53 cm. Inv. No. M6 470

In the 17th and 18th centuries such three-
tiered corner cupboards decorated with
painted, mostly companion, panels were
in great vogue in Europe. The upper part
of the present cupboard with ledged
shelves features insets of genuine Chinese
lacquers of the late 17th century with
painted images of kylin, the fabulous
Chinese animals of a favour-invoking character. The doors were painted by European
masters in chinoiserie style (derived from
the French *chine* – Chinese), which was
in fashion in the Rococo period. The cupboards bear the mark of the French cabinet-maker Etienne Doiarat (1670–1732).
*From the Museum of the Baron A. Stieglitz
School of Technical Design, Leningrad,
1933.*

Armchair

Ca. 1749. Master N.-Q. Foliot. France, Paris.
Oak, carving, gilt, velvet, silver thread
embroidery. 113 x 77 x 90 cm. Inv. No. M6 411

In the 18th century furniture pieces, especially for sitting, were mostly made for
comfort. The French ébenistes created a
wide variety of elegant armchairs with soft
spacious seats. This armchair was part of
the set commissioned by Louise-Elizabeth,
daughter of Louis XV, Princess of Parmes,
for the Count's palace in Parmes. The furniture was made by Nicolas-Quinibert Foliot,
Purveyor to the Royal Court. Two similar
armchairs are in the collection of the
Metropolitan Museum of Art in the USA
and in a private collection in Paris.
The authentic upholstery embroidered
in silver threads, however, has survived
only on the Hermitage piece.
From the Museum of the Baron A. Stieglitz
School of Technical Design, Leningrad, 1933.

Secretaire

Last quarter, 18th century. France, Paris.
Mahogany, porcelain, bronze.
156 x 116 x 51.5 cm. Inv. No. Э 279

In the late 18th century, the era of Neo-
classicism, the cabinet-makers came to
use classical motifs in decoration. The gilt
bronze mounts in the frieze part of the
Hermitage secretaire represent the scenes
of Bacchanalias. The porcelain plaques,

made at the Sèvres Porcelain Manufactory
in the technique evolved by the British
potter Josiah Wedgwood, imitate antique
cameos with white ceramic paste in relief
pressed on a blue (or sky-blue) ground.
The scene of the central plaque is *The
Rape of Helen*. Due to the elegant decor
and magnificent execution, the secretaire
can be ranked among the finest examples
of decorative and applied art.
From the Main Collection of the Winter Palace.

Chair

Last quarter, 18th century. England. *Satinwood, painting, weaving (seat). 93 x 51 x 45 cm. Inv. No. Э 285*

The Neo-classical style in England found vivid expression in simple and elegant furniture pieces, often of satinwood, decorated with exquisite carving and fine painting. The publication, in 1788, of the *Cabinet-Maker and Upholsterer's Guide* by George Hepplewhite (d. 1786) resulted in a particular demand for the chairs with heart-, shield- or oval backs. Though the decor of the Hermitage chair has no direct analogies in Hepplewhite's edition, it provides a notion of the style evolved by the famous British cabinet-maker.
From the collection of the Oliv family, Petrograd, 1923.

Bureau-pupitre with a small cabinet

1785. D. Roentgen. Germany. *Thuyawood, bronze. 118 x 142 x 96 cm. Inv. No. Э 5090*

The celebrated German cabinet-maker David Roentgen (1743–1807) was a purveyor to many European courts. His sensational success in France at the court of Louis XVI attracted the attention of Catherine II, and from 1784 on he received commissions from Russia. One of the deliveries to the court of the Russian Empress included a bureau-pupitre which resembles a monumental piece of architecture with columns, a frieze and a stepped top serving as a pedestal for a bronze sculpture. Like most of Roentgen's famous works, the bureau is complete with numerous pigeonhole compartments provided with secret locks and a special device to raise the tabletop and turn it into a standing pupitre.
From the Main Collection of the Winter Palace.

TAPESTRIES

Tapestry: *The Vision of the Virgin* **from the series** *The Story of the Virgin of Le Sablon*

1518–19. After a cartoon by B. van Orley. Workshop of P. van Aelst. Flanders, Brussels. Wool, silk. 345 x 543 cm. Inv. No. T 2976

In the 15th and 16th centuries the best tapestries were produced in Flanders and Brabant, the southern provinces of the Low Countries, with a centre in Brussels. The *Vision of the Virgin* from the well-known series *The Story of the Virgin of Le Sablon* is one of the finest in the Hermitage tapestry collection. Commissioned by François Tourne de Taxis, the Chief Postmaster of the Habsburg Empire, it was woven in Brussels. Bernard van Orley (1492 ?–1541), the designer of the series, invested the Brussels tapestries with a monumentality and idealization typical of the Italian Renaissance. The *Story of the Virgin of Le Sablon* is one of the early works by the celebrated artist. The cartoons in the series are based on the legend of an old nun, Beatrice, to whom the Virgin Mary appeared in her dream, telling her to bring a sculptural image of the Virgin from Antwerp to the Sablon Cathedral in Brussels. In the foreground of the central part are the Duke of Brabant and Tourne de Taxis, in front of them are the kneeling Beatrice and the courtiers dressed in rich clothes. In the upper and lower borders are the woven unrolled scrolls with Latin inscriptions explaining the subject of the composition.

From the Museum of the Baron A. Stieglitz School of Technical Design, Petrograd, 1923.

Tapestry: *The Wedding of Constantine* **from the series** *The Story of the Emperor Constantine*

1633–68. After cartoons by P.P. Rubens. Manufactory of R. de La Planche. France, Paris. Wool, silk. 445 x 470 cm. Inv. No. T 15606

At the turn of the 17th century, at the invitation of Henri IV who had cherished the dreams to restore the production of tapestries, two Flemish masters, François de La Planche (Franz van der Planken; 1573–1627) and Marc de Comans (1563–before 1650), arrived in France. They established a tapestry manufactory in the old Gobelins family dyeworks on the outskirts of Paris. When François de La Planche died, it passed to his son Raphael who started the production of tapestries on his own while de Comans retained the Gobelins workshop.

Competing with each other, the two factories created outstanding works, enlisting the services of such eminent artists as Peter Paul Rubens. The theme of the Baroque series of tapestries *The Story of the Emperor Constantine*, the cartoons for which Louis XIII commissioned from Rubens, was closely related to the epoch of the Reformation and the Wars of Religion waged throughout the Europe in the first half of the 17th century. The Roman emperor Constantine, who advocated the freedom of religious belief, was famous for his adherence to Christianity and his piety. During his reign, the ancient city of Byzantium was renamed Constantinople and made the capital of the Roman Empire.

From the A. Polovtsev collection, Leningrad, 1926.

Gobelins tapestry:
May. Saint Germain-de-Près.
The King and the Dames Promenading
from the series *Royal Residences*
Late 17th–early 18th century. Cartoons
designed by Ch. Le Brun. The Royal Gobelins
Manufactory. France, Paris. *Wool, silk.*
318 x 291 cm. Inv. No. T 2953

In 1667 the famous manufactory in the
Gobelins workshop, in fact already passed
to the Crown in 1662, was given the formal
status of the Royal Manufactory. However,
it retained the name Gobelins as the more
familiar and habitual one, now often used
as a generic word for tapestry. The artist
Charles Le Brun (1619–1690), the first
Director of the Royal Manufactory, considered the glorification of Louis XIV's reign his
main objective. He designed such celebrated series as *The Child Gardeners*, *The
Seasons*, *The Life of Louis XIV* and *Royal
Residences*, engaging the eminent
French artists to work on them. The *Royal*

Residences series was to reflect the
magnificence of the Royal Court. Its
tapestries (equal to the number of months
in a year) depict twelve royal palaces.
The series was a tremendous success.
Represented in the background of the
royal châteaux are the scenes of promenades and hunting of the King and his
suite; in the foreground, as a setting,
are the balustrades adorned with carpets
and garlands, precious vessels and baskets
of fruit and flowers. The artist, however,
focuses not so much on the changes
in the natural environment or the agricul-
tural works peculiar to different seasons
as on the King's amusements. The tapestry
May shows the residence built in 1612–22
for Marie de' Medici, the widow of Henri IV,
who had chosen the wooded area on the
left bank of the Seine (near the Saint-
Germain Abbey) to lay out the famous
Luxembourg Gardens there.
*From the Museum of the Baron A. Stieglitz
School of Technical Design, Petrograd, 1923.*

Gobelins tapestry: *The Feast of Esther* from the series *The Story of Esther*
1764. After cartoons by J.-F. de Troy.
The Royal Gobelins Manufactory, workshop of Cozette. France, Paris. *Wool, silk.*
445 x 540 cm. Inv. No. T 15582

The Hermitage owns four Gobelins tapestries from the series *The Story of Esther* for which Jacque-François de Troy (1679–1759) created seven cartoons in 1737–40. The bordering of the tapestries imitates the framework of painted canvases, a device widely used in the late 18th century when the weaving technique itself made the tapestries look more like paintings.
From the Main Collection of the Winter Palace.

Tapestry: *The Dancer*
(detail of the tapestry *Sacrifice to Pan* from the series *Grotesques Against the Yellow Background*)
First quarter, 18th century. France, Beauvais.
Wool, silk. 391 x 172 cm. Inv. No. T 2957

Another famous tapestry manufactory, located in Beauvais (Picardy, northern France), was established by two Flemings, Louis Hinar and Phillippe Behagle, in 1664. While the Royal Gobelins Manufactory catered only for the Royal Court, the Beauvais enterprise remained in private possession, though under the King's patronage. The commissioners of the works were mostly the French nobles. The six-tapestry series *Grotesques Against the Colour of Spanish Tobacco* (*Grotesques Against the Yellow Background*) was created in 1689 to be reproduced more than one hundred times in a variety of versions. The Hermitage tapestry has a woven border imitating a golden frame with depictions of coloured stones, peacock feathers and flowers.
From the Museum of the Baron A. Stieglitz School of Technical Design, Petrograd, 1923.

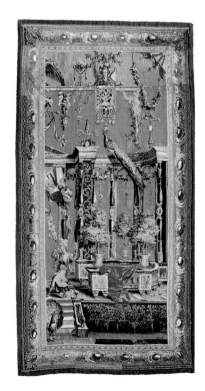

SILVER AND BRONZE

Lidded goblet

Late 16th century. Germany, Nuremberg.
Silver, gilt, coloured stones. Height 25.5 cm.
Inv. No. Э 13038

In addition to Augsburg and Dresden,
the Swabian city of Nuremberg was one of
the largest centres of silverware production
in northern Europe. This type of formal
Nuremberg lidded goblet is characterized
by a fancy-pattern base, embossed surfaces with or without ornament, and a rich
plant decor. Lavishly decorated with
arabesque motifs, the Hermitage goblet
is a brilliant example of the German
jeweller's art.
From the Counts Sheremetev collection,
1930.

Aquamanile

1650s–80s. Sicily, Trapani. *Copper, bronze,*
gilt, corals. Height 20 cm. Inv. No. Э 2708

The Hermitage aquamanile (a vessel
used for washing the hands at table),
made of copper in Trapani, Sicily, is
a typical Baroque piece notable for its
rich figurative ornamention and bright
colours. During the 17th century the
Trapani masters specialized in making
icons, vessels for holy water, goblets
and sculptural groups of gilded bronze
adorned with coral insets and coloured
enamel.
From the Main Collection of the Winter Palace.

Soup tureen from the Paris Service

1758–59. Master F.-T. Germain. France.
Silver, gilt. Height 30 cm. Inv. No. Э 7209

François-Thomas Germain, son of the famous jeweller Thomas Germain (1675–1748), continued his father's business and became Court Master to Louis XV. He created works in the Rococo style and catered for the French court as well as the Russian and Portuguese sovereigns. The Paris Service was commissioned by Elizabeth Petrovna in 1757.
From the Main Collection of the Winter Palace.

The Chesme inkset

1775. Master B.-A. de Mailly. France, Paris.
Bronze, silver, ebony, enamel, gilt.
57.2 x 77 x 55 cm. Inv. No. ЗИ 1450

This inkset by Barnave-Augustine de Mailly (1732–ca. 1793), an eminent Neo-classical enameller and jeweller from Paris, was commissioned by Catherine II to decorate the Round table in the Chesme Palace where the holders of the St George Cross held their sittings. The sophisticated composition includes enamel miniatures depicting episodes from the Russo-Turkish War (1768–74), notably the battle of Chesme (1770), in which the Russian squadron defeated the Turkish fleet.
From the Main Collection of the Winter Palace.

LIMOGES ENAMELS

Plaques: *The Kiss of Judas*
and *The Flagellation of Christ*
from the *Passion* **series**
Mid-16th century. France, Limoges. *Copper,
enamel. 22 x 19 cm. Inv. No. Ф 286*

The craftsmanship of enamellers from
Limoges – the city in central France –
was highly reputed throughout Europe
in the 15th–17th centuries. The famous
Limoges pieces were executed on copper
plaques painted in opaque coloured
enamels with each layer fired separately.

The Hermitage boasts a magnificent
collection of enamels from the 15th
and 16th centuries, which includes works
by the leading Limoges masters of both
the Old and New schools. The *Passion*
series of twelve plaques is attributed to
the Old Limoges school, which followed
the Gothic tradition. The compositions
and the characters are presumably
borrowed from engravings by Lucas
van Leyden.
From the A. Basilewsky collection, Paris, 1885.

Cup with a depiction of round dance
Late 16th–early 17th century. Master
J. Limosin. France, Limoges. *Copper, enamel.
Height 18 cm. Inv. No. Ф 316*

Jean Limosin (d. after 1646) is one of
the last Limoges masters of importance.
The Hermitage cup is remarkable for its
subject: a depiction of women dancing
in a circle is quite untypical for a master
who specialized in hunting scenes. His
saturated colour schemes combined with
a wealth of ornaments were generally
characteristic of the Limoges enamels
at the final stage of their development.
From the A. Basilewsky collection, Paris, 1885.

The Nativity of Christ

15th century. Master G. della Robbia. Italy, Florence. *Majolica. 262 x 167 cm.*
Inv. No. Н. ск. 337

The name 'majolica' comes from the island of Majorca where the Valencian pottery, bound to France and Italy, was transhipped. The wide use of majolicas in the 15th century for the creation of sculptural reliefs, portraits and multifigure compositions is associated with the name of Luca della Robbia (1400–1482), who established his celebrated workshop in Florence.
The relief *The Nativity of Christ*, executed by his grand-nephew Giovanni (1469–1529), is illustrative of the style evolved by Luca della Robbia.
From the A. Basilewsky collection, Paris, 1885.

Bowl with the scene of the *Feat of Marcus Curtius*

Ca. 1515. Master N. da Urbino. Italy, Urbino. *Majolica. Diameter 30.5 cm. Inv. No. Ф 365*

About 1500 in Faenza, the most important pottery centre in Italy, the istoriato style of decorated majolicas came into being. Popular in Europe throughout the 16th century, it made use of decorative painting on biblical, historical and mythological themes. The key exponent of this style was Nicolo da Urbino who worked in the well-known workshops of Urbino and Castel Durante. The painting of the Hermitage bowl is modelled on an engraving by Raimondi after a Raphael's composition.
From the A. Basilewsky collection, Paris, 1885.

Dish with the scene of *Joshua Stopping the Sun* and ornamentation in grotesque style

1560s–80s. O. Fontana Workshop, Italy, Urbino. *Majolica. Diameter 44.2 cm. Inv. No. Ф 3019*

The evolution of decorative painting in majolicas led to the development of the style of ornament known as the grotesque (from the Italian *grotte* – grottoes).
Its emergence was connected with the excavations in Rome, in 1509, that revealed the remains of the Golden House of Nero (Domus Aurea) with intact ancient murals. These, in turn, inspired Raphael to create the famous frescoes in the Vatican. Thanks to Raphael this ornamental style became incredibly popular and was widely used in the most diverse kinds of decorative and applied art. The Fontana Workshop in Urbino was the first to use grotesques in the decor of majolica tableware.
From the Museum of the Baron A. Stieglitz School of Technical Design, Leningrad, 1933.

PORCELAIN AND FAIENCE

Lady with a Pugdog
1737. Master J.J. Kändler. Meissen Manufactory, Germany. *Porcelain, overglaze painting.* *Height 15.5 cm. Inv. No. 23839*

Before the early 18th century Chinese porcelain in Europe was enormously expensive because the recipe of its manufacture was kept in strict secrecy. The Saxonian ceramists Johann Friedrich Böttger and Erenfried Walter von Tschirnhausen were the first to create the recipe for the production of hard porcelain in Europe, following which the famous factory was opened in Meissen in 1710. It was in the 1730s that the factory began to produce porcelain figurines very popular in the Rococo period. Evolved by the eminent master Johann Joachim Kändler (1706–1775), the series, which includes the Hermitage *Lady with a Pugdog* was given the name 'crinoline figures' as its main characters were the elegant ladies wearing crinolines.
From the Museum of the Baron A. Stieglitz School of Technical Design, Leningrad, 1926.

Chariot-shaped clock
Mid-18th century. Meissen Manufactory, Germany. *Porcelain, bronze, overglaze painting, gilt. Height 52 cm. Inv. No. 23674*

Such items combining modelled porcelain and bronze, usually of functional purpose with incorporated clocks or chandeliers, were very popular in the Rococo period. The lavish floral decoration of the clock is made of 'soft' (less kaolin) porcelain at the French factory in Vincennes, near Paris, specializing in such products.
From the Museum of the Baron A. Stieglitz School of Technical Design, Leningrad, 1926.

Wineglass stand
Ca. 1730. Vienna Porcelain Manufactory, Austria. Porcelain, overglaze painting, gilt. Height 19.6 cm. Inv. No. 20400

In 1719 the Dutchman Claudius Inno-centius du Pacquier (d. 1751), assisted by the Meissen masters, established a porce-lain enterprise in Austria, the celebrated Vienna Manufactory, which existed until 1864. The most famous ornamental motifs of the 'du Pacquier period' were *indianis-che Blumen* (a floral ornament in an Oriental style), *deutsche Blumen* (a floral ornament echoing the Dutch still life) and *Schwarzlot* (the monochrome linear design). This wineglass stand is a magnifi-cent example of the *Schwarzlot* painting executed by Jakobus Helchis, the most eminent artist of the Vienna Manufactory's early period (active in the 1740s).
From the Museum of the Baron A. Stieglitz School of Technical Design, Leningrad, 1926.

Items from the Green Frog Service
1773–74. The Wedgwood Etruria Manufactory, England. Faience. Height of the ice-creamer 34.5 cm. Inv. Nos. ГЧ 8472, 20835, 20832

Josiah Wedgwood (1730–1795), an out-standing British Neo-classical potter, invented high-quality faience pastes (creamware, jasperware, basaltware) and founded his famous manufactory in 1769. In the late 1760s Wedgwood creamware was recognized far beyond England. In 1770 the Russian consul in London was instructed to commission from Wedgwood a large table service for Catherine II.

The complete delivery totalled 944 pieces with 1,222 views of Great Britain. The serv-ice was intended for the Chesme Palace situated on the road from St Petersburg to Tsarskoye Selo in the locality called Kekereeksinen, or Frog swamp in Finnish. Hence the specific coat of arms in the form of a green frog on each item of the service. In line with the increasing romantic trends and the interest in antiquity and medieval relics, many landscapes deco-rating the service reproduce with docu-mentary precision the old English estates and famous parks.
From the English Palace, Peterhof, 1912.

Vase

Late 18th century. The Sèvres Manufactory.
France. *Porcelain, bronze, gilt. Height 190 cm.*
Inv. No. Э 6716

In 1756 the production of porcelain
was transferred from Vincennes to Sèvres,
a Paris suburb, to continue under the
patronage of Mme de Pompadour,
a favourite of Louis XV, who had a residence in Sèvres. Mme de Pompadour
engaged the most eminent French artists,
including François Boucher and Etienne-
Maurice Falconet, the chief designer of
the Sèvres Manufactory from 1757 to 1766.

This enterprise enjoyed particular fame
for its sculptures of biscuit porcelain and
its use of variously coloured glazes, which
made the Sèvres products easily recogniz-
able. The huge Hermitage vase with
mounts of gilded bronze is a masterpiece
of the Sèvres Manufactory. It was purchased by the Russian Vice-Chancellor
Prince Alexander Bezborodko who prided
himself on this 'unicum' and often mentioned it in his letters. The travellers visiting
the Russian capital in the late 18th century
considered the vase one of St Petersburg's
sights.
From the Paskevich collection, Petrograd, 1915.

GLASS

Beaker

Last quarter, 16th century. Italy, Venice.
Glass, Venetian thread. Height 30.5 cm.
Inv. No. Φ 477

When the Crusaders seized Constantinople in 1204, Byzantine glassmakers fled to other cities on the Mediterranean. Part of them settled in Venice where the production of glass had already existed. In 1291 the glass furnaces were moved to the island of Murano in the Venetian lagoon, which turned into a celebrated centre of the Venetian glassmaking. It was in Murano that the unique technique of latticinio was invented: an interglass filigree which consisted in embedding thin opaque white (less frequently of different colour), often intertwined, glass threads into a matrix of hot, still liquid clear glass. In the process of blowing a glass worker gave the threads the necessary direction.
From the A. Basilewsky collection, Paris, 1885.

Beaker and cover

1725–30. Master I. Preissler. Germany, Kronstat (Bohemia). *Glass, painting, gilt. Height 19.5 cm. Inv. No. 16118*

The Hermitage collection includes examples from almost all celebrated centres of German glassware. Before the 18th century the principal glassware decoration techniques were engraving and multicoloured enamel painting, in which German masters were equal to none. By the early 18th century, due to the changing fashions, the multicoloured enamel painting was used alongside the Schwarzlot monochrome painting especially practised by the Bohemian glasshouses. The Schwarzlot painting with touches of gold brought fame to two Bohemian masters – Daniel Preissler and his son Ignaz (1676–?).
The form and the decorative plant motifs of the Hermitage beaker tend toward the Baroque style. Ignaz Preissler has added to the ornament so-called chinoiserie subjects, fanciful scenes from Chinese life, very popular in the Rococo period.
From the Shuvalov Palace, Leningrad, 1925.

FIRST FLOOR

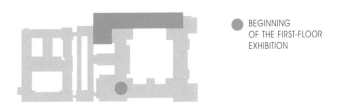

BEGINNING
OF THE FIRST-FLOOR
EXHIBITION

FRENCH ART. 15th–18th CENTURIES

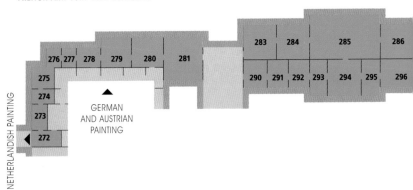

NETHERLANDISH PAINTING

276 277 278 279 280 281

283 284 285 286

290 291 292 293 294 295 296

275

274

273

272

▲
GERMAN
AND AUSTRIAN
PAINTING

SECOND FLOOR

BEGINNING
OF THE SECOND-FLOOR
EXHIBITION

FRENCH ART. 19th–20th CENTURIES

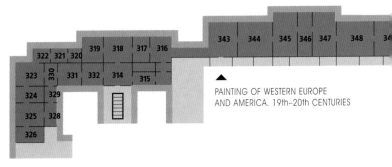

322 321 320 319 318 317 316

343 344 345 346 347 348 34

323 330 331 332 314 315

324 329

325 328

326

▲
PAINTING OF WESTERN EUROPE
AND AMERICA. 19th–20th CENTURIES

FRENCH PAINTING AND SCULPTURE.
15th–20th CENTURIES

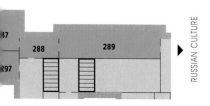

RUSSIAN CULTURE

EASTERN ART

The Hermitage takes pride in its collection of French art which covers a period of five centuries and occupies over 50 rooms on the first and second floors of the Winter Palace. The exhibition of 15th- to 18th-century French art, arranged on the first floor, features not only masterpieces of painting but also the finest examples of sculpture, furniture and porcelain. 19th-century works and modern French paintings produced by the Impressionists, Post-Impressionists and the leading exponents of other trends in the last quarter of the 19th to the early 20th century are displayed on the second floor of the Winter Palace and on the new exhibition premises in the General Staff building on Palace Square (see pp. 308–315).

PAINTING.
15th–18th CENTURIES

MASTER OF THE THUISON ALTARPIECE
Second half, 15th century
The Entry into Jerusalem
Oil on panel. 116.5 x 51.5 cm.
Inv. No. 5699

Chronologically the French visual arts
represented in the Hermitage date back
to the second half of the 15th century.
Works of this period are very rare – even
the Louvre has only several 'primitives'.
The Entry into Jerusalem was painted by

an anonymous master of the school
of Amiens, known as the Master of the
Thuison Altarpiece, and the Hermitage
panel is probably one of its parts (according to the opinion voiced by Vladimir
Loewinson-Lessing in 1973). In its refined
painting the panel bears a close affinity
with other works characteristic of the art
of northern France, which was strongly
influenced by the Netherlandish school.
*Acquired in 1919; formerly in the A. Gagarin
collection, Petrograd.*

MASTER OF ST SEBASTIAN
Active 1493–1505/8
**St Sebastian in Front of the Emperors
Diocletian and Maximilian**
Oil on panel. 80.5 x 56 cm. Inv. No. 6745

The painter was so named after an
altarpiece with scenes from the life of
St Sebastian, ascribed to him. Other panels
of the altarpiece are found in various
collections in the Netherlands, Italy and
the USA. On the strength of its expressive,
summary painting and its effects of perspective and lighting, the panel can be
referred to the southern French school of
the second half of the 15th century which
made wide use of the discoveries of Italian
artists. The costumes and hairdos of the
characters along with the architectural
details evoke the atmosphere of medieval
France rather than the Rome of the
Emperor Diocletian's era (243–313/316).
*From the State Museum Reserve, 1931;
formerly in the V. Volkonskaya collection,
Leningrad.*

ANONYMOUS PAINTER
Portrait of Henri, Duke of Anjou (?)
*Second half, 16th century. Oil on panel.
48.5 x 32 cm. Inv. No. 1255*

16th-century French painting is represented in the Hermitage by a number of portraits. The portrait genre had flourished in
France during the Renaissance period, but
from the second quarter of the 16th century it started to undergo changes. The generalized image of Man-thinker, Man-creator
gave way to the subtle psychological
characterization which found its most
conspicuous reflection in the works of the
celebrated portraitist François Clouet, to
whom some researchers ascribe this portrait. The face of the sitter bears the stamp
of disquiet and tension typical for the
atmosphere of the French court during
the Wars of Religion. There is also a later
inscription: *Duke of Alençon.* A compara-
tive analysis, however, does not allow us to
identify the sitter with François Valois, who
was titled Duke of Alençon and was the
youngest of Catherine de'Medici's three
sons, although an obvious family likeness
testifies to the fact that the man depicted
was one of the last representatives of the
ruling Valois dynasty.
*From the collection of L.-A. Crozat
Baron de Thiers, Paris, 1772.*

JACQUES BELLANGE
Active 1602–1617
Lamentation
Oil on canvas. 115 x 175 cm. Inv. No. 10032

In Nancy, the central city of the independent Duchy of Lorraine (until 1633), an art school emerged in the early 17th century. Its founders were two eminent masters – Jacques Callot (in drawing) and Jacques Bellange (in engraving and painting), who developed the artistic ideas of 16th-century Mannerists. Reflecting the crisis of the humanistic culture of the Renaissance and the advent of the reaction of the 1530s, Mannerism was characterized by a highly emotional portrayal of mysterious images through elongated, intricate forms. Bellange was a gifted portrait painter and he has proved it in his representation of an anonymous donor in the right-hand part of the canvas.
Acquired in 1967.

VALENTIN (DE BOULLOGNE)
1594–1632
Christ Driving the Money-Changers from the Temple
Oil on canvas. 192 x 266.5 cm. Inv. No. 1214

Valentin was a French follower of Caravaggio whose work marked the flourishing of realism in 17th-century art. Like Caravaggio, the artist boldly treats complex foreshortenings and uses sharp contrasts of light and shade. In this work Christ appears not so much as the Redeemer as a daring reformer.
From the collection of L.-A. Crozat, Baron de Thiers, Paris, 1772.

SÉBASTIEN BOURDON
1616–1671
The Death of Dido
*After 1637. Oil on canvas. 158.5 x 136.5 cm.
Inv. No. 1247*

The picture was produced after the artist's return from Italy where he lived from 1634 to 1637. Its Baroque manner, standing in sharp contrast to Bourdon's portrait paintings, is an obvious debt to Italian masters. In Roman mythology, Dido is the founder of the city of Carthage and her image derives from Grecian or Phoenician sources (the Carthaginians venerated her as a goddess). According to Virgil (*Aeneid*), Dido, by the will of Venus fell in love with the Trojan hero Aeneas, who had fled to Africa. When, fore-ordained by Jupiter, Aeneas had departed from Carthage in order to become the forefather of Rome's founders, Dido built a funeral pyre and slew herself on it, having pre-dicted the enmity between Carthage and Rome.
From the collection of L.-A. Crozat, Baron de Thiers, Paris, 1772.

LOUIS LE NAIN
1593–1648
The Milkmaid's Family
*1640s. Oil on canvas. 51 x 59 cm.
Inv. No. 1152*

The realistic tendencies of French art in the first half of the 17th century found their most articulate expression in the work of Louis Le Nain. The *Milkmaid's Family* is quite concrete, devoid of any idealization and rendered in an uniform greyish-silvery colour scale. It dates from Le Nain's flourishing period when his specific 'peasant' genre came into its own. The painting lacks any entertaining or narrative elements characteristic of Dutch genre scenes. The low line of the horizon – a discovery made by the Italian artists of the Renaissance era – and the spreading flat landscape impart a majestic, even epic quality to this painting unpretentious in subject-matter.
Acquired between 1763 and 1774.

NICOLAS POUSSIN
1594–1665
Tancred and Erminia
1630–31. Oil on canvas. 98.5 x 146.5 cm.
Inv. No. 1189

The consolidation of absolutism and suc-
cesses in the Thirty Years' War (1618–48)
determined the mood of French society on
the eve of the period of France's political
hegemony in Europe. French artists sought

lofty ideals consonant with the spirit of
the time in classical antiquity. The work
of Poussin and Lorrain, those great French
classicists of the 17th century, reflected
in full measure the atmosphere of that
epoch. In *Tancred and Erminia*, based
on an episode from Torquate Tasso's
Jerusalem Delivered (1580), Poussin extols
the heroes ready to sacrifice themselves
in the name of civic ideals.
From the J. Aved collection, Paris, 1766.

NICOLAS POUSSIN
1594–1665
Landscape with Polyphemus
1649. Oil on canvas. 150 x 199 cm.
Inv. No. 1186

An illustration for the *Metamorphoses* by the
Latin poet Ovid (43 B.C.–ca. 18 A.D.), this landscape embodies the artist's dream of a harmonious orderly world. Before us is an integral
and elevated image of nature drawn from
the 'golden age' of Hellenic culture.

The river god and the nymphs form an inseparable whole with the realm of water they
rule; a satyr is sneaking up to them from
behind the bush and a ploughman is seen
in the far distance. And above this picture
of peace and harmony towers the figure of
the cyclope Polyphemus playing a reed-pipe.
The companion painting, *Landscape with
Hercules Wrestling with Cacus*, is in the
Pushkin Museum of Fine Arts, Moscow.
*From the collection of the Marquis
de Conflans, Paris, 1772.*

SIMON VOUET
1590–1649
Allegorical Portrait of Anne of Austria
Oil on canvas. 202 x 172 cm. Inv. No. 7523

Vouet, First Painter to King Louis XIII, became famous mainly for his large-scale decorative schemes for royal palaces. He spent many years far from Paris – in England, Turkey (Constantinople), at the court of Sultan Akhmed, and in Italy. He was Principe of the Accademia di St Luca in Rome. Vouet produced numerous paintings on religious, mythological and allegorical subjects, and also portraits. The French Queen Anne of Austria (1601–1660), wife of Louis XIII and regentress under the infant Louis XIV, is represented as Minerva. The portrait is a characteristic example of court art in the time of King Louis XIII. *From the Antiquariat, Leningrad, 1931.*

CLAUDE GELLÉE, CALLED LORRAINE
1600–1682
Rest on the Flight into Egypt (Noon)
Between 1651 and 1661. *Oil on canvas.*
113 x 157 cm. Inv. No. 1235

The artist was born in Lorraine, hence his nickname 'Lorraine'. He went to Rome as a youth and lived there for the rest of his life. Lorraine made his name as a landscape painter, though small figures in his works were usually painted by other artists. Contemporaries admired the subtlety of his lighting effects and his skilful use and construction of aerial perspective. The idealized landscapes *Morning, Noon, Evening* and *Night* from the *Four Times of Day* cycle reflecting the artist's striving for harmony and beauty. Each painting is on a biblical subject which, however, is perceived as something secondary. All the figures in the paintings were presumably executed by the Italian artist F. Lauri (1623–1694).
From the Empress Joséphine collection, Malmaison, 1814.

ANTOINE WATTEAU
1684–1721
**The Capricious Girl
(La Boudeuse)**
*Ca. 1718. Oil on canvas. 42 x 34 cm.
Inv. No. 4120*

A refined colourist and a master of elegant compositions, Watteau created a specific genre, fêtes galantes, where cavaliers and ladies converse, make music and flirt with one another in the lap of nature, entirely absorbed in their own emotions and interests. The spectator thus acts as a sort of detached observer of their lives passing in a beautiful poetic world of love and sensual pleasures.
From the Stroganov Palace, Petrograd, 1923; formerly in the H. Walpole, Strawberry Hill, England.

ANTOINE WATTEAU
1684–1721
Savoyard with a Marmot
*Ca. 1716. Oil on canvas. 40.5 x 32.5 cm.
Inv. No. 1148*

The painting depicts a strolling musician from Savoy, the poorest province of France. Such musicians wandered in the towns and villages with a street organ and a trained marmot in search of a living. The image of the smiling boy standing on a deserted square in the small town of Beauvais is amazingly realistic and humane. Watteau often used sketches from nature for his paintings. A drawing in charcoal and red chalk for the *Savoyard* is in the Musée des Beaux-Arts in Paris.
Acquired before 1774; formerly in the C. Audran collection, Paris.

NICOLAS LANCRET
1690–1743
La Camargo
Oil on canvas. 45 x 55 cm. Inv. No. 1145

Watteau's novel artistic idiom was emulated by his younger contemporaries and the following generation of artists. During the regency of Philippe d'Orleans (1715–30), when the exquisite manners of the French court at Versailles set the tone for the whole of Europe, painting became more and more refined. The present picture, treated as a gallant scene or a scene from theatrical life, is actually a portrait of the famous French dancer Marie-Anne de Cupis, called La Camargo (1710–1770). Several similar versions are known, for example, one in the Wallace collection, London, and another in the Musée des Beaux-Arts, Nantes.
Acquired between 1763 and 1774.

FRANÇOIS BOUCHER
1703–1770
Pastoral Scene
Oil on canvas. 61 x 75 cm. Inv. No. 1275

François Boucher, Director of the Royal Academy of Painting and Chief Painter to Louis XV, left a large number of pictures, drawings and engravings. He was the key exponent of the French Rococo, which, according to a contemporary apt remark, was intended to 'be liked'. Boucher made sets for theatrical performances, illustrated books, produced ceiling paintings and decorative panels and made designs for Gobelins tapestries. He frequently turned to the pastoral, a new genre which was in vogue in the 18th century, and painted Venuses and Cupids in the form of idealized shepherds and shepherdesses. Such pictures beautifully matched the interiors of French aristocratic mansions.
Acquired between 1763 and 1774.

FRANÇOIS BOUCHER
1703–1770
Landscape near Beauvais
Early 1740s. Oil on canvas. 49 x 58 cm.
Inv. No. 5734

This idealized landscape is painted in a conventional greyish-blue tonality, very characteristic of the artist's landscapes in general, whose painterly manner derives from his theatrical sets.
From the collection of E. and M. Oliv, Leningrad, 1925.

JEAN-HONORÉ FRAGONARD
1732–1806
The Stolen Kiss
Oil on canvas. 45 x 55 cm. Inv. No. 1300

Fragonard was one of the most outstanding exponents of the French Rococo, a pupil of Chardin and Boucher. In his late period he was attracted to the genre painting of the 17th-century Minor Dutchmen, which was particularly liked by members of the third estate.
Acquired in 1895; formerly in the collection of Polish king Stanisław Augustus in the Łazienki Palace, Warsaw

JEAN-BAPTISTE GREUZE
1725–1805
Paralytic Tended by His Children
1763. Oil on canvas. 115.5 x 146 cm.
Inv. No. 1168

In the 1760s Greuze enjoyed a great vogue. Contemporaries praised his didactic-cum-sentimental canvases best attuned to the ideal of the Enlightenment.

One of Greuze's most important paintings, the *Paralytic* was perceived as a protest against the frivolity of Rococo art. It was bought from the artist in 1766 for Catherine II on Denis Diderot's advice. After the French revolution, didactic art lost its attraction, giving way to official Classicism and, later, to Romanticism. *Acquired in 1766.*

JEAN-BAPTISTE SIMÉON CHARDIN
1699–1779
Still Life with the Attributes of the Arts
1766. Oil on canvas. 112 x 140.5 cm.
Inv. No. 5627

Commissioned by Catherine II for the Conference Hall of the Academy of Arts, this *Still Life* was completed and brought to Russia in 1766. The empress liked it so much that instead of the Academy it was left in her private apartments in the Winter Palace. In the centre of the composition

is Pigalle's famous statue *Mercury*, around it are the attributes representing the main genres of art. Architectural plans and medals, commemorating the founding of various institutions, symbolize Architecture, the statue of Mercury, patron of the arts – Sculpture while the easel with brushes and paints allude to Painting. It is generally accepted that the painting was brought to St Petersburg by the French sculptor Falconet who had been invited to work on an equestrian statue of Peter I. *Acquired in 1766.*

JEAN-BAPTISTE PERRONNEAU
1715–1783
Boy with a Book
Mid-1740s. *Oil on canvas. 63 x 52 cm.*
Inv. No. 1270

The 18th-century in French painting was marked by the flourishing of the portrait genre and the emergence of a number of outstanding portraitists. François-Hubert Drouais, Jean-Marc Nattier, Louis Tocqué and the Van Loo family, who are represented in the Hermitage, were instrumental in shaping the main characteristics of the genre during the Rococo epoch and the entire succeeding period when Rococo gave way to Neo-classicism, Sentimentalism and Romanticism which found their vivid reflection in the works of Jean-Baptiste Greuze and Elisabeth Vigée-Lebrun. *Boy with a Book*, painted in a soft manner characteristic of Perronneau, who preferred pastels favoured by many 18th-century portraitists, is the artist's only work to be found in the Hermitage and in Russia. The catalogue of the 1746 Salon in Paris listed a painting by Perronneau under the title *Portrait in Oil of a Schoolboy, the Artist's Brother, with a Book*. This, in all probability, was the Hermitage picture.
From the A. Teplov collection,
St Petersburg, 1781.

HUBERT ROBERT
1733–1808
Ruins of a Terrace in a Park
Early 1780s. *Oil on canvas. 59 x 87 cm.*
Inv. No. 5647

The outstanding French landscape painter Hubert Robert is represented in the Hermitage by more than 50 works. In addition to the large decorative compositions intended for aristocratic salons and mansions, which are now exhibited in the White Hall of the Winter Palace, they include cabinet paintings in which the artist's fantasies coexist with reality. Such paintings were very popular in the late 18th century. *Ruins of a Terrace in a Park* is a characteristic example of the decorative landscape using motifs sketched from life. The sculptural group *The Horse-Tamers* by Guillaume Coustou, with its companion on the same theme, decorated the terrace of the park at Marly in the 18th century; it now crowns the pylons of the entrance from Place de la Concorde to the Champs Elysées. However, neither the architecture of the depicted terrace nor the character of the surrounding landscape has anything in common with the park at Marly.
From the Yusupov Palace, Leningrad, 1925.

ÉTIENNE-MAURICE FALCONET
1716–1791
Cupid
1766–69. Marble. Height 85 cm.
Inv. No. H.ск. 1856

SCULPTURE. 18th CENTURY

Before going to Russia and creating his
celebrated equestrian monument to Peter I
in St Petersburg, Falconet was best known
for his elegant statuettes in marble and
porcelain. The world-famous statue
The Menacing Cupid, done in 1757,
was commissioned by the Marquise de
Pompadour. It was to be installed in the
round Temple of Love pavilion at Versailles,
hence the singular composition and
the round pedestal. With amazing ease
Falconet has conveyed the charm, natural
grace and tender forms of the child's
body. The statue enjoyed immense popularity and was repeated several times in
marble, bronze and porcelain. Executed
for Count Stroganov, the Hermitage
version was kept in the Stroganov Palace
in St Petersburg.
From the Stroganov Palace,
Leningrad, 1931.

JEAN-ANTOINE HOUDON
1741–1828
Voltaire Seated in an Armchair
1781. Marble. Height 138 cm. Inv. No. H.ск. 9

The great French writer and philosopher
Voltaire (Marie François Arouet, 1694–1778)
posed for Houdon when he was 84 years
old. The sculptor has recorded every wrin-
kle on his face, emphasizing his brittle fin-
gers and toothless mouth. Yet Houdon has
managed to achieve something that only
a genius is capable of – his Voltaire is not
just a very old man but one blessed with a
keen mind and an inner flame that did not
fade until his death. The statue was commissioned by Catherine II, who considered
herself a pupil of the great philosopher.
In 1784 it was sent to Russia and cere-
moniously installed in a grotto at Tsarskoye
Selo together with other sculptures from
the Empress's collection. In 1805 it was set
up on the ground floor of the block of
the Raphael Loggie, where books from
Voltaire's library were kept at that time.
Another version of the statue decorates the
foyer of the Comédie Française in Paris.
From Tsarskoye Selo, 1805.

PAINTING. 19th–20th CENTURIES

ANTOINE-JEAN GROS
1771–1835
Napoleon at Arcole
After 1797. Oil on canvas. 134 x 104 cm.
Inv. No. 5669

Napoleon Bonaparte (1769–1821), first consul, then the emperor of France (1804–14, 1815), defeated the Austrian troops in the battle at Arcole, which took place on November 15–17, 1796. In this battle Napoleon demonstrated his great military genius and heroism, winning the respect of the army and the whole of France. The Hermitage canvas is a replica of the painting of 1797 which is in the palace at Versailles.

From the State Museum Reserve, 1924; formerly in the collection of Duke Nicolas of Leuchtenberg, St Petersburg.

FRANÇOIS GERARD
1770–1837
Portrait of Joséphine Beauharnais
1801. Oil on canvas. 178 x 174 cm.
Inv. No. 5674

This is a characteristic example of the representative portrait of the Consulate period (1799–1804), painted by the brilliant exponent of Neo-classicism François Gerard, who was the most fashionable portraitist of Napoleon's court. Joséphine (1763–1814), wife of General Alexandre Beauharnais in the first marriage and of Napoleon in the second (1796–1809), is shown sitting in the park of her suburban residence – the Malmaison Palace near Paris.
From the State Museum Reserve, 1919; formerly in the collection of Duke Nicolas of Leuchtenberg, St Petersburg.

JACQUES-LOUIS DAVID
1748–1825
Sappho and Phaon
1809. Oil on canvas. 225.3 x 262 cm.
Inv. No. 5668

A celebrated Neo-classical artist, David first searched for civic virtues in antiquity, then extolled the ideals of revolutionary France through the images of the heroes of the early Roman republic. He became a jacobin and a Deputy and painted his famous canvas *The Death of Marat*. During the Consulate and First Empire periods he was Court Painter to Napoleon and again turned to classical antiquity, now giving preference not to heroic but amorous-mythological or allegorical subjects. This painting commissioned by Nikolai Yusupov (1751–1831) depicts the love-story of the ancient Greek poetess Sappho and the beautiful Phaon.
From the Yusupov Palace, Leningrad, 1925.

JEAN AUGUSTE DOMINIQUE INGRES
1780–1867
Portrait of Count Nikolai Guryev
1821. Oil on canvas. 107 x 86 cm.
Inv. No. 5678

The portrait was painted in Florence when Count Nikolai Dmitryevich Guryev (1792–1849) served as the Russian envoy in Rome and Naples. An ardent devotee of Neo-classicism, an admirer of Raphael and a superb draughtsman, Ingres treats this portrait of the Russian diplomat in a manner peculiar to Romantic artists: the landscape before the storm creates a sense of anxiety.
From the State Museum Reserve, 1922; formerly in the A. Naryshkina collection, Petrograd.

FERDINAND VICTOR EUGÈNE DELACROIX
1798–1863
Arab Saddling His Horse
1855. *Oil on canvas. 56 x 47 cm.*
Inv. No. 3852

The leader of the French Romantic school, Delacroix painted this work twenty years after his trip to Morocco. For Romantic artists the horse was an embodiment of freedom, and this scene of the saddling of a horse anticipates a headlong race towards freedom. To achieve his goal, that is, to show the emotional state of his heroes, the artist makes use of impetuous brushstrokes, ignoring the rules of anatomy and distinct drawing. He experiments with complementary colours and builds the composition upon the contrasts of numerous grey and red hues, thereby enhancing the dramatic aspect of the scene.
From the Museum of the Academy of Arts, Petrograd, 1922; formerly in the Kushelev Gallery, St Petersburg.

FERDINAND VICTOR EUGÈNE DELACROIX
1798–1863
Lion Hunt in Morocco
1854. *Oil on canvas. 74 x 92 cm.*
Inv. No. 3853

The canvas was painted from memory, inspired by the trip to Morocco in 1832. The only one of this contemporaries to remain faithful to the ideals of Romanticism, Delacroix has filled this hunting scene with a passionate emotionality.
From the Museum of the Academy of Arts, Petrograd, 1922; formerly in the Kushelev Gallery, St Petersburg.

THEODORE ROUSSEAU
1812–1867
Market Place in Normandy
1832 (?). *Oil on panel. 29.5 x 38 cm.*
Inv. No. 3950

Rousseau created his paintings relying on studies from life. His primary concern was to convey the charm and peculiarity of unprettified nature. *Market Place in Normandy* is an example of the urban landscape genre rarely tackled by the artist. He unfolds the composition, juxtaposing the volumes of several buildings and expressively emphasizing the silhouettes of their roofs by a small piece of the sky. The summarily treated human figures are part of the landscape, obeying its rhythm and mood.

From the Museum of the Academy of Arts, Petrograd, 1922; formerly in the Kushelev Gallery, St Petersburg.

CHARLES-FRANÇOIS DAUBIGNY
1817–1878
The Seashore at Villerville
1875. *Oil on canvas. 85 x 149 cm.*
Inv. No. 5694

In the 1830s a group of artists, including Daubigny, settled in the village of Barbizon, not far from Paris, and devoted themselves to painting the quiet, rural scenery. The artists, who came to be called the Barbizons (besides Daubigny, the group included T. Rousseau, J. Dupré, N.-V. Díaz and C. Troyon), aimed to embrace the scenery on the spot and to convey their personal attitude to nature. This makes them, to a large extent, the precursors of Impressionism.

From the Anichkov Palace, Petrograd, 1918; formerly in the collection of Alexander III, St Petersburg.

CONSTANT TROYON
1810–1865
On the Way to the Market
1859. *Oil on canvas. 260.5 x 211 cm.*
Inv. No. 3966

A member of the Barbizon group, this marvellous landscape and animal painter has been able to convey here the illusion of a moving herd and the effect of sunlight breaking through the morning haze.
From the Museum of the Academy of Arts, Petrograd, 1922; formerly in the Kushelev Gallery, St Petersburg.

JEAN-FRANÇOIS MILLET
1814–1875
Peasant Women Carrying Brushwood
Ca. 1858. Oil on canvas. 37.5 x 29.5 cm.
Inv. No. 3924

Millet was an outstanding painter and draughtsman whose work reflected the socially attuned trend in French realistic painting. There is an obvious link between Millet's art and the realistic traditions of the 17th-century Dutch school.
From the Museum of the Academy of Arts, Petrograd, 1922; formerly in the Kushelev Gallery, St Petersburg.

JEAN-BAPTISTE CAMILLE COROT
1796–1875
Peasant Woman Pasturing a Cow on the Edge of a Forest
1865–70. Oil on canvas. 47.5 x 35 cm.
Inv. No. 7166

Corot painted genre scenes and portraits but he was particularly famed for his landscapes permeated with subtle lyricism and harmony. He lovingly depicted the quiet and externally unpretentious scenery in a greyish-silvery colour scheme with a characteristic transparent veil of mist and twilight. The artist also worked out a special technique for the rendition of atmospheric effects: juxtaposing the differently lit patches of one colour he sometimes resorted to scores of gradations.
From the State Pushkin Museum of Fine Arts, Moscow, 1930.

GUSTAVE COURBET
1819–1877
Landscape with a Dead Horse
1850s. Oil on canvas. 46 x 56 cm. Inv. No. 3897

Echoing the tastes of the Second Empire of Napoleon III (1852–70), the Paris salons abounded in paintings peopled with odalisques, bacchantes and nymphs. Courbet also paid tribute to such subjects, although he reached his creative apogee in his realistic works. Marked by a restrained dramatic quality, *Landscape with a Dead Horse* may serve as a challenge to the aesthetic views of the period.
From the Museum of the Academy of Arts, Petrograd, 1922; formerly in the Kushelev Gallery, St Petersburg.

ALFRED SISLEY
1839–1899
Villeneuve-la-Garenne on the Seine
1872. Oil on canvas. 59 x 80.5 cm.
Inv. No. 9005

The son of a rich English merchant who settled in Paris, Alfred Sisley, at the age of 18, was sent to London to prepare for a commercial career. But the young man, fascinated by the work of Constable and Turner, dreamed of making a completely different career. He visited museums and exhibitions and upon his return to France was allowed to enter the École des Beaux-Arts under Gleyre, where he met Monet, Renoir and Bazille. In the 1870s Sisley took part in the Impressionist exhibitions that baffled the Parisian public. He painted mainly *en plein air* in the new Impressionist manner and his works are marked by a delicate and refined colouring. The canvas depicting Villeneuve-la-Garenne is the only example of the coulisse construction of space in Sisley's work.
From the State Museum of Modern Western Art, Moscow, 1948; formerly in the P. and S. Shchukin collection, Moscow.

CLAUDE OSCAR MONET
1840–1926
Lady in the Garden (Sainte-Adresse)
1867. Oil on canvas. 82.3 x 101.5 cm.
Inv. No. 6505

At his father's insistence, Monet spent the summer of 1867 at Sainte-Adresse, in the house of his aunt. In his landscapes created there, he achieved the unusually powerful effects of sunlight. These landscapes were a revelation to contemporaries. Full of light, pure tones and amazing reflections, which seemingly had never been noticed in nature, they sometimes frightened the spectators by their novelty.
In the present painting Monet's main concern was to convey the white colour of the lady's dress and perhaps for this reason he painted over the male figure to the right of the lady. Another part of this garden appears in the *Garden in Blossom* (Musée d'Orsay) and *Terrace at Sainte-Adresse* (Metropolitan Museum of Art, New York), produced at the same time. The lady depicted was Jeanne-Marie Lecadre, wife of Monet's cousin.

From the State Museum of Modern Western Art, Moscow, 1930; formerly in the S. Shchukin collection, Moscow.

CLAUDE OSCAR MONET
1840–1926
Poppy Field
1887. Oil on canvas. 59 x 90 cm.
Inv. No. 9004

From the end of the 1880s Monet's work was gaining recognition which made him a well-to-do man. His *Poppy Field* dates from this period, forming part of a series that Monet painted at different times of day, exploring the changes of colour under various lighting conditions.
From the State Museum of Modern Western Art, Moscow, 1948; formerly in the M. Morozov collection, Moscow.

CLAUDE OSCAR MONET
1840–1926
Waterloo Bridge (Effect of Mist)
1903. Oil on canvas. 65 x 100 cm.
Inv. No. 6545

The absence of a detailed drawing and the use of free, as it were carelessly applied brushstrokes of pure colour, account for that summary impression which Money's landscapes produce from a distance, in streams of light, through a veil of air. Monet made three visits to London (1899, 1900 and 1901), where he always stayed at Hôtel Savoy on the Victoria Embankment. The window of his room looked out to a beautiful view on the Thames with the Charing Cross and Waterloo bridges. The *Waterloo Bridge* series, connected with these trips, totals 41 pieces. It took several years to complete. When creating this series the artist aimed to record the changing states of weather conditions and illumination, to catch the fleeting impression.
From the State Museum of Modern Western Art, Moscow, 1930; formerly in the I. Morozov collection, Moscow.

CAMILLE PISSARRO
1830–1903
Boulevard Montmartre in Paris
1897. Oil on canvas. 73 x 92 cm.
Inv. No. 9002

In the winter and spring of 1897 Pissarro worked on a series of town views under the title *Boulevards of Paris*. The series attracted the attention of critics who linked his name with the technique of painting known as Divisionism. Pissarro made sketches from the window of his room in the Hôtel de Russie and completed them in his studio at Eragny. This series is the only one in Pissarro's legacy in which he strove to record all sorts of weather and lighting conditions.
From the State Museum of Modern Western Art, Moscow, 1948; formerly in the M. Riabushinsky collection, Moscow.

EDGAR DEGAS
1834–1917
Woman Combing Her Hair
1885. Pastel on cardboard. 53 x 52 cm.
Inv. No. 42154

Degas received an academic education at the École des Beaux-Arts in Paris and in addition to the study of the old European masters, he took a liking to Japanese engraving. *Woman Combing Her Hair* was inspired by prints of beauties at their toilette by the early 19th-century Japanese artist Utamaro. But unlike the Japanese master whose images are rather stylized and generalized in character, Degas has created here a more concrete, yet poeticized image.
From the State Museum of Modern Western Art, Moscow, 1935; formerly in the S. Shchukin collection, Moscow.

PIERRE-AUGUSTE RENOIR
1841–1919
Child with a Whip
1885. *Oil on canvas. 105 x 75 cm.*
Inv. No. 9006

Renoir painted four portraits of Senator Goujon's children. *Child with a Whip* is apparently a portrait of the youngest son, conceived as a pendant to *Girl with a Hoop* (Goujon's daughter, now in the National Gallery of Art, Washington). Despite a certain difference in height, the canvases have a similar landscape background and the figures complement one another compositionally.
From the State Museum of Modern Western Art, Moscow, 1948; formerly in the I. Morozov collection, Moscow.

PIERRE-AUGUSTE RENOIR
1841–1919
Girl with a Fan
1881. *Oil on canvas. 65 x 50 cm. Inv. No. 6507*

Girl with a Fan is considered a portrait of Alphonsine Fournaise, daughter of the owner of the floating restaurant, La Grenouillére, at Chatou where the *Oarsmen's Breakfast* (National Gallery of Art, Washington) was painted. Many art historians point out that Renoir's female models look remarkably alike in his canvases: the artist paid particular attention to details of the dress and hairdos, omitting the individual features of the appearance of his models.
From the State Museum of Modern Western Art, Moscow, 1930; formerly in the I. Morozov collection, Moscow.

PIERRE-AUGUSTE RENOIR
1841–1919
Woman in Black
Ca. 1876. *Oil on canvas. 65.5 x 55.5 cm.*
Inv. No. 6506

It is not known who sat for the painting. Some researchers believe that the model was Mme Hartmann, wife of a music publisher, while others identify the woman with a certain 'belle Anna' whom Renoir depicted in several canvases. The person of the model, however, is not of great importance: the artist is much more concerned with the study of the pictorial effects of the colour black than the psychological characterization of his model.
From the State Museum of Modern Western Art, Moscow, 1930; formerly in the I. Morozov collection, Moscow.

PIERRE-AUGUSTE RENOIR
1841–1919
Portrait of the Actress Jeanne Samary
1878. Oil on canvas. 174 x 101.5 cm.
Inv. No. 9003

The 1870s–80s were marked by the highest achievements in the long creative career of Renoir – one of the leading exponents of modern French painting. During this period he created such masterpieces as *La Loge, The Swing, Dancing at the Moulin de la Galette, Oarsmen's Breakfast, Girl with a Fan* and portraits of Jeanne Samary. An actress of the Comédie-Française,

Jeanne Samary (1853–1890) performed the parts of maids and soubrettes in Molière's plays. According to the artist's son, the portrait was done at the request of Jeannes' parents, who lived nearby. Legend has it that Renoir so much hurried to capture all the charm of his model that before the sittings he even forgot to say 'hello' snatching up his brush. This portrait was apparently the last painted representation of the actress.
From the State Museum of Modern Western Art, Moscow, 1948; formerly in the I. Morozov collection, Moscow.

PAUL CÉZANNE
1839–1906
Still Life with Curtain
1894–95. Oil on canvas. 55 x 74.5 cm.
Inv. No. 6514

Still Life with Curtain is one of Cézanne's best works in this genre. By virtue of its beautiful and harmonious painting and its perfectly balanced parts the canvas can be regarded as a masterpiece of world painting.
From the State Museum of Modern Western Art, Moscow, 1930; formerly in the I. Morozov collection, Moscow.

PAUL CÉZANNE
1839–1906
Mont Sainte-Victoire
Ca. 1896–98. Oil on canvas. 78.5 x 98.5 cm.
Inv. No. 8991

Mont Sainte-Victoire, towering above the outskirts of Aix-en-Provence, where Cézanne was born and died, increasingly attracted him at the sunset of his life. For Cézanne it was an embodiment of the grandeur, simplicity and indestructibility of nature – everything that formed the basis of his world perception. The bend of the road in the foreground is a motif constantly recurring in Cézanne's later landscapes; it supposedly reflects the artist's meditations on the end of his life path.
From the State Museum of Modern Western Art, Moscow, 1948; formerly in the I. Morozov collection, Moscow.

PAUL CÉZANNE
1839–1906
The Smoker
Ca. 1890–92. Oil on canvas. 92.5 x 73.5 cm.
Inv. No. 6561

Paul Cézanne is often called the 'father of modern painting' – his discoveries in the realm of colour and form exerted a well-nigh decisive influence on the development of Post-Impressionism, the term covering all artistic trends which surpassed the framework of Impressionism in the late 19th century. In his later period (from the 1890s) the artist created a number of masterpieces notable for their highly generalized and profound imagery and a virtuoso painterly manner unrestrained by any technique. This portrait of a Provence peasant with a pipe, *The Smoker*, is one of a series of smokers and card players which Cézanne painted in the early 1890s. The artist sought to stress the aloofness of his characters from the hustle and bustle of everyday life. It is interesting to note that the smoker is depicted against the background of Cézanne's still lifes. These 'pictures in a picture' reflect his world outlook, creating both colouristic and conceptual accents and serving as allegorical and symbolical elements. There are two versions of the *Smoker* in the Pushkin Museum of Fine Arts, Moscow, and the Kunsthalle, Mannheim (Germany).
From the State Museum of Modern Western Art, Moscow, 1931; formerly in the I. Morozov collection, Moscow.

PAUL SIGNAC
1863–1935
The Port of Marseilles
Ca. 1906–07. Oil on canvas. 46 x 55.2 cm.
Inv. No. 6524

Paul Signac was a follower of Georges Seurat, who invented a new method of painting, Divisionism, by the use of tiny dots of pure colour. This technique was also known as Pointillism (from the French, *point*). Mixed in the spectator's eye, the pure primaries and complementary colours ensured a far greater brightness of representation. Seurat and his followers referred to their fellow artists as 'romantic' Impressionists and to themselves as 'scientific' Impressionists, since their experiments were based on scientific discoveries made in the field of optics. Pissarro associated with this group and in the 1900s this method attracted the attention of Matisse and Derain.
From the State Museum of Modern Western Art, Moscow, 1930; formerly in the I. Morozov collection, Moscow.

ALBERT MARQUET
1875–1947
The Bay of Naples
1909. Oil on canvas. 62 x 80.3 cm.
Inv. No. 9150

Having completed his studies at the École dex Beaux-Arts in the 1890s, Marquet did not become a salon painter. In 1905 he exhibited at the original Fauve show, yet never turned into a genuine Fauve himself. Using the flat patterns and colour patches characteristic of Fauvism, Marquet, however, would never pass beyond a reality coloured by his mood and world perception.
From the State Museum of Modern Western Art, Moscow, 1948; formerly in the I. Morozov collection, Moscow.

VINCENT VAN GOGH
1853–1890
Women of Arles
1888. *Oil on canvas. 73 x 92 cm. Inv. No. 9116*

In the 1880s Van Gogh moved from Paris to the South where under the blazing Provence sun he painted daily two or three pictures from nature, working in a state of extreme excitement. The artist's paintings are built upon the decorative patches of colour, each dynamic stroke having its own importance. Van Gogh believed that an artist should be preoccupied not so much with the characterization of the depicted objects as with the problem of how to bring out the state of his soul. In this 'psychologism' lies Van Gogh's aesthetic, the source of the intensity of lines and colours in his expressive pictures. Van Gogh left a deep mark on twentieth-century art, particularly Fauvism and Expressionism.
From the State Museum of Modern Western Art, Moscow, 1948; formerly in the S. Shchukin collection, Moscow.

VINCENT VAN GOGH
1853–1890
Cottages
1890. *Oil on canvas. 60 x 73 cm. Inv. No. 9117*

In May 1890 Van Gogh, already gravely ill, left Provence for Auvers-sur-Oise in northern France, where he lived in the house of his friend and patron Dr. Gachet. There he painted dynamic, heartfelt landscapes in the environs of the town. One of the artist's last works, *Cottages* is rendered by an avalanche of brushstrokes surging upward (the sky) and downward (the hill slope almost merging with the cottages).
From the State Museum of Modern Western Art, Moscow, 1948; formerly in the I. Morozov collection, Moscow.

**HENRI ROUSSEAU,
CALLED LE DOUANIER**
1844–1910
**In a Tropical Forest: Struggle Between
Tiger and Bull**
*Ca. 1908–09. Oil on canvas. 46 x 55 cm.
Inv. No. 6536*

On the back of the canvas is the following inscription: *Combat du tigre et du taureau. Reproduction de mon tableau exposé au Salon des Indépendants. 1908. Henri Rousseau*. The picture mentioned by Rousseau is now in the Cleveland Museum of Art, USA; the Hermitage painting is its replica. The iconography of the painting derives from the etching *Royal Tiger Attacking a Bull*, published in the magazine *L'art* in 1906. *In a Tropical Forest* is one Rousseau's famous series of hunting scenes set in fantastic jungles. The artist painted his exotic landscapes in the secluded corners of the Jardin des Plantes in Paris, where stuffed animals were on view. The plants with their isomorhic, snake-like forms suggest that the present work is one of Rousseau's later 'tropical' landscapes, which were admired by André Breton and the Surrealists.
From the State Museum of Modern Western Art, Moscow, 1930; formerly in the S. Shchukin collection, Moscow.

**HENRI ROUSSEAU,
CALLED LE DOUANIER**
1844–1910
**The Luxembour Gardens.
The Chopin Memorial**
*1909. Oil on canvas. 38 x 47 cm.
Inv. No. 7716*

Rousseau's artistic vision, paradoxical even for the turn of the century, was bitterly critisized for a long time. It was only after the Salon d'Automne of 1905, where Rousseau exhibited with the Fauves, that he was ranked among the cult masters of avant-garde painting. *The Luxembourg Gardens* is one of his most famous Parisian landscapes.
From the State Museum of Modern Western Art, Moscow, 1934; formerly in the S. Shchukin collection, Moscow.

PAUL GAUGUIN
1848–1903
**Woman Holding a Fruit
(Eu haere ia oe)**
*1893. Oil on canvas. 92.5 x 73.5 cm.
Inv. No. 9120*

The Maori title of the painting is translated as "where are you going"? With such question the Tahitians greet passers-by. Researchers believe that the woman depicted is Tehura, Gauguin's Tahitian wife. Her calm, dignified figure is perceived as the Eve of Oceanian Paradise. The fruit she is holding is a pumpkin for carrying water, hence the fruit acquires a symbolic meaning since water is a symbol of life. The Tahitian woman with a child in the middle distance alludes to Tehura's pregnancy at the time Gauguin worked on the painting. For him Tahiti was a harmonious world unspoiled by civilization, a world where man is at one with nature. For this reason, Gauguin repeatedly used the same figures and details in his paintings. The colour combinations of his canvases reflected not so much the natural qualities of objects as the symbolic meaning of images.
From the State Museum of Modern Western Art, Moscow, 1948; formerly in the I. Morozov collection, Moscow.

PAUL GAUGUIN
1848–1903
**Sacred Spring: Sweet Dreams
(Nave Nave Moe)**
1894. Oil on canvas. 74 x 100 cm. Inv. No. 6510

Painted in Paris, the picture is woven from memories of Oceania and populated with images of the artist's first Tahitian period. The female figures can be perceived as the Virgin Mary (with a halo) and Eve (with a fruit). Christian symbols and Maori beliefs are thus fused together. The similarity of Maria's and Eve's features is symbolized by the dualism invested in the image of the Tahitian girl with a fruit: her purity coexists with her disposition to sensual temptation. The lily personifies tropical nature and Maria's chastity. The spring is a Christian symbol of purity. The Tahitian women in the background perform a ritual dance around a gigantic idol, devoted to the Moon Goddess Hina.
From the State Museum of Modern Western Art, Moscow, 1931; formerly in the I. Morozov collection, Moscow.

HENRI MATISSE
1869–1954
The Red Room
(La Desserte. Harmony in Red)
1908. *Oil on canvas. 180 x 220 cm.*
Inv. No. 9660

Matisse's first one-man show was organized
by Ambroise Vollard in 1904. At the Paris
Salon d'Automne of 1905, the works of a
number of artists were hung together in the
seventh hall which a critic dubbed a 'cage
of the wild beasts' (in French, *Les fauves*).
Matisse came to be regarded as the
leader of the new Fauvist movement.
His oeuvre consists of monumental decorative compositions permeated with bright
saturated colours in the most unusual
combinations.
From the State Museum of Modern
Western Art, Moscow, 1948; formerly
in the S. Shchukin collection, Moscow.

HENRI MATISSE
1869–1954
The Artist's Family
1911. *Oil on canvas. 143 x 194 cm. Inv. No. 8940*

In this work Matisse for the first time
endeavoured to depict a genre scene:
his wife Amélie is doing embroidery, his
daughter Marguerite is entering the room
and his sons Pierre and Jean are playing
draughts. But the main 'hero' of the painting is colour. The squares of the chess-
board in the centre link together the oriental carpet, the figures and the ornament.
The most conspicuous spots of colour are
the boys' red shirts and the girl's black
dress. Working on this complicated composition, Matisse derived inspiration from
Persian miniatures, acknowledging that
they had helped him to "go beyond intimate painting".
From the State Museum of Modern
Western Art, Moscow, 1948; formerly
in the S. Shchukin collection, Moscow.

HENRI MATISSE
1869–1954
The Dance
1909–10. Oil on canvas. 260 x 391 cm.
Inv. No. 9673

Representations of round dances occurred in the work of such European artists as Cranach, Rubens and Goya. The Symbolists and modernists also frequently used the enclosed form of the round dance, being attracted by flexible, bending lines. Charged with dynamism, Matisse's *Dance* has none of their fragile refinement. Like its companion panel, *Music*, it was intended for decorating the stairway in Sergei Shchukin's Moscow mansion. Matisse wrote: "I like the dance very much, it is an amazing thing: life and rhythm. It makes my life easy. When I had to do a dance for Moscow I simply went to the Moulin de la Galette on Sunday. I watched how they danced, especially the farandole... which is very joyful. The dancers, joining hands, run through the hall, surrounding and even slightly stunning the people... On coming back home, I composed my dance on a four-metre surface, humming the tune I had heard in the Moulin de la Galette, so that the whole composition, all the dancers are moving in an uniform rhythm..."
From the State Museum of Modern Western Art, Moscow, 1948; formerly in the S. Shchukin collection, Moscow.

HENRI MATISSE
1869–1954
Portrait of Madame Henri Matisse
1913. Oil on canvas. 145 x 97 cm.
Inv. No. 9156

The French poet Guillaume Apollinaire regarded this portrait as an embodiment of Parisian charm. Even many years later Louis Aragon recollected how strongly it had fascinated him. The artist's wife Amélie is represented as an elegant Parisian lady, wearing a fashionable feathered hat and a costume with a scarf. Her face looks like a mask with sharply delineated, deliberately exaggerated features. This sharpness along with the vacillating colour modulations produce an impression of phantasmagoria.
From the State Museum of Modern Western Art, Moscow, 1948; formerly in the S. Shchukin collection, Moscow.

PABLO PICASSO
1881–1973
The Absinthe Drinker
1901. Oil on canvas. 73 x 54 cm.
Inv. No. 9045

Born in Málaga, Picasso studied at the
Academy of San Fernando in Madrid
and associated with a circle of Barcelona
artists and poets who met in the *Four Cats*
cabaret. In October 1899 he visited Paris
for the first time. *The Absinthe Drinker*

dates from his Blue period related to
Barcelona and Paris. Already in Barcelona,
Picasso started to treat the theme of a
lonely woman sitting in a café. In the present canvas, painted in Paris, he rejected
all Impressionist elements. For Picasso, the
café is a shelter for the homeless. In the
novel by the singer Yvette Gilbert, immor-
talized by Toulouse-Lautrec, we find a
description of one such café: "These
happy unemployed comics, these jokers in
the streets, these singers, declaimers and
eccentric dancers, all those who in the
evenings, under lights, tomorrow, perhaps,
in some run-down place will share laughter
and joy with a public that believes them
to be happy and envies them... And they
come here every day, to the Chartreuse,
seeking any engagement, eyes open for
the agent who will enter the premises...
in need... of a soliloquist or a singer...
"For there are also the women. Poor girls!
Livid in the bright day's cruelty, with an
obligatory smile, fugitive or frozen, reddened or grape-coloured, pallid from
cheap powder, their eyelids blue, their
eyes encircled by pencilled dark specta-
cles, they, too, standing on the sidewalk,
attend upon the pleasure of the showman,
who will be kind enough to make use
of a youthfulness almost gone and
a dying voice."
From the State Museum of Modern
Western Art, Moscow, 1948; formerly
in the S. Shchukin collection, Moscow.

PABLO PICASSO
1881–1973
Boy with a Dog
1905. Gouache and pastel on cardboard.
57 x 41 cm. Inv. No. 42158

In 1904 Picasso finally moved to Paris and
settled in Monmartre. In the winter 1904–05
he worked on a huge canvas depicting
travelling circus artists. At present the
Family of Saltimbanques (National Gallery
of Art, Washington) is well known as the
milestone of his Pink (Monmartre) period.
Boy with a Dog, a study for it, closely
resembles the large gouache, *Two Acrobats
with a Dog* (Museum of Modern Art, New
York) which is generally believed to be a
direct response to Charles Baudelaire's
verse, *Les Bons Chiens*: "I sing the dirty
dog, the poor dog, the homeless dog, the
stray dog, the dog saltimbanque, the dog
whose instinct, like that of the beggar, the
bohemian and the comedian, is so wonderfully sharpened by necessity, this kind
mother, this real patron of all intelligence!"
From the State Museum of Modern
Western Art, Moscow, 1948; formerly
in the S. Shchukin collection, Moscow.

PABLO PICASSO
1881–1973
Guitar and Violin
1913. *Oil on canvas. 65 x 54 cm.*
Inv. No. 9048

By its high artistic standard and scope,
the Hermitage collection of works from
Picasso's Cubist period (1908–14) is virtually
the world's best. His incessant experiments
with the construction of space and the
modelling of form led Picasso to analytical
and, later, to synthetic Cubism. From 1912
to 1914 the artist produced a large number of 'synthetic' compositions devoted
to music. In other words, he attempted
to create a collective image of musical art
with tangibly rendered musical instruments.
From the State Museum of Modern
Western Art, Moscow, 1948; formerly
in the S. Shchukin collection, Moscow.

PABLO PICASSO
1881–1973
Woman with a Fan (After the Ball)
1908. *Oil on canvas. 150 x 100 cm. Inv. No. 7705*

Woman with a Fan is an example of
Picasso's analytical Cubism. The portrait
is modelled from the figured planes of simple geometric configurations. Despite its
openly formal treatment, the canvas is
charged with a deep emotion. The plastic-
ity of the figure and the colour scheme of
the painting show an influence of primitive
art, particularly the art of African peoples
which Picasso studied for a long time.
From the State Museum of Modern
Western Art, Moscow, 1934; formerly
in the S. Shchukin collection, Moscow.

MAURICE DE VLAMINCK
1876–1958
View of the Seine
Ca. 1906. Oil on canvas. 54.5 x 65.5 cm.
Inv. No. 9112

One of the leading landscape painters of the Fauve group, Vlaminck revealed his vigorous temperament even in his earliest works. The 1901 Van Gogh exhibition gave him a fresh impetus to create highly emotional and expressive paintings. He made use of large slashing brushstrokes, pure colours and contrasting tonal values. When working on his pictures, including this *View of the Seine*, Vlaminck squeezed the tube, forcing the paints out directly onto the canvas. This picture was produced in Chatou, a Paris suburb, where Vlaminck shared a studio with Derain. The contours of the Chatou bridge can be discerned in the background.
From the State Museum of Modern Western Art, Moscow, 1948; formerly in the I. Morozov collection, Moscow.

CORNELIS THEODORUS MARIE VAN DONGEN, CALLED KEES
1877–1968
Woman in a Black Hat
Ca. 1908. Oil on canvas. 100 x 81.5 cm.
Inv. No. 6572

The artist repeatedly used the effect produced by the green of the dress and the black of the hat. The woman depicted resembles the artist's wife but some of her features bear an affinity with other models, from which we can conclude that before us is a sort of collective image, the femme fatale.
From the State Museum of Modern Western Art, Moscow, 1931; formerly in the S. Shchukin collection, Moscow.

ANDRÉ DERAIN
1880–1954
**Portrait of an Unknown Man Reading
a Newspaper (Chevalier X)**
1911–14. *Oil on canvas. 162.5 x 97.5 cm.*
Inv. No. 9128

This *Portrait of an Unknown Man,* or
Chevalier X, as Guillaume Apollinaire
dubbed it, shows a synthesis of different
sources which influenced Derain's work:
Negro art, the formal portrait, the late
medieval miniature and modern painting,
for instance the *Portrait of the Artist's
Father with a Newspaper* by Cézanne.
Sharply contrasting the large planes and
small patterned surfaces (cf. floor and
newspaper) Derain achieves a pronounced
decorative effect. As follows from an
extant photograph, a real newspaper was
pasted on the canvas, which calls to mind
the collages of Picasso and Braque.
*From the State Museum of Modern
Western Art, Moscow, 1948; formerly
in the S. Shchukin collection, Moscow.*

FERNAND LÉGER
1881–1955
Carte Postale
1932–48. Oil on canvas. 92.3 x 65.4 cm.
Inv. No. 9726

Produced in the 1930s–40s, the monumental decorative canvases of Léger, who
briefly fell under the influence of Cubism,
are painted in a life-asserting spirit.
His experiments with line and colour led
to the development of a specific manner
which enabled the artist to poeticize
the life of industrial cities.
Gift of Fernand Léger's pupils, 1953.

SCULPTURE.
19th–20th CENTURIES

AUGUSTE RODIN
1840–1917
Eternal Spring
After 1884. *Marble. Height 77 cm.*
Inv. No. Н.ск. 1298

August Rodin was the first of the 19th-century sculptors to reject the academic conventions. His realistic idiom came under violent attack, critics even accused him of using life-casts. Many of his later sculptures echo, to a certain extent, the works of his contemporaries-Impressionists. Attracted by light-and-shade effects, Rodin frequently resorts to the soft modelling of marble. He achieves an extraordinary smoothness of gradations which virtually convey the warmth of the tender body. The contours of the figures are fused together by an airy haze and the rough block of marble appears as the breathing flesh of two youthful beings merging in a love embrace.
From the Yeliseyevs collection,
St Petersburg, 1923.

PABLO PICASSO
1881–1973
Jug
1950s. *Painted clay. Height 33.5 cm.*
Inv. No. 27359

In the 1950s Picasso lived in Antibes and Vallauris – the ceramic centre in the South of France – where he did a large number of decorative ceramics. This jug in the form of a female head is a marvellous interpretation of the Mediterranean pottery of the archaic era which Picasso studied at length.
Gift of N.P. Léger, 1976.

ÉMILE ANTOINE BOURDELLE
1861–1929
Eloquence
1917. *Bronze. Height 47 cm.*
Inv. No. H.ск. 2430

In 1912 Bourdelle was commissioned to create a monument to the national hero of Argentine, General Carlos Maria Alvear, which was to be erected in Buenos Aires. The Hermitage *Eloquence* is the model of a head for one of the four allegorical statues which adorn the monument. In his work Bourdelle was inspired by archaic and Gothic art, striving to achieve the maximum of expression by the sparing use of expressive means.
From the Yeliseyevs collection, St Petersburg.

FIRST FLOOR

● BEGINNING
OF THE FIRST-FLOOR
EXHIBITION

RUSSIAN CULTURE OF THE FIRST HALF
OF THE 18th CENTURY

RUSSIAN CULTURE OF THE SECOND HALF
OF THE 18th CENTURY

RUSSIAN INTERIOR DECORATION
OF THE 19th CENTURY

CULTURE OF PRE-MONGOL RUS'.
9th–13th CENTURIES

CULTURE OF MUSCOVITE RUSSIA.
15th–17th CENTURIES

PORTRAIT GALLERY OF THE ROMANOVS

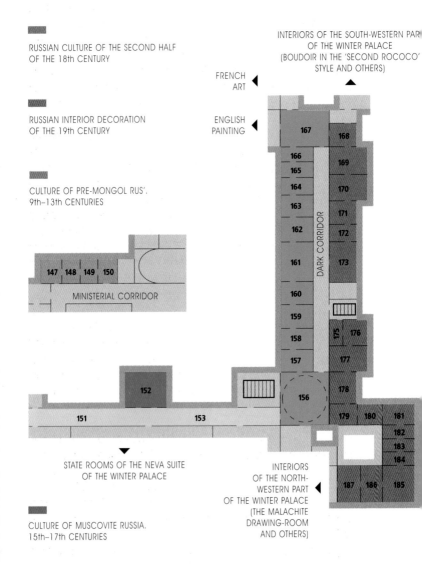

FRENCH
ART ◀

ENGLISH
PAINTING ◀

INTERIORS OF THE SOUTH-WESTERN PART
OF THE WINTER PALACE
(BOUDOIR IN THE 'SECOND ROCOCO'
STYLE AND OTHERS) ▲

167 168
166 169
165
164 170
163
162 171
172
161 173

DARK CORRIDOR

160
159
158 175 176
157 177
152
156 178
151 153 179 180 181
182
183
184
187 186 185

MINISTERIAL CORRIDOR

147 148 149 150

▼
STATE ROOMS OF THE NEVA SUITE
OF THE WINTER PALACE

INTERIORS
OF THE NORTH-
WESTERN PART ◀
OF THE WINTER PALACE
(THE MALACHITE
DRAWING-ROOM
AND OTHERS)

RUSSIAN CULTURE. 9th–19th CENTURIES

There was a Russian Department even in the Imperial Hermitage where works by Russian masters made up the bulk of the museum collections and the interior decoration of the Winter Palace. Once most of the canvases by Russian artists were transferred to the newly opened Emperor Alexander III Russian Museum in 1898, the department ceased to exist, although numerous items of Russian art remained in the Winter Palace. The events of 1917 led to the nationalization of private mansions in St Petersburg and the creation, on their basis, of the museums of the culture of the nobility, closed in the 1920s–1930s. As the mansions were placed under the jurisdiction of public and state institutions, the problem arose of where to put the enormous collections which included numerous first-rate items of Russian culture amassed by the Stroganovs, Shuvalovs, Yusupovs and Bobrinskys. In 1941 it was decided to place them under the jurisdiction of the State Hermitage. Today, over 300, 000 exhibits that are found in the Department reflect the history of Russian culture from the 9th–early 20th centuries. The best of them are displayed at the permanent exhibition divided into several sections, namely, Art of Pre-Mongol Rus' of the 9th–13th Centuries, Russian Art of the 15th–17th Centuries, Art of the First Half and the Middle of the 18th Century, Art of the Second Half of the 18th Century and Russian Interior Decoration of the 19th Century. Amply represented in the collection is the work of Western European masters, who were invited to Russia to fulfil rapidly growing commissions in European styles unfamiliar to Russian artists. This had been practised throughout the Petrine era and at a later date until a brilliant galaxy of Russian artists as competent as their European teachers stepped forward. The foreign masters who worked in Russia invariably fell under the influence of Russian culture. The symbiosis of the two cultures brought forth an original phenomenon that art experts term 'Rossica'. An outstanding part in the exhibition is the collection of Peter I's tools and lathes, indicative of his reforms in the realm of Russian culture. A gallery extending along the Neva suite of rooms is used for a special exhibition of portraits of Russian emperors and empresses (rooms 151, 153, pp. 22, 23). It is similar to the former Romanovs Gallery in the Small Hermitage.

CULTURE OF PRE-MONGOL RUS'. 9th–13th CENTURIES
(rooms 147–150)

Necklace

10th century. *Silver, filigree, granulation.*
Diameter 11 cm. Inv. No. 973/18

The culture of Rus' before the Mongol invasion is represented by a number of unique artefacts including this famous silver necklace of ten large beads, made in filigree and granulation techniques. The necklace used to be part of a woman's festive costume. This one was found in a hoard dated to the 11th century and given the name of Shalakhovsky after the site of its discovery (the village of Shalakhovo, now in the Pskov Region). Before the Mongol invasion an important trade route passed through this area, linking the cities of Polotsk and Novgorod.

From the Archaeological Commission, 1893.

Kolt

12th–13th centuries. *Gold, cloisonné enamel.*
5.5 x 5.6 cm. Inv. No. 635/7

Part of a hoard found in Kiev in 1885, this fine golden kolt is decorated with two small figures of mythical Syrins, birds with female heads, the most widespread personages in the ancient Russian legends of Byzantine origin. Since time immemorial the headdress of a Slav woman has included the so-called temple rings. Usually these decorations were either plaited in the hair or suspended from the headdress. Each Eastern Slav tribe had its distinctive type of temple rings and these have been found in quantities during the excavations of ancient Slav settlements. The kolts are similar in form to the temple rings of the Viatichi and Krivichi, the Slav tribes from the upper reaches of the Dnieper, Volga and Oka Rivers, and evidently were used by rich townswomen. They differ from the temple rings by their higher artistic workmanship and by the presence of two convex plates put together to form a cavity for possible use as incense containers.

From the Archaeological Commission, 1888.

The Tmutarakan' stone

11th century. *Marble. 45 x 110 x 24 cm.*
Inv. No. ЭРА 38/1

Tmutarakan' (the Taman gorodishche) was a town situated on the southern border of Rus'. The inscription carved in marble is one of the most ancient examples of the Russian written language (1068). It says that Prince Gleb of Tmutarakan' "fared across the sea on the ice from Tmutarakan' to Korchev [Kerch]". Discovered on the Taman peninsula in 1792.

Acquired from the Kerch Archaeological museum, 1851.

Cross of Patriarch Philaret

First third, 17th century. *Gold, silver, filigree, enamel, niello. 15.9 x 10.6 cm.*
Inv. No. РП 1303

An outstanding item of the decorative and applied arts of 17th-century Muscovite Russia, this golden cross belonged, as legend has it, to Patriarch Philaret (before taking his monastic vows, Fiodor Nikitich Romanov, 1554/55–1633, father of Mikhail Fiodorovich, the first Russian Tsar of the Romanov dynasty). The pectoral cross was worn over the clothes and used as a reliquary at the same time.
From the Pavlovsk Palace-Museum, 1958.

**CULTURE OF MUSCOVITE RUSSIA.
15th–17th CENTURIES**
(room 152)

Shroud of St Sylvester

17th century. *Canvas, satin, damask, silk, gilded and silver threads. 192 x 83 cm.*
Inv. No. РП 1387

The interior decoration of Russian churches included works of so-called facial embroidery (images of saints executed in embroidery technique). In the 17th century, the heyday of this art, the icon-painters joined the master-embroideresses, renowned for their virtuoso craftsmanship, in the creation of embroidered shrouds, palls and veils. The shroud with an image of St Sylvester is a typical example of this unique handicraft. The wide border, enframing the central part of the shroud with the image of the saint, resembles an ornamental frieze and carries liturgical texts.
From the church in the village of Voznesenskoye near Yaroslavl, 1974.

Bowl

Last quarter, 17th century. Sol'vychegodsk.
Silver, painting on enamel, cloisonné enamel.
Diameter 14.5 cm. Inv. No. PO 6874

The so-called Usolsk (formerly Sol'vychegodsk) enamels were particularly noted among the items of applied art of pre-Petrine Russia due to large plant patterns painted on white enamel backgrounds. The manufacture of Usolsk enamels is associated with the Stroganov family of merchants and factory-owners. The famous workshops – including the enamelling ones – built on their vast Archangel estates, produced a variety of silver utensils.
From the State Ethnographical Museum, Leningrad, 1941.

**PETER THE GREAT'S
MEMORIAL ITEMS**
(rooms 157–161)

BARTOLOMEO CARLO RASTRELLI
1675–1744
Bust of Peter I
1723–29. Bronze. Height 102 cm.
Inv. No. PCк 162

The Baroque bust of Peter I by Bartolomeo
Carlo Rastrelli is the acme of the sculptor's
work, now displayed in the portrait gallery
of the Romanov family (room 151). The
Emperor is portrayed with an ermine mantle thrown over his armour. The sculptor
and chasers have managed to reproduce
in bronze a strikingly fine variety of textures:
the openwork of lace, the silkiness of the
order's ribbon, the hardness and lustre of
the cuirass. Surpassing the traditional
framework of the representative portrait,
Rastrelli has conveyed the strong will and
spiritual grandeur of Peter I.
*From the Main Collection
of the Winter Palace.*

Ring sundial of universal use

Late 17th–early 18th century. Master C. Metz. Amsterdam. *Brass. Diameter 9.8 cm. Inv. No. PTx 704*

The most remarkable items among the exhibits representing the Petrine era are the navigational devices and instruments. One of the most popular kind of portable instruments for measuring time, the sundial, can be folded and carried in a flat box. By virtue of its universal construction it can be used at any geographic latitude.
From the Main Collection of the Hermitage (Gallery of Peter the Great).

Travelling medicine chest of Peter I

Ca. 1613–15. Masters T. Leucker and H. Georg I Brenner. Germany, Augsburg. *Wood, metal, glass, fabric, trimming, oil on copper, gilt. 39.5 x 41 x 32.5 cm. Inv. Nos. PTx 1389–1424*

Apart from flasks and silver gallipots for medicines and their components, the chest contains a set of simple tools for preparing medicines: scales, pestle and mortar, funnel, spatula, etc. The case of the chest is finished with ebony, the doors and numerous drawers are decorated with silver plates. The copper plate fixed on the inside of the top cover carries a painted image of a pharmacy or a chemist's laboratory.
From the Main Collection of the Hermitage (Gallery of Peter the Great).

Globe

17th century. Spain. *Silver, gilt. Height 34.9 cm, diameter 19.6 cm. Inv. No. Э 55*

A common item in the studies of 17th-century scholars, the globes reflected the scope of knowledge about the universe at that time. This tabletop globe is a true masterpiece of applied art in the Baroque style. The sculptural group serving as its base features the characters from classical mythology – Neptune and Amphitrite.
From the Main Collection of the Hermitage (Gallery of Peter the Great).

Lateral duplicate lathe

1711. Master F. Singer. Italy, Florence (?).
Wood, iron, copper alloys. 205 x 127 x 83 cm.
Inv. No. PTx 648

In the late 17th century a lathe workshop
known as the Turnery was set up
at the Peter's court. According to the 1741
inventory the Turnery included twenty-four
lathes for industrial purposes and twenty-
seven lathes for artistic handicrafts.
In 1712 Peter I invited Franz Singer, who had
already distinguished himself at the court
of the Duke of Tuscany, to St Petersburg.
In Russia Singer was made the head of
the Turnery to elaborate new types of the
lathes and devices for the artistic tooling
of metals, precious wood species and
ivory. Lateral duplicate lathes were used
for making relief copies on the side surfaces of cylindrical items following the
bronze master forms. By virtue of special
mechanical couplings the master form
transferred all peculiar features of the relief
onto the cutting tool which reproduced
the image in its 'positive' form.
From the Main Collection of the Hermitage
(Gallery of Peter the Great).

Lateral duplicate lathe

1718–29. Masters F. Singer, A. Nartov.
St Petersburg. Wood, steel, bronze, silver.
Height 228 cm. Inv. No. PTx 649

Andrei Nartov (1693–1756), an eminent
Russian mechanic and Court Turner to
Peter I, was the tsar's choice for the most
important and sophisticated commissions.
In 1718 Nartov visited Prussia, France and
England to improve his skills and demonstrate the Turnery's achievements. When
Singer died in 1723 he became the head
of the Turnery. Nartov invented the unique
mechanism of a lateral duplicate lathe
with the developed support system substi-
tuting the operator's hand in his work.
This invention marked the transition from
manual labour to machine production.
From the Museum of the Institute
for the History of Natural Science
and Technology of the USSR Academy
of Sciences, Leningrad, 1941.

Relief medallion commemorating the foundation of St Petersburg

1720s. St Petersburg. Wood. Diameter 12.5 cm. Inv. No. РД 98

This relief medallion was fashioned by the medal-making lateral duplicate lathe in Peter I's Turnery after the low relief by Rastrelli. It represents symbolically the foundation of St Petersburg with a Russian warrior holding a brick in his hands and a landowner taking from his pocket the money intended for the building of the city.
From the Main Collection of the Hermitage (Gallery of Peter the Great).

Medallion with a relief image of St Andrew

1720s. St Petersburg. Ivory, wood, gesso, gilt. Diameter of the medallion 14 cm, diameter from the outer extreme of the 'radiance' – 44 cm. Inv. No. РК 593

Similar medallions with 'radiance' were a common production by the lathe workshop of Peter I. Medallions with an image of St Andrew, who was considered the patron saint of the Russian Navy, were often created to decorate the covers of compasses.
From the State Ethnographical Museum, Leningrad, 1941.

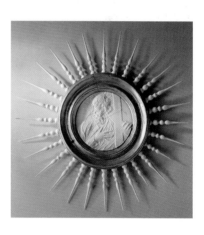

Church chandelier

1723. St Petersburg. Ivory, wood. Height 225 cm. Inv. No. РК 976

This church chandelier is the most significant decorative item produced in the Turnery with the participation of Peter I himself. The multi-tiered construction of bent rods, with oblong grooves made of ivory, mammoth tusks and wood, is decorated with rosettes and flowers fashioned by special lathes – the so-called rose-making machines. On the cylinder in the centre of the stem are the carved relief scenes of the *Crucifixion* and the *Last Supper*. As legend has it, on seeing this remarkable chandelier a foreign visitor commented that he would not spare millions to buy it. He was proudly answered that "Russia has got enough millions but a chandelier like this is the only one".
From the Main Collection of the Hermitage (Gallery of Peter the Great).

PAINTING.
17th–EARLY 19th CENTURIES

LOUIS CARAVAQUE
1684–1754
The Battle of Poltava
1717–18. Oil on canvas. 281 x 487 cm.
Inv. No. РЖ 1913

Louis Caravaque, a native of Marseilles, lived and worked in St Petersburg from 1716 to his last day. He was famous as a skilled portrait-, battle- and scene-painter.

This painting is one of the earliest depictions of the Battle of Poltava (1709) when the Russian troops led by Peter I dealt a crushing blow to the armies of King Charles XII of Sweden. A brilliant example of the battle-painting of the period, it was repeatedly copied.
From the State Tretyakov Gallery,
Moscow, 1946.

BOLMS AND LUTZ
The Battle of Lesnaya
1829–31. Copy from the original painting by P.-D. Martin the Younger. Oil on canvas.
100 x 200.5 cm. Inv. No. 4181

Commissioned by Tsesarevich Konstantin Pavlovich, this canvas is a copy by the artists Bolms and Lutz from the original painting by Pierre-Denis Martin the Younger, an artist of the Gobelin Tapestry Manufactory. The original painting was, in turn, a repro-

duction of the Martin's cartoon for a series of tapestries commissioned by Peter I and dedicated to Russian victories in the Great Northern War. Peter I himself is depicted on horseback in the right foreground surrounded by his suite and trabants. The battle scene is very authentic because Martin used to refer to the battle plans specially sent by Peter I from Russia.
From the Main Collection
of the Winter Palace.

ANDREI MATVEYEV
1704–1739
Portrait of Peter I
After 1725. From the original
painting by K. de Moor (1717).
Oil on canvas. 78 x 61 cm.
Inv. No. 4257

Peter I regarded the
Europeanization of Russian painting as one of the most important
aims of his reforms. For this purpose
he established grants ("pensions") for
the most talented artists and sent them
to Europe for retraining at the Crown's
expense. Andrei Matveyev, one of the first
"pensioners" trained for eleven years in
Amsterdam, was made the head of the
painting shop of the College for
Construction in St Petersburg in 1730. He
evidently made this copy from the portrait
by Karel de Moor as soon as he returned
from Holland to Russia in 1727.
*Acquired in 1851; formerly in the Shuvalovs
collection, St Petersburg.*

KAREL DE MOOR
1656–1738
Portrait of Yekaterina Alexeyevna
1717. Oil on canvas. 81 x 64 cm.
Inv. No. РЖ 2429

The portrait of Yekaterina Alexeyevna, the
second wife of Peter I, made Empress of
Russia in 1725, is a pendant to the above
portrait of Peter I. Both were painted by
Karel de Moor in The Hague in 1717.
*Acquired in 1956; formerly in the F. Kurakin
collection, St Petersburg.*

IVAN NIKITIN
Mid-1680s–after 1742
**Portrait of Grand Duchess
Elizabeth Petrovna as a Child**
Ca. 1712. Oil on canvas. 54 x 43 cm.
Inv. No. РЖ 1401

Ivan Nikitin was trained in Florence under
Tommazo Redi in 1716–19 when he had
already reached a mature age. He painted this portrait of Elizabeth Petrovna,
the daughter of Peter I and Yekaterina
Alexeyevna, before going to Italy.
*From the State Ethnographical Museum,
Leningrad, 1941; formerly in the Gorchakovs
collection, St Petersburg.*

GEORG-CHRISTOPH GROOTH
1716–1749
**Portrait of Grand Duchess
Yekaterina Alexeyevna**
Ca. 1745. Oil on canvas. 106 x 85 cm.
Inv. No. РЖ 2474

The German artist Grooth worked in Russia
as a court painter from 1741. This portrait
shows the young Grand Duchess Yekaterina
Alexeyevna, the future Empress Catherine
the Great, wearing a star and a sash of
the Order of St Catherine.
From the Pavlovsk Palace-Museum, 1958.

UNKNOWN ARTIST
Portrait of a Girl
Mid-18th century. Oil on canvas. 108 x 86.5 cm.
Inv. No. РЖ 1795

Towards the mid-18th century many Russian artists fully imbibed the lessons of the European school, but some masters still adhered to the traditions of national primitive painting. One of the most expressive examples of the individual manner they have evolved is this charming portrait of a child by an unknown artist.
From the State Ethnographical Museum, Leningrad, 1941.

IVAN VISHNIAKOV
1699–1761
Portrait of Mikhail Yakovlev
After 1756. Oil on canvas. 90.5 x 72 cm.
Inv. No. РЖ 340

Ivan Vishniakov, a talented and original portrait painter, was very popular in the mid-18th century. His works combine the icon-painting devices of the decorative and constrained *parsuna* composition with a realistic treatment of the image. Mikhail Yakovlev – a son of Savva Yakovlev, the noted Petersburg lease-holder and the Urals factory owner – is represented in a luxurious costume. The carefully painted details point to the artist's thorough approach to and his deeply rooted admiration for the material world.
The Hermitage collection has a companion portrait of Mikhail Yakovlev's wife.
From the State Ethnographical Museum, Leningrad, 1941; formerly in the Yakovlevs collection.

ALEXEI ANTROPOV
1716–1795
Portrait of Fiodor Dubiansky
1761. Oil on canvas. 99.5 x 76.5 cm.
Inv. No. РЖ 2639

Alexei Antropov, a portraitist and decorator, was a pupil of Pietro Rotari, Louis Caravaque, Andrei Matveyev and Ivan Vishniakov. He painted murals in the Summer, Winter and Anichkov Palaces in St Petersburg. His works bear a close affinity with the Russian artistic traditions. In the portrait of archpriest Fiodor Dubiansky, the confessor of Elizabeth Petrovna, the masterly rendition of the materials' texture prevails over the treatment of form and perspective.
Acquired in 1932.

IVAN ARGUNOV
1727–1802
Portrait of Count Piotr Sheremetev
(Portrait of Sheremetev with a Dog)
1753. Oil on canvas. 135 x 103 cm.
Inv. No. РЖ 1867

Count Piotr Borisovich Sheremetev, a senator and owner of the richest estates, patronized the arts and founded the famous theatre of serf actors on his Ostankino estate. *Portrait of Sheremetev with a Dog* is one of Argunov's early attempts to create a nobleman's representative portrait against a landscape background. Ivan Argunov has reproduced here the compositional scheme of the well-known portrait of Alexander Kurakin by Jean-Marc Nattier.
From the State Ethnographical Museum, Leningrad, 1941; formerly in the Sheremetevs collection, St Petersburg.

UNKNOWN ARTIST OF THE 18th CENTURY
Portrait of Anna Sheremeteva
Ca. 1766. Oil on canvas. 138 x 87 cm.
Inv. No. РЖ 1872

Anna Sheremeteva, a daughter of Piotr Sheremetev, is depicted as Bellona wearing a costume evidently made for the carrousel which took place on 16 June 1766. This famous merry-making at the court of Catherine II bore a pronounced theatrical character. Very fashionable in Russia during the reign of Catherine II, these royal court fancy-dress merry-makings originated from the famous Carrousel of Louis XIV, a grandiose theatricalized performance deriving from the medieval knight tournaments staged on the square in front of the Louvre in 1662.
From the State Ethnographical Museum, Leningrad, 1941.

CARL LÜDWIG CHRISTINECK
1730/32–ca. 1794
Portrait of Count Alexei Bobrinsky as a Child
1769. Oil on canvas. 90 x 73.5 cm.
Inv. No. РЖ 1407

Count Alexei Bobrinsky (1762–1813), a bastard son of Catherine II and Count Grigory Orlov, is represented in a court costume, holding a cocked hat with lace trimming. This portrait by Carl Lüdwig Christineck, treated in a slightly dry manner typical of German painting, is notable for its delicate colouring of green and silver.
From the State Ethnographical Museum, Leningrad, 1941; formerly in the Bobrinskys collection, St Petersburg.

DMITRY LEVITSKY
1735–1822
Portrait of Mikhail Krechetnikov
1776–79. Oil on canvas. 63 x 49.5 cm.
Inv. No. РЖ 1897

A magnificent flowering of Russian portraiture took place during the reign of Catherine II. One of the major artistic highlights of the period was the work of Dmitry Levitsky who depicted nearly all the eminent statesmen of Catherine's time, raising Russian painting to the very top of European art. The portrait of Mikhail Krechetnikov, a military chief and governor of several cities in Malorossia, is a generalized image of a dignitary of the enlightened empress: the appearance of this elegant, experienced courtier betrays his inner strength and self-confidence.
From the State Ethnographical Museum, Leningrad, 1941.

JOHANN-BAPTIST LAMPI THE ELDER
1751–1830
Portrait of Yekaterina Samoilova
1790s. Oil on canvas. 104.5 x 82.5 cm.
Inv. No. РЖ 1890

An impeccable mastery marks the works of Johann-Baptist Lampi, an Austrian artist who lived in Russia for a short time, but managed to paint an enormous number of portraits. The portrait of the General-Procurator Alexander Samoilov's wife, a lady-in-waiting to Catherine II, is one of his best.
From the State Ethnographical Museum, Leningrad, 1941.

JOHANN-BAPTIST LAMPI THE ELDER
1751–1830
Portrait of Prince Alexander Bezborodko
1794. Oil on canvas. 121 x 95 cm.
Inv. No. 8382

Alexander Bezborodko (1747–1799), one of
the eminent Russian statesmen in the reign
of Catherine II, owed his brilliant career
exclusively to his own talents. His diplomatic gift manifested itself to the full during
the signing of the Jassy Peace Treaty
ending the Russo-Turkish War of 1787–91.
Bezborodko was the only minister to retain
his importance at the court even after the

death of Catherine II. Paul I granted him
the title of Most Serene Prince and the
rank of State Chancellor, the highest in the
Empire. Bezborodko was also a renowned
collector and patron of the arts. On the
Lampi's portrait he is shown wearing a sash
and a star of the Orders of St Alexander
Nevsky and St Vladimir, First Class, and the
cross of the Order of St Alexander Nevsky
on the neck ribbon. For its pictorial qualities this portrait by Lampi the Elder is considered one of his best.
From the Stroganov Palace-Museum,
Petrograd, 1923; formerly in the collection
of Prince V. Kochubei, Kiev.

VLADIMIR BOROVIKOVSKY
1757–1825
**Portrait of Grand Duchess
Yelena Pavlovna**
Before 1799. Oil on canvas. 72 x 58 cm.
Inv. No. РЖ 599

Vladimir Borovikovsky was the most prominent figure in the Russian portraiture of the
second half of the 18th century. The artistic outlook of the painter, a pupil of Dmitry
Levitsky and Johann-Baptist Lampi, took
shape under the influence of Sentimentalism
in Russian literature. Grand Duchess
Yelena Pavlovna, one of the six daughters
of Paul I, is shown before her marriage
to the Prince of Mecklenburg-Schwerin
in 1799.
From the State Ethnographical Museum,
Leningrad, 1941.

18th-CENTURY ARTISTIC GLASSWARE

Lidded cup with a portrait of Elizabeth Petrovna

Mid-18th century. St Petersburg Glassworks.
Glass, engraving, gilding. Height 41 cm.
Inv. No. PC 25

In the mid-18th century the Imperial Glassworks of St Petersburg, founded in the 1730s, won fame for its production of lidded cups, goblets and *shtof*-bottles of colourless transparent glass with portraits, coats of arms and monograms of eminent customers engraved in a fine frosted technique.
From the Main Collection
of the Winter Palace.

Lidded compotier

Second half, 18th century. St Petersburg Glassworks. Ruby glass, painting in gold. Height 18.5 cm. Inv. No. PC 147 a, б·

During the reign of Catherine II the St Petersburg Glassworks was famed for its coloured glassware: 'golden ruby', violet, turquoise, yellow, green (emerald) and opal glass. Its manufacture became possible owing to the experiments carried out by Mikhail Lomonosov, his pupils and followers. The composition of the glass named 'golden ruby' included gold. This glassware was in vogue in the 18th century.
From the Leningrad Customs, 1941.

MIKHAIL LOMONOSOV
1711–1765
Mosaic portrait of Peter I
1754. St Petersburg, Ust-Ruditsa Factory.
Iron base, smalt. 89 x 69 cm.
Inv. No. PKм 673

Mikhail Lomonosov is credited with the revival of Russian mosaic art. Elizabeth Petrovna granted him a monopoly for the production of coloured glass in Russia, and for this purpose a factory in Ust-Ruditsa outside Petersburg was built. This unique mosaic portrait of Peter I, composed by Lomonosov himself, was presented to the Empress in 1754.
From the Institute for the History of Science and Technology, Leningrad, 1941.

18th-CENTURY MOSAICS AND ENAMELS

UNKNOWN ARTIST
Portrait of Catherine II holding the text of the *Nakaz*
1770s. Copper, enamel, painting. 8 x 10.7 cm.
Inv. No. PP 8014

In the second half of the 18th century the portrait miniature achieved the status of a self-sufficient art. Its technique was extremely sophisticated: once the image had been outlined on the golden or red copper convex plates coated with a white enamel ground, these were painted in colour enamels with a very fine brush of ermine furs. The plates were subsequently fired in kilns, each colour corresponding to a certain temperature. Catherine II is shown writing the *Nakaz*, or *Instruction*, a philosophical and legal treatise, which she prepared in 1767 for the deputies of the legislative commission for drawing up a new Legal Code (*Ulozhenie*).
Acquired in 1978; formerly in the Orlovs-Davydovs collection, St Petersburg.

ANDREI CHORNY (?)
Portrait of Count Grigory Orlov
Late 1760s–early 1770s. Copper, enamel, painting. 7.2 x 5.3 cm. Inv. No. PP 8013

The portrait of Count Grigory Orlov (1734–1783) was evidently executed by Andrei Chorny, an outstanding miniaturist and a master at the Imperial Porcelain Factory. The miniature shows a favourite of Catherine II who played an active part in her accession to the throne, wearing the dress-coat of an officer of the Cavalry Guards Corps and the ribbon of the Order of St Andrew the First-Called.
Acquired in 1978.

18th-CENTURY ARTISTIC SILVERWARE

Ship-shaped cup

1706. St Petersburg. *Silver, moulding, chasing, engraving, gilt. 30.5 x 12 x 37 cm.*
Inv. No. PO 6928

This is one of the most original jewellery pieces of the early 18th century. To all appearances, it was executed to commemorate the victory of the Russian Navy squadron under the command of Vice-Admiral Cornelius Cruys in the Baltic Sea in 1705. The cup is shaped like a sail warship carrying four guns. Of the nineteen sailors' figures on the deck the highest one presumably represents the Emperor Peter I. The cup was made from the first heat of silver extracted in the Zabaikalye area.
From the Main Collection
of the Winter Palace.

Presentation dish

1720s. St Petersburg. *Silver, gilding, chasing, engraving, chiseling. Diameter 49 cm.*
Inv. No. PO 4596

Silver presentation dishes were a common feature in the everyday life of the grand princes of Muscovite Rus'. They were used in offering of the Russian customary bread and salt to a visitor and of various gifts including the diplomatic ones. This dish is decorated with a relief on the biblical subject: *The Meeting of Abraham and Melchizedek.* It might be the dish presented to Peter I after the Senate had approved his title of Emperor. This suggestion is confirmed by an engraved inscription: *Long Live the Most Serene Sovereign Peter the Great, the Emperor and Autocrat of All the Russias.*
From the Main Collection of the Hermitage.

Dipper granted to Mikhail Pankratovich Orlov, Ataman of the Don Cossacks

1752. St Petersburg. *Silver, chasing, chiseling, engraving, gilding. 10.2 x 28.3 x 15 cm.*
Inv. No. PO 4556

By the turn of the18th century the boat-like dippers were no longer used for practical purposes and were offered to eminent Russian statesmen for their various services. Called 'granted' and made, as a rule, of precious metals, they were decorated with dedicatory inscriptions, often with a list of the awarded person's services.
From the Main Collection of the Hermitage.

Plat de ménage

1739–40. Master I. Liebmann. St Petersburg.
Silver, casting, chasing, engraving.
15 x 70 x 58 cm (tray), 30 x 32 x 32 cm (vase),
25 x 9 x 9 cm (incense burners), 16 x 6 x 6 cm
(sauce-boats). Inv. Nos. PO 4723–4732

The plat de ménage is a table decoration
shaped like a fancy tray with candelabra
to carry fruit vases, various cruet-stands
and wine decanters. The Hermitage piece
was part of a service commissioned by

Empress Anna Ioannovna for the State
Chancellor Prince Cherkassky and
created by the Petersburg silversmith
Ivan Liebmann. After her death, Empress
Elizabeth Petrovna ordered to buy the service and decorate the plat de ménage
with Imperial crowns and her own monograms. The high relief of casting, asymme-
try and excessive decor impart a certain
heaviness to the exhibit.
From the Main Collection
of the Winter Palace.

Presentation dish

1762. Masters A. Gerasimov, A. Polozov.
Moscow. *Silver, gilding. 46.3 x 57.5 cm.*
Inv. No. PO 5058

The oval silver dish has an ornamental
relief decoration *en rocaille* with a monogram of the Empress Catherine II and
an Imperial crown in the centre.
From the Main Collection of the Hermitage.

Egg-shaped clock

1764–67. Master I. Kulibin. Nizhny Novgorod.
Silver, gilding. Height 9.5 cm, diameter
5.6 cm. Inv. No. PO 7318

This famous clock "of an egg figure", created by Ivan Kulibin (1735–
1818), the master genius from
Nizhny Novgorod, was intended
as a gift to Catherine II. The clock's
mechanism totals 427 details. In
the lower part of the body are the
face and hands, on one side – a small

opening to the 'chamber' where tiny figures used to play every hour the scene
of the Resurrection of Christ to the
accompaniment of the melody
Christ has arisen repeated three
times. The clock struck every
quarter and half an hour and
every day at noon it played
the melody of a cantata composed by Kulibin in honour
of Catherine II.
From the Main Collection
of the Hermitage.

18th-CENTURY PORCELAIN

Snuff-box: *Pugdogs*

1752. Master D. Vinogradov. Porcelain Manufactory. St Petersburg. Porcelain, gold, painting. 4.8 x 7.7 x 6.2 cm. Inv. No. PФ 150

First made in Europe in 1710 and produced by several manufactories in Germany and France, porcelain remained an invaluable material and its recipe was kept in strict secrecy. It was only after the Russian chemist Dmitry Ivanovich Vinogradov (1720?–1758) became the head of research work at the Porcelain Manufactory in St Petersburg founded by order of Elizabeth Petrovna that the multiple attempts to invent the Russian porcelain-making recipe proved successful. The first porcelain items produced before the 1750s, when a large kiln was constructed at the Nevskaya Porcelain Manufactory, were small-sized. The snuff-box *Pugdogs* is an example of the manufactory's first output. The miniature image of the dogs on the lid was executed by the talented artist Andrei Chorny. The snuff-box was presented to Empress Elizabeth Petrovna and she liked it so much that the artist has reproduced the painting on two more similar items.
From the Main Collection of the Hermitage.

Items from the Orlov Service

1760s. Imperial Porcelain Factory. St Petersburg. Porcelain, painting, gilding, silvering, guilloche. Height of the teapot 22.5 cm. Inv. Nos. PФ 8280–8282, 8284 a, б, 8291, 8294

Placed under the patronage of Empress Catherine II and renamed the Imperial Porcelain Factory, the Porcelain Manufactory rapidly developed and its output soon acquired its distinctive idiom. The Orlov Service is one of the most perfect examples of early Russian porcelain manufacture. Made at the Imperial Porcelain Factory, it was commissioned by Catherine II as a gift to her favourite, Count Grigory Orlov. A monogram under the Count's crown is placed on each item. The service is adorned with miniature battle scenes, trophies and emblems painted after Gavriil Kozlov's sketches.
Purchased at Christie's, Geneva, 1981.

Wine-glass stand from the Cabinet Service

1793–95. Imperial Porcelain Factory. St Petersburg. *Porcelain, overglaze painting, gilding. 12.5 x 28 x 17 cm. Inv. No. РФ 343*

The items of the Cabinet service made for Count Bezborodko are decorated with views of Rome within oval medallions and the garlands of wild flowers on a gilded ribbon.
From the Expert-Purchasing Commission of the Hermitage, 1953.

Figurines from the *Peoples of Russia* series

1780s–90s. Master J.-D. Rachette. Imperial Porcelain Factory. St Petersburg. *Porcelain, painting, gilding. Height 20.7 cm, 20.2 cm. Inv. Nos. РФ 176, 178*

This sculptural series is based on the *Description of the peoples inhabiting the Russian Empire...* by Johann-Gottlieb Georghi (1729–1802), a well-known ethnographer, traveller and researcher who summarized the data gathered by numerous travellers and scientists in various territories of Russia.
From the State Ethnographical Museum, Leningrad, 1941.

Vase: *Gossips*

1807. Mould after the sketch by J.-D. Dugour. Imperial Porcelain Factory. St Petersburg. *Porcelain, coloured mat coating, gilding, guilloche. Height 95 cm. Inv. No. РФ 7354 а, б*

The vase's handles take the form of two gilded women's figures standing on consoles with feminine mascarons and leaning on the vase's rim. The stepped base is decorated with bands of plant ornaments in relief guilloche on gilt, relief gilded masks on a black ground and four chimeras (a mythological monster with a lion's head, goat's body and serpent's tail) on the corners. This is one of two companion vases which were presented to Emperor Alexander I by the Director of His Imperial Majesty's Cabinet Count Guryev.
From the Main Collection of the Winter Palace.

18th-CENTURY BONE-CARVING

Table-top cabinet
Mid-18th century. Kholmogory. *Bone, wood.*
54.5 x 34 x 15.5 cm. Inv. No. PK 830

The art of bone-carving was flourishing
in the 18th century. In the Archangel area,
St Petersburg and Moscow, skilled masters
created works of high artistic standard –
boxes, vases, sculptural groups, portrait-
plates. The execution of the Hermitage
cabinet with all its thorough carving
heightened with mineral paints is typical
for the masters of the Russian North.
*From the State Ethnographical Museum,
Leningrad, 1941.*

Vase: *Seasons*
Late 18th century. Master N. Vereshchagin.
Archangel. *Bone, carving. Height 31 cm.
Inv. No. PK 836*

The vase, executed by Nikolai Vereshchagin
(1770–ca. 1814), has an austere classical
silhouette and a wealth of ornamental
motifs. Its openwork top features four
medallions with engraved allegories
of seasons treated as genre scenes.
The *Winter* medallion, for instance, shows
two men and a woman warming themselves at a fire.
*From the State Ethnographical Museum,
Leningrad, 1941; formerly in the Main
Collection of the Hermitage.*

Mug
1774–75. Master O. Dudin. St Petersburg. *Bone,
horn, silver. Height 25 cm. Inv. No. PK 834*

Osip Dudin (1714–1780), a native of
Archangel province and one of the most
notable bone-carvers of the 18th century,
worked for a long time in St Petersburg.
One of his masterpieces is this mug
adorned with 58 portraits of Russian tsars
and princes from Riurik to Catherine II: due
to its scale and location in the centre of
the composition, her portrait is particularly
distinctive. The representations are placed
in four tiers against the background of
the open lacework of the finest carving.
The crown and the orb on top of the lid
are the symbols of sovereignty.
*From the State Ethnographical Museum,
Leningrad, 1941.*

TULA STEELWORK

Chess casket and chessmen
1782. Master A. Sukhanov. Tula. *Steel,
bronze, gilding, silver and golden inlay.
17 x 50 x 31 cm (casket), 9.4 x 3 cm (king),
8.2 x 2.8 cm (queen), 4.8 x 2.6 cm (knight).
Inv. Nos. PM 4578, 4580, 4602, 4622*

Famous throughout Russia and beyond,
the work of the goldsmiths of Tula has long
been synonymous with the Russian craftsmanship, fine taste and deep appreciation
of beauty. In addition to weapons, the Tula
craftsmen made steel caskets, vases, mirrors, candlesticks and seals. The armourers
were allowed to do 'particular' works as a
privilege for the obligatory delivery of arms
to the state. The heyday of such production dates back to the last quarter of the
18th century. The finishing effect of the
Tula articles was based on the combination of gilded bronze and the silvery mirror-
like polished or blue steel. Especially popular was the use of steel beads as "facet
diamonds" distributed over the surface of
an item in hundreds of glittering jewels. The
inimitable example of this craft is this steel
chess casket containing eighty chessmen.
It was presented to Catherine II in the
1780s. In the 18th century the chess was
kept in the Hermitage Cabinet of Curios
and in the 19th century – in the Jewellery
Gallery.
*From the Main Collection of the Hermitage
(Jewellery Gallery).*

Table-top mirror
*Ca. 1801. Tula. Steel, bronze, gilding.
Height 70 cm. Inv. No. PM 7498*

The openwork top of the mirror features
a monogram of Empress Maria Feodorovna,
wife of Paul I, to whom it was presented
about 1801.
*From the Main Collection of the Hermitage
(Jewellery Gallery).*

18th-CENTURY ARTISTIC FURNITURE

Table

Early 18th century. Archangel. *Wood, gesso, tempera. 770 x 287 x 205 cm. Inv. No. PM6 201*

Of all the decorative and applied arts of Peter's time, it was the furniture-making closely connected with the new urban interior decoration that underwent the greatest changes. This oval table made in Archangel for Peter I can serve an example of an original combination of new and traditional forms in furniture. Folded flaps and collapsible legs resemble the famous English constructions of the late 17th century. The painting of stylized acanthus leaves and medallions with images of birds, executed in traditional Russian gesso technique, imitates an inlaid wood veneer. *From the Yekaterininsky Palace, Tsarskoye Selo, 1907.*

Fancy-pattern settee

Second quarter, 18th century. St Petersburg. *Wood, gilding, damask (upholstery). 128 x 178 x 65 cm. Inv. No. PM6 24*

An astonishingly high artistic standard marked the best works of Russian serf masters. The lavish decor of the settee upholstered in green damask with gilt thread is characteristic of Elizabeth Petrovna's reign. *From the State Ethnographical Museum, Leningrad, 1941.*

Fancy-pattern commode

1762–65. Ust-Sysert (?). *Wood, ivory, onyx, brass, zinc. 76 x 88 x 45 cm. Inv. No. PM6 37*

The commode of a curved, wavy silhouette is lavishly inlaid with valuable wood, ivory plates and milky-toned onyx. The tabletop features an inlaid monogram of Catherine II and a coat of arms of Siberia. *From the State Ethnographical Museum, Leningrad, 1941.*

Armchair for the President of the Military College

Ca. 1784. St Petersburg. Wood, carving, gilding, velvet upholstery with gilded trimming. 153 x 75 x 68 cm. Inv. No. PMб 109

This armchair was evidently intended for Count Grigory Potiomkin, who headed the Military College in the 1780s, hence the choice of decor themes: the armchair's supports are shaped like the lictor's sheaves of spears with a Hercules's club, a sword, a bow and an arrow and laurel leaves under a classical helmet in between.
From the State Ethnographical Museum, Leningrad, 1941; formerly in the Military College, St Petersburg.

Bean-shaped table

1780s-90s. M. Veretennikov Workshop. St Petersburg. *Valuable wood, ivory. 71 x 96 x 58 cm. Inv. No. PMб 544*

Tables with bean-like tops were very popular in the second half of the 18th century. A cabinet-maker from the Matvei Veretennikov Workshop has brilliantly adorned this item with pieces of valuable wood (intarsia) and ivory mosaic.
From the State Ethnographical Museum, Leningrad, 1941.

Corner cupboard

1787. Master Ch. Meyer. St Petersburg. *Wood, metal, mosaic. 92 x 43 x 43 cm. Inv. No. PMб 70*

According to archival records, the Hermitage had quite a few corner cupboards by Christian Meyer in the late 18th century. Nearly all of them were altered by the furniture factory-owner Tour in 1847. However, several cupboards, kept in other collections at that time, have retained their original appearance.
From the State Ethnographical Museum, Leningrad, 1941.

Armchair

1784. After the drawing by Ch. Cameron.
Master J.-B. Charlemagne. St Petersburg.
Wood, carving. 119 x 77 x 73 cm.
Inv. No. PM6 1193

The furniture 'in Chinese taste' was made after the drawings of Charles Cameron for the Chinese Room in the Yekaterininsky Palace in Tsarskoye Selo. An armchair from this set has delicately carved arms with carved wooden lizards and an original top of the back in the form of two intertwined serpents supporting a basket of flowers.
From the Counts Shuvalov collection,
St Petersburg; formerly in the Yekaterininsky
Palace, Tsarskoye Selo.

Throne of Paul I
from the Maltese Capella

1798–1800. St Petersburg. After sketches by G. Quarenghi. *Wood, carving, gilding, embroidery. 156 x 115 x 96 cm (throne), 23 x 64 42 cm (stool). Inv. No. PM6 108 / 4, 5*

In 1798 Emperor Paul I became the Magister of the Maltese Order of St John of Jerusalem. In this connection the architect Giacomo Quarenghi built a capella for the sittings of the Maltese knights in Count Vorontsov's palace in Sadovaya Street in St Petersburg. From that capella come the throne formerly owned by Paul I and other items of the capella's ritual decoration executed after Quarenghi's sketches.
From the State Ethnographical Museum,
Leningrad, 1941.

Bureau

1795–1815. Master H. Gambs. St. Petersburg.
Mahogany, bronze. Height 175 cm.
Inv. No. PM6 249

Large lots of furniture were purchased by Catherine II and her courtiers abroad and in St Petersburg from foreign furniture-makers. The Hermitage owns a fine piece by Heinrich Gambs (1765–1831), a pupil of David Roentgen, the famous furniture-maker. The bureau resembles an architectonic structure and its sophisticated mechanisms make it possible to open drawers and caches. The built-in mechanical organ plays Mozart's melodies.
Acquired in 1817.

19th-CENTURY RUSSIAN INTERIOR DECORATION
(rooms 175–187)

Drawing-room with furniture pieces of Karelian birch

In the early 19th century furniture sets of Karelian birch were in vogue in Russia.

Neo-Classical masters using simple forms and frugally decorated surfaces valued Karelian birch for its unusual texture accounting for especially decorative aspect of the objects produced.

Rosewood cupboard
1846. Designed by A. Stackenschneider. Master G. Alexander. Gambs Furniture Factory. St Petersburg. *Rosewood, bronze, porcelain, painting. Height 186 cm.*
Inv. No. PM6 696

The cupboard is executed in the Rococo style which experienced a second revival in Russia from the 1840s onwards. Such direct address to the previous styles, as was typical for the arts in the 19th century, was partly due to the absence of a new artistic vocabulary which could have replaced the Empire style. The furniture pieces that the best masters were able to create within the retrospective framework of the so-called 'historical styles', were unique indeed. This rosewood cupboard with inlaid porcelain decorations depicting gallant scenes from the everyday life of 18th-century nobility, was made by Gavriil Alexander after a design by Andrei Stackenschneider at the Gambs Furniture Factory for the Pink Drawing-Room of the Winter Palace.
From the Main Collection of the Winter Palace.

18th-CENTURY TAPESTRIES

Tapestry: *The Battle of Poltava*

1722. Masters Ph. Behagle, I. Kobyliakov.
Imperial Tapestry Manufactory. St Petersburg.
Wool, silk. 300 x 315 cm. Inv. No. PT 16181

The Imperial Tapestry Manufactory was
founded by Peter I in St Petersburg in
1716–17. Russian handicraftsmen were
quick to master the skills of tapestry weaving, so that contemporaries even compared works by Petersburg masters with
the best pieces from the famous Gobelins
Manufactory. *The Battle of Poltava* tapestry
was intended to commemorate the tenth
anniversary of the Poltava victory. Begun
in 1719 under the supervision of the French
master Philippe Behagle, the tapestry
took nearly three years to complete due to the
laborious technology of weaving. The cartoon for the tapestry was apparently made
by the famous artist Louis Caravaque after
his own painting.
*From the Assembly of the Nobility,
St Petersburg, 1914.*

Tapestry: *Hector Reproaching Paris*

1773. Imperial Tapestry Manufactory.
St Petersburg. *Wool, silk. 400 x 500 cm.
Inv. No. PT 16184*

The second half of the 18th century
proved to be the most productive period
for the Imperial Tapestry Manufactory when
both individual tapestries and entire
ensembles for the decoration of halls were
created. Under the increasing influence
of Classicism in the 1770s the classical
themes came to the fore. One of the
earliest works of its kind, the *Hector
Reproaching Paris* is based on Homer's
Iliad. By virtue of its clear composition,
high emotionality and superbly treated
architectural background, the tapestry can
be classed among the best pieces produced by the manufactory at that time.
*From the Court Equerry Museum,
after 1917.*

18th-CENTURY COURT CARRIAGES

Coronation carriage

1720s. Paris. *Wood, metal, glass, leather, silk, cloth, wood carving, gilding, embroidery, painting. Length 7 m. Inv. No. 686*

The carriage was presumably commissioned by Peter I during his visit to Paris in 1717. The Imperial regalia on the roof of the carriage body indicate that it was intended for coronations. It may have been used in the ceremonial coronation of Catherine II. The decor and allegorical paintings *Wisdom, Fidelity, Minerva, Authority, Triumph of Amphitrite* comply with the purpose of the carriage. The painting of the body is attributed to the famous French artist François Boucher (1703–1770). An analysis of the decor and construction of the carriage, however, warrants the assumption that it was made in the first quarter of the 18th century. Should this be the case, Boucher would have taken part in its painting at the earliest stage of his career when his manner had not yet taken shape. It is on display in the Field Marshals Hall (room 193).
From the Museum of Toys, Moscow, 1929.

Carnival sledge

Mid-18th century. St Petersburg (?). *Wood, iron, gilding. 174 x 350 x 116 cm. Inv. No. 472*

The carnival sledge is shaped in the form of the dragon slain by St George who is considered the patron saint of the Romanov dynasty. Carved from a solid block of wood, the sledge is a fine example of the Baroque sculpture dynamically unfolded in space. It is lavishly gilded and its seat is upholstered with velvet.
From the Court Equerry Museum, after 1917.

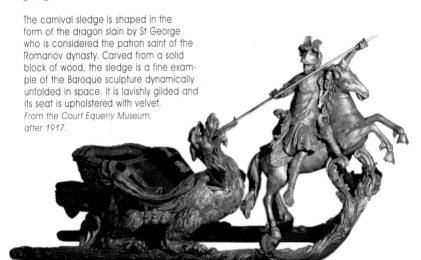

GROUND FLOOR

● BEGINNING
OF THE GROUND-FLOOR
EXHIBITION

▲ ENTRANCE

NICHOLAS STAIRCASE

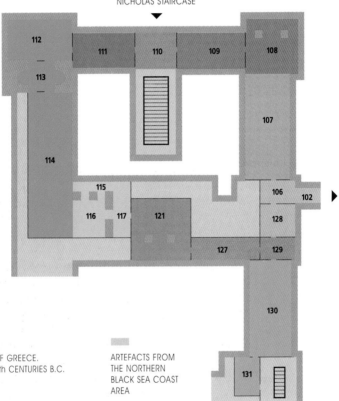

ART OF ANCIENT EGYPT

ART OF GREECE.
7th–5th CENTURIES B.C.

ARTEFACTS FROM
THE NORTHERN
BLACK SEA COAST
AREA

ART OF GREECE.
5th–4th CENTURIES B.C.

ART
OF ANCIENT
ITALY

DECORATIVE SCULPTURE
OF GREECE.
4th–3rd CENTURIES B.C.

ROMAN
SCULPTURAL PORTRAITS
OF THE REPUBLIC
AND IMPERIAL PERIODS,
APPLIED ARTS OF ROME

ART OF THE HELLENISTIC
PERIOD

ROMAN SCULPTURE.
1st–4th CENTURIES

ROMAN RELIEFS
AND SCULPTURE.
2nd CENTURY

The collection of art works from Ancient Greece, Etruria, Rome and the Greek colonies in the northern Black Sea coast area began to take shape in the reign of Peter I, and the process especially gained in scale under Catherine II who was a great admirer of carved stones, or 'antiquities'. In 1787 the empress purchased a collection of ancient sculptures from G. Lyde Browne, director of the British Bank, which formed the nucleus of the Hermitage collection of antique sculpture. The largest and most valuable acquisition was made in Rome in 1862 from the museum of the celebrated collector Marquis Gian-Pietro Campana who had spent away a fortune on buying antiquities. This acquisition brought in about 100 sculptures and more than 600 painted vases. The huge statues of Augustus enthroned and Jupiter sitting, as well as the hydria known as the 'Queen of the Vases', became the highlights of the museum collection. In 1884, the Hermitage experienced a new 'antique boom', now connected with the purchase of a unique collection of Tanagra terracottas gathered by the Russian ambassador to Athens, Piotr Saburov. With the beginning of large-scale archaeological excavations the Hermitage turned into a repository for multifarious artefacts unearthed in the former Greek colonies on the north coast of the Black Sea, including pieces of jewellery, fabrics, articles of wood, bone and metal, painted vases, sculptures and terracottas. At present, the Hermitage houses more than 113,000 works of antique art. Chronologically the exhibition begins in the rooms situated on both sides of the Main (Nicholas) Staircase in the New Hermitage.

ART OF GREECE.
8th–5th CENTURIES B.C.
(rooms 108, 109, 111–114)

Amphoriskos
Second quarter, 6th century B.C. Corinth.
Clay, painting. Height 16.8 cm.
Inv. No. Б 2775

During the archaic period Corinth was one of the most important production centres of painted ceramics. It was the birthplace of black-figured vases. The style of arranging depictions on vases in friezes came to be called the 'carpet style.'
From the Archaeological Commission, 1901.

Amphora with depiction of a deer
6th century B.C. Asia Minor, Clazomenae.
Clay, painting. Height 32 cm. Inv. No. Б 3222

Clazomenae, alongside other cities in Asia Minor and islands in the Aegean Sea (Rhodos, Samos, Chios), was famous for its pottery workshops which catered mainly for export. By the mid-6th century B.C. vase-painters in Clazomenae lost interest in the carpet style considering it to be too archaic, and began to decorate their works with depictions of single animal figures. The silhouette of the grazing deer stands out graphically from the light background of the vase body.
From the excavations in Taman, 1914.

Lekane
6th century B.C. By Protomas Painter. Boeotia.
Clay, painting. Height 26.9 cm. Inv. No. Б 3143

The problems connected with the Universe were among the basic ones in the culture of Antiquity. They were not alien to vase-painters both in Corinth and Asia Minor. During the archaic period vase-painters in Boeotia and Attica considered man to be the hub of the Universe and endowed him with the features of a mythological hero. This Hermitage lekane is notable for the skill with which a man's figure is inscribed into the vessel bottom as a decorative element.

The outer sides of the lekane body carry depictions of a goat and a wild boar.
From the Gokhmann collection, Odessa, 1905.

Amphora: *Rider and Warriors*
6th century B.C. By Amasis Painter. Athens.
Clay, painting. Height 31 cm. Inv. No. Б 161

Ceramists in Athens brought the black-
figured style of vase-painting to the acme
of perfection. The frieze-type decoration
gave way to separate story-telling pictures
while ornament remained only on the
stems and joints of the mouth and the
body. Masters of black-figured vases preferred to depict scenes of leaving for
campaigns, battles and victorious home-
comings. The subject-matter of feast vessels corresponded to the mood of heroic
songs sung at feasts.
From the Pizzati collection, Rome, 1834.

Pelike: *The Arrival of a Swallow*
Ca. 510 B.C. Euphronios' workshop. Attica.
Clay, painting. Height 37.5 cm.
Inv. No. Б 2352

Around 530 B.C. black-figured vase-painting
gave way to the red-figured style. Now it
was the background that was coated with
black varnish while human figures and other
objects retained the reddish colour of clay.
This red-figured pelike depicting the arrival
of the first swallow was found in Vulci in Italy.
This discovery was at once featured in the
magazine of the Archaeological Institute
in Rome. Then the pelike disappeared
from the public view and eventually was
acquired by the Russian diplomat Nikolai
Guryev who brought it to Moscow. Afterwards
it found its way to the collection of the
Minister of Finance, A. Abaza, whose widow
sold it in 1901 to the Hermitage. The pelike
with a swallow is one of the pieces produced by the workshop of Euphronios,
an outstanding Greek potter.
From the A. Abaza collection,
St Petersburg, 1901.

Psykter: *Hetaerae Feasting*

505–500 B.C. By Euphronios. Attica.
Clay, painting. Height 34 cm. Inv. No. Б 1653

This psykter, a jar for cooling wine, was painted by Euphronios who won acclaim for his skill of rendering intricate movements through a simple but very expressive arrangement of figures. One of a few extant vases signed by Euphronios, the psykter features depictions of four hetaerae whose names are inscribed in purple colour next to their figures. The women are playing cottabus. The players were to throw the last drop of wine into an empty bronze vessel placed on a stand in the distance. While doing this, the player had to say some words in honour of her lover. The inscription on the psykter says: "I throw this [drop] for you, Leagros."
From the collection of Marquis G.-P. Campana, Rome, 1862.

Lekythos: *Artemis and Swan*

5th century B.C. By Pan Painter. Athens.
Clay, painting. Height 38 cm. Inv. No. Б 2363

In such vessels the Greeks used to keep olive and fragrant oil. Quite often these slender small vases were used for funerary purposes as well. A lekythos painted against a white background is a rather rare piece. It depict Artemis feeding a swan. Red-figured ornaments alternate with the painting in which the bodies of the goddess and the swan rendered in white colour, stand out clearly from the cream-coloured background. Stripes of gold-coloured diluted varnish are introduced into the graphic painting of the vase.
From the A. Abaza collection, St Petersburg, 1901.

Figured kantharos

Early 5th century B.C. Attica. *Clay, painting. Height 18.9 cm. Inv. No. Б 4504*

The form and painting of this kantharos demonstrate a brilliant fusion of coroplastic and vase-painting. The vessel is made in the shape of two woman's heads, white and black.
From the collection of Marquis G.-P. Campana, Rome, 1862.

Mirror stand: *Aphrodite and Eroses*
5th century B.C. The Island of Aegina.
Bronze. Height 28.5 cm.
Inv. No. B 815

This is an example of the output of the famous bronze casters of Aegina. The figure of the goddess of love, serving as the stand for her mirror, is surrounded with winged eroses personifying love and passion. Aphrodite stands on a stool-like base, its legs ending in hooves. She is coquettishly lifting the edge of her robe with one hand and holding a pine cone by the other.
From the A. Bludov collection,
St Petersburg, 1888.

Kouros with a dedicatory inscription
590–570 B.C. Island of Samos.
Bronze. Height 13 cm. Inv. No. B 616

This statue of a young athlete is one of the most brilliant pieces in the Hermitage collection. It belonged to the Venetian doge Nani and became famous thanks to the inscription on its base saying: *Polycrates has dedicated me.* This inscription is associated with Polycrates, tyrant of Samos, who ruled in 538–522 B.C. The stylistic peculiarities of the statuette, however, speak of an earlier date of execution. Judging by an opening in the athlete's head, the statue might have served as a stand.
From the M. Pourtalès collection,
Paris, 1865.

Kitharedos
5th century B.C. Greece. *Bronze.*
Height 12 cm. Inv. No. B 613

The plastic image of a youth playing kithara goes back to the lost statue by the sculptor Pythagoras from the city of Rhegium in Italy. The half-naked youth playing kithara is represented sitting on a rock. His eyes were once inlaid with silver. It was a common practice among ancient masters to reproduce large statues by their famous contemporaries in small bronze figurines.
From a private collection, 1863.

Head of Athena

Roman copy after the original of
the 5th century B.C. by Cresilas.
Marble. Height 65 cm. Inv. No. A 47

The majestic nobility and lucid beauty of
the ideal images of Man – these qualities
distinguished the classical sculpture of
Phidias and his contemporary Cresilas.
This head of the goddess, found in Rome
in the 18th century, attracted Johann
Winckelmann's attention, and he decided
to acquire it. However, the sculpture found
its way to the collection of the English
banker G. Lyde Browne.
*From the G. Lyde Browne collection,
London, 1787.*

Athena (The Campana Athena)

Roman copy after the original of
the 5th century B.C. by Phidias (?).
Marble. Height 224 cm. Inv. No. A 364

The statue of the Campana Athena,
called so after the name of its former
owner, goes back to the Promachos
Athena made by the great Phidias in the
5th century B.C. This lifelike depiction of
the goddess in the pose of a calm standing woman is one of the most important
achievements of the art of the period.
The majestic goddess of wisdom and war,
holding a spear, is represented dressed
in a peplos, a ceremonial robe of Greek
women with a cloak thrown
upon it. On her breast is an
aegis with a Medusa's
head. The head of
the statue was lost in
ancient times and
the statue is now
topped with a
head from another
antique statue
of Athena.
*From the collection
of Marquis
G.-P. Campana,
Rome, 1862.*

Head of a doryphorus

Roman copy after the original of *ca.* 440 B.C.
by Polyclitus. *Basalt. Height 26 cm.
Inv. No. A 292*

This is a green basalt copy of the bronze
original by Polyclitus of Argos. The polished
surface of the stone has retained its play
of light typical for metal surfaces. The statue of a doryphorus (an athlete with a
spear) was considered a model sculpture.
Polyclitus himself called it 'canon', just like
his treatise devoted to it.
From the collection of Tsarskoye Selo, 1850.

Head of Ares
Roman copy after the original of *ca.* 420 B.C.
by Alcamenes. *Marble. Height 57 cm.*
Inv. No. A 105

This head of the Greek god of war, Ares,
was sculpted by the younger contemporary of Phidias, Alcamenes. In the 18th
century it was thought to be a depiction
of Achilles as identified by the famous
artist Anton Raphael Mengs. At present
the Hermitage statue is regarded as a
copy of the *Borghese Ares* (Louvre, Paris).
*From the collection of Tsarskoye Selo,
1850; formerly, in the collection
of Count I. Shuvalov.*

Relief: *Slaughter of Niobids*
Roman copy after the original
of the 5th century B.C. by Phidias.
Marble. Height 48 cm, length 194 cm.
Inv. No. A 434

The original relief adorned the throne of
the statue of Zeus at Olympia. The statue
was made of gold and ivory. The relief
was very popular: a copy of it adorned
the door of the temple of Apollo Palatine
in Rome. Even artisans who decorated
sarcophagi imitated Phidias' creations.
*From the collection of Marquis
G.-P. Campana, Rome, 1862.*

Portrait of Socrates
Roman copy after the original
of the 4th century B.C. by Lysippus.
Marble. Height 34 cm. Inv. No. A 402 a

The original is considered to be the work
of Lysippus from Sicyon, an outstanding
sculptor of the second half of the 4th century B.C., a representative of late classical
art and Court Artist to Alexander the
Great. In the words of his contemporaries,
Socrates, who studied the problems of
ethics, "took down philosophy from Heaven
to earth". The tall wrinkled forehead and
the gaze of the thinker, absorbed in
his thoughts, betray the intense work
of the intellect.
*From the collection of Marquis
G.-P. Campana, Rome, 1862.*

Eros with a bow
Roman copy after the original of ca. 335 B.C.
by Lysippus. *Marble. Height 133 cm.
Inv. No. A 199*

Marble copies from Lysippus, sculptures
of eroses with a bow are housed in various
museums of the world. But only in the
Hermitage copy the position of Eros' right
hand fully corresponds to the original: it
depicts Eros drawing a bow-string but not
shooting an arrow.
Acquired from Pope Pius IX, 1851.

Satyr Resting

Roman copy after the original of the
mid-4th century B.C. by Praxiteles. *Marble.
Height 168 cm. Inv. No. A 154*

Among the Greek sculptors of the 4th century B.C. Praxiteles occupied an outstanding position, on a par with Phidias and
Polyclitus. The image of the *Satyr Resting*,
known only from marble copies, is so striking for its sensual beauty and refinement
that it gave rise to numerous imitations
and copies. The Hermitage alone has
five copies.
From the Demidovs collection, 1851.

Aphrodite (Venus of Taurida)

Roman copy after the original of
the 3rd-century B.C. from Praxiteles' circle.
Marble. Height 169 cm. Inv. No. A 150

This statue is the first work of classical art
to arrive in Russia. The so-called Venus of
Taurida is a cult statue of the goddess of
love. It was Praxiteles who for the first time
attempted to represent Aphrodite in the
nude: to this end the sculptor had to intro-
duce an everyday moment into his work:
the goddess is going to take a bath. With
her hands (not extant) she chastely covered her breast and bosom. Beside her,
on an incense vessel, one can see her
clothes. Thus looked Praxiteles' statue in
the Aphrodite Temple in Cnidus. It was
greatly admired in ancient times.
*From the Taurida Palace, St Petersburg, 1850;
formerly in the collection of Peter I.*

ART OF THE HELLENISTIC PERIOD
(room 121)

Aphrodite and Eros

3rd century B.C. Tanagra. *Clay, painted.
Height 18.5 cm. Inv. No. Г 440*

This charming Tanagra statuette may have
been inspired by a poem by the ancient
poetess Sappho, in which a young girl tells
her mother that she cannot spin any more
as her soul pines for Eros. The sculptor
seems to reopen the door leading into
the woman's half of a Greek house, which,
as a rule, was kept closed to strangers.
The young spinner, immersed in her work,
has not noticed the moment when the
playful Eros appeared in her lap.
From the P. Saburov collection, 1884.

Dionysus and Cora

*Roman copy after a Greek original
of the 4th–3rd century* B.C. *Marble.
Height 207.5 cm. Inv. No. A 104*

This ancient statue which decorated
the park of Catherine II in Tsarskoye
Selo in the 18th century was extolled
by Alexander Pushkin in one of his
youthful verses:

> *There is Bacchus peaceful
> and perennially young!
> A thyrsus in his hand,
> A grape wreath yellowing
> In his black curly hair.*

The god of wine-making is depicted
before an ancient idol of the goddess
of virginity, Cora. This statue matched
beautifully the decoration of the park.
From the collection of Tsarskoye Selo, 1780.

Head of a satyr

*Roman copy after a Greek original of
the 3rd-century* B.C. *Marble. Height 30 cm.
Inv. No. A 853*

This head of a satyr goes back to the works
of Pergamum sculptors from the Hellenistic
period. The image is full of restrained suffering. It is worthy of note that Catherine II's
son, Tsesarevich Paul Petrovich (the future
Emperor Paul I), chose this head to decorate the throne room in the Gatchina
Palace, his suburban residence. The image
of a suffering youth was marvellously in
tune with the spiritual mood of the 'Russian
Hamlet', whom his mother denied
the throne.
From the Gatchina Palace, 1925.

Cameo: *Ptolemy II and Arsinoë* (The Gonzaga cameo)

3rd century B.C. Alexandria. *Sardonyx.*
15.7 x 11.8 cm. Inv. No. Ж 291

The Gonzaga cameo, called so after the name of its owner in the Renaissance period, is a real 'icon' of the dynastic cult in the Hellenistic era. Royal luxury was necessary to the rulers of Egypt to create the cult of the Ptolemy dynasty. This paired portrait of Ptolemy Philadelphus and his wife, Arsinoë – the kingly brother and sister – has recorded their 'sacral wedding', which made this couple akin to the Olympic gods – Zeus and Hera, who were brother and sister, too. *From the Empress Joséphine collection, Malmaison, 1814.*

Cameo: *Zeus*

3rd century B.C. Alexandria. *Sardonyx.*
Diameter 6.1 cm. Inv. No. Ж 292

One of the most beautiful ancient cameos to come down to us, this is a rare example of 'painting in stone', as the art of engraving in multi-layered polychrome sardonyx was called. Using transparent layers of the stone the carver has achieved a painterly effect of light-and-shade modelling and colour contrasts. The light silhouette of the face stands out against the golden background and dark curly hair. The carver has been able to impart a pathetic character to the image. Before the Napoleonic wars the cameo was in the Doge's Palace in Venice for hundreds of years. *From the Duchess Ye. Golitsina collection, St Petersburg, 1850.*

Intaglio: *Nymph Aura*
1st century B.C. By Dioskourides.
Amethyst. 3.5 x 3 cm. Inv. No. Ж 1251

The art of carving on coloured stones
experienced its third flourishing during the
rule of Emperor Augustus (63 B.C.–14 A.D.).
After the fall of Ptolemy Egypt, many outstanding stone-carvers moved to Rome.
This intaglio on a large convex amethyst,
with the nymph Aura personifying favourable
sea-breeze, was carved by the master
Dioskourides in the 1st century B.C. The
nymph Aura was particularly worshipped
during the reign of Augustus, as official
ideologists asserted that it was she who
filled out the sails of Roman ships when
they defeated the fleet of Cleopatra
and Mark Antony.
From the Mallia collection, Vienna, 1813.

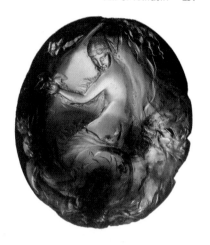

Amphora: *Triumph of Love*
1st century. Rome. *Sardonyx.*
Height of the body 5.5 cm. Inv. No. Ж 361

This miniature amphora made in cameo
technique is a unique piece of applied art.

In the Renaissance period it was in the col-
lection of Francis I at Fontainebleau, and
in the 17th century it passed to Cardinal
Mazarin, Prime Minister of France.
*From the collection of Baron A. Nikolai,
St Petersburg, 1800.*

ARTEFACTS FROM THE NORTHERN BLACK SEA COAST AREA
(rooms 115–117)

Stamnos
6th century B.C. Miletus. *Clay, painting.*
Height 41.5 cm. Inv. No. Б 408

A splendid example of the carpet style of vase-painting, this stamnos may have been made by ceramists from Miletus. Bulls, panthers and hounds, depicted on the friezes, alternate with purely ornamental motifs, such as meanders and plaited patterns. The impression of a motley carpet is enhanced by the flower-like ornaments scattered around the animals' figures.

From the excavations on the island of Berezan near Ochakov, 1914.

Amphora with depiction of comastes
550–540 B.C. Samos. *Clay, painting. Height 30.2 cm. Inv. No. Б 62-1*

The amphora features a characteristic ornament of floral and geometric motifs organically inscribed into the shape of the vessel. The depiction of feasting youths on the central frieze is schematic and purely decorative.
From the excavations on the island of Berezan near Ochakov, 1962.

Hydria: *Dispute of Athena and Poseidon*
4th century B.C. Athens. *Clay, painting.*
Height 51 cm. Inv. No. П 1872.130

The painting of this vase has proved to be a priceless source for the reconstruction of the ruined sculptural group by Phidias with which he decorated one of the pediments of the Parthenon in Athens. According to legend, Athena and Poseidon contested for Attica. Poseidon caused salt-water to spring up on the Acropolis by throwing his tridents into the ground. Athena planted an olive tree by the stroke of her spear. She was crowned with a laurel wreath by Nike as the winner.
From the excavation of the Panticapeum necropolis, Kerch, 1872.

Sphinx-shaped lekythos

Late 5th century B.C. Attica. *Clay, painting, gilding. Height 21.5 cm. Inv. No. Φα 1869.7*

This vessel is magnificent example of classical pottery. Its marvellously preserved painting provides insights into the lost polychromy of Greek sculpture. It was a truly original idea to make an incense vessel in the form of an antique monster with the head of a beautiful fair-haired woman. The lekythos was found in 1869 among other artefacts in the grave of a Greek woman in Phanagoria (Taman peninsula). *From the Archaeological Commission, 1869.*

Lekythos in the form Aphrodite's torso in a shell

Late 5th century B.C. Attica. *Clay, painting, gilding. Height 17 cm. Inv. No. Φα 1869.9*

This lekythos was found in the same grave as the sphinx-shaped one reproduced above. It is made in the same style and technique. According to legend, Aphrodite was born of sea-foam and carried in a shell to the shore of the island of Cyprus. The goddess' face and body adorned with precious stones are shaded in so delicate pinks that the beautiful Aphrodite seems to be lit with the first rays of the raising sun. *From the Archaeological Commission, 1869.*

***Isis* Ship** (fragment of painting)
3rd century B.C. Northern Black Sea coast area. *Fresco, sgraffito. Length 120 cm. Inv. No. HФ 82526*

This depiction of a really existing ship of the 3rd century B.C. arriving in Nymphaea from Alexandria is perceived as a rare historical record. The drawing was discovered on an inner wall of a temple. It is made in sgraffito technique, i.e. scratched on the top layer of plaster, revealing the lower layer of another colour. There are numerous inscriptions that add to our knowledge about the culture, history and daily life of Nymphaea.
From the excavations of the temple complex in Nymphaea, 1982.

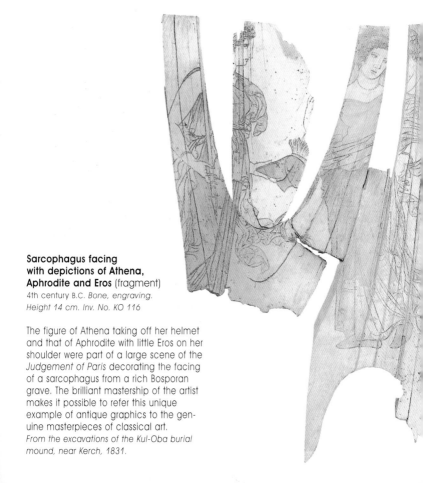

Sarcophagus facing with depictions of Athena, Aphrodite and Eros (fragment)
4th century B.C. *Bone, engraving. Height 14 cm. Inv. No. KO 116*

The figure of Athena taking off her helmet and that of Aphrodite with little Eros on her shoulder were part of a large scene of the *Judgement of Paris* decorating the facing of a sarcophagus from a rich Bosporan grave. The brilliant mastership of the artist makes it possible to refer this unique example of antique graphics to the genuine masterpieces of classical art.
From the excavations of the Kul-Oba burial mound, near Kerch, 1831.

Pyxis

3rd century. Eastern Mediterranean coast area.
Silver. Height 16.5 cm. Inv. No. P 33

This slender vessel with a loose handle
is decorated with chased figures of eroses
carrying garlands with a mask of Medusa
Gorgon. There are also torches and butter-
flies in their hands, possibly, the attributes
of Psyche who was usually depicted in
the guise of a butterfly by classical artists.
However, this rather complex set of symbolic images can be interpreted in a
variety of ways. It is commonly accepted
that such vessels were used for keeping
women's adornments.
*From the excavations of the Panticapeum
necropolis, Kerch, 1837.*

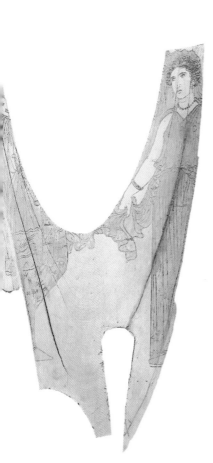

Portrait of Dynamia

Late 1st century B.C. Northern Black Sea
coast area. *Bronze, silver inlay. Height 24 cm.
Inv. No. ПАН 1726*

It is a rare portrait of the granddaughter
of Mithradates VI, Queen of the Bosporus
Kingdom in the 1st century B.C. The Phrygian
tiara on her head is inlaid with silver and
red copper. The queen, with her typically
Roman hairdo, is portrayed in her mature
years. The identification of the portrait was
suggested by the historian M. Rostovtsev
in 1916.
From the excavations near Novorossiysk, 1898.

ART OF ANCIENT ITALY
(rooms 130, 131)

Amphora
6th century B.C. Etruria. *Clay. Height 86.8 cm.*
Inv. No. Б 1374

Thin-walled earthenware vessels of the
7th–6th centuries B.C., made of black clay,
bucchero, are a specific type of Etruscan
ceramics. Apparently intended for burial
and cult purposes, they imitated the forms
and decor of bronze and silver vessels.
The sculptural and moulded decorations
were usually made by hand while the
relief – with the aid of stamp. The polished
surface of the amphora increases its
likeness to a metal piece. The cover
is crowned with the figure of a cock.
From the collection of Marquis
G.-P. Campana, Rome, 1862.

Holmos
Second half, 7th century B.C. Etruria.
Clay. Height 130 cm. Inv. Nos. Б 1324, 1324 a

It is an extremely rare example of Etruscan
burial vessels made in impasto technique
from unglazed and polished clay. Usually
they had a geometric or, sometimes,
Oriental ornament. This holmos, featuring
lion's heads on its body, with the red paint
rubbed into its surface, is put on a four-
part stand. Its form is an imitation of
Syrian and Urartu vessels.
From the collection of Marquis
G.-P. Campana, Rome, 1862.

Tripod-incense burner

6th century B.C. Etruria, Vulci. *Bronze.*
Height 53 cm. Inv. No. B 486

This tripod is a remarkable example of the
output of the bronze-casting workshops of
Vulci, the capital of Etruria. Etruscan masters liked to decorate their works with moving figures, usually rendered in an intricate
foreshortening. This tripod is adorned with
miniature relief compositions which represent the fairly expressive scenes of the
twelve labours of Heracles, namely, his
fightings with the Nemean Lion, the Cretan
Bull and the Erimanthian Boar. The legs,
shaped like lion's paws, support the vessel
body. This is one of the finest examples
of antique tripods.
*From the collection of Marquis
G.-P. Campana, Rome, 1862.*

Head of a lion (fragment of a statue)

6th century B.C. Etruria. *Bronze. Height 26 cm.*
Inv. No. B 493

Etruscan bronze casters were second to
none, and their works were rated very highly even in Greece. This lion's head is a
fragment of a rather large funeral sculpture. Such figures were frequently placed
at the entrance to a burial-vault guarded
by a ferocious lion. This beast is represented angrily growling, ready to jump.
The statue is remarkable for its conventional ornament and overt expressivity typical
for Etruscan art from the archaic period.
*From the collection of Marquis
G.-P. Campana, Rome, 1862.*

Funeral urn

Mid-4th century B.C. Etruria. *Bronze.*
Height 42 cm, length of the base 69 cm.
Inv. No. B 485

*From the collection of Marquis
G.-P. Campana, Rome, 1862.*

Etruscans ascribed magic qualities to the
depictions of the dead whose soul did not
die with the body. As a rule, the masters
who made sculptures to crown the urns
with the ashes, sought to reproduce the
portrait likeness of the dead. Usually the
deceased person was represented reclin-
ing and holding a bowl (in this case
the bowl did not survive), which was
to symbolize 'eternal feast'.
The urn was found in
Perugia in 1843.

Mirror with depiction of Priam, Hecuba, Thetis, Diomedes and Cassandra

Ca. 300 B.C. Etruria. *Bronze. Diameter 18 cm. Inv. No. B 509*

Decorating the mirror back is a scene with the heroes of the Trojan War whose names are engraved along the edge. The Etruscan master has interpreted the Old Greek subject in his own way, creating a work with no analogies in the world.
From the collection of Marquis G.-P. Campana, Rome, 1862.

Amphora with depiction of sea creatures

4th century B.C. Etruria. *Clay, painting. Height 39 cm. Inv. No. Б 313*

The Etruscan vase-painter, who evidently did not experience the influence of Greek masters, abstained from the depiction of ornamental bands and friezes and represented the amphora as a huge drop of water with sea creatures inhabiting it. They include both real animals (dolphins and starfishes) and fantastic ones (hippocampi and sea dragons).
From the Pizzati collection, Rome, 1834.

Amphora with depiction of Orestes, Iphigenia and Pylades

4th century B.C. By Ixion Painter. Campania. *Clay, painting. Height 62.2 cm. Inv. No. Б 2080*

The subject is taken from the tragedy *Iphigenia in Tauris.* According to legend, Iphigenia was to make a horrible sacrifice to Artemis – to kill two strangers on the altar of the virgin goddess. But when she recognized in them her brother Orestes and his bosom friend Pylades, the pristess fled with them.
From the collection of Marquis G.-P. Campana, Rome, 1862.

Crater: *Gigantomachy*
4th century B.C. By Lycurgus Painter.
Apulia. *Clay, painting. Height 105 cm.*
Inv. No. Б 1714

Enormous, one-metre-high craters were
intended for the funeral cult. The battle
of the giants and Olympic gods, in which
the gods won the day, instilled hopes of
the victory of light over darkness. The
painting is centred on Zeus in a quadriga
driven by Victory. Athena and Artemis,
standing on top of the mountain, are
throwing spears and arrows while, below,
on the earth, Heracles is fighting the
giants. The Apulian vases differ from
their Athenian counterparts by large
dimensions and lavish decor.
From the collection of Marquis
G.-P. Campana, Rome, 1862.

**Hydria with scenes from the Eleusinian
mysteries (Queen of the Vases)**
4th century B.C. Campania. *Clay, painting;*
reliefs. Height 62.2 cm. Inv. No. Б 1659

This luxuriously adorned hydria, called the
'Queen of the Vases' by the archaeologists, was found at Cumaea. Its shoulders
are decorated with relief scenes from the
Eleusinian mysteries. Demeter is shown
sitting on the throne and Cora, with a
torch in her hand, is standing at her side.
In a chariot driven by snakes, we see
Triptolemus, the first man who was taught
by the goddesses to till the soil. The polychrome reliefs stand out graphically from
the black varnish background.
From the collection of Marquis
G.-P. Campana, Rome, 1862.

ART OF ANCIENT ROME.
1st CENTURY B.C.–4th CENTURY A.D.
(rooms 101, 102, 106, 107, 110, 127–129)

Portrait of an unknown man

1st century B.C. By the master of Leningrad Bronze. Rome. *Bronze. Height 39 cm.
Inv. No. B 2067*

The 'Master of Leningrad Bronze', as an anonymous sculptor was named by modern researchers, created an image striking for its tragic expressivity. The face of a Roman bears the stamp of his bitter thoughts. Two deep wrinkles mark the wearily lowered corners of his mouth. There is a supposition that this is a portrait of Sextus Pompeius Magnus, a political opponent to Augustus, who died in 36 B.C.

From the State Museum Reserve, 1928.

Emperor Augustus as Jupiter

1st century. Rome. *Marble.
Height 187 cm. Inv. No. A 399*

The Roman sculptor who made this posthumous portrait of the idolized Emperor Augustus took as his model the famous statue of Zeus by Phidias at Olympia. The appearance of the Roman ruler shows no trace of old age and senility – henceforth he is destined to be always young.
From the collection of Marquis G.-P. Campana, Rome, 1862.

Marble plate with depiction of bucrania

1st century. *Marble. Height 87 cm.*
Inv. No. A 65

Façades of Roman buildings in the early imperial period used to be decorated with carved marble reliefs. On display in the Hermitage is a marble plate with depiction of bucrania (skulls of sacrificial bulls), garlands and sacral vessels. Judging by the character of the relief, the plate was part of the decor of a temple or a magnificent funeral structure of the 1st century.

From St Michael's Castle where it was brought by Paul I from Tsarskoye Selo.

Painted amphora

1st century. *Glass, painting. Height 20 cm.*
Inv. No. П 1910.38

This is a unique work of antique glassmakers, painted with coloured enamels. Polychrome vines, with fluttering birds amongst them, are depicted against a bright emerald-coloured background. Another similar amphora was found on Cyprus.
From the excavations of the Panticapeum necropolis, Kerch, 1912.

Cameo: *Constantine the Great and Tyche of Constantinople*

4th century. *Rome. Sardonyx. 18.5 x 12.2 cm.*
Inv. No. Ж 146

Chronologically the gems of the 4th century A.D. complete the Hermitage collection of antiquities. Among them is the cameo known in literature under the erroneous name of the Trajan Cameo. Specialists have established, however, that the gem represents Emperor Constantine and the goddess of fortune, Tyche, crowning him with a laurel wreath. Tyche was the guardian of Constantinople which was declared the capital of the world by Constantine.
From the N. Khitrovo collection presented to Alexander I, 1805.

Jupiter

Late 1st century. Rome. *Marble, stucco, gilding. Height 347 cm. Inv. No. A 362*

This colossal marble statue was found in the ruins of the villa of Emperor Domitian (51–96) in Castel Gandolfo. The Roman sculptor took as the model the statue of Zeus at Olympia, made by Phidias in ivory and gold. This statue of Jupiter is executed in acrolithic technique: the drapery and attributes are made not of marble, but of metal and coloured stones.
From the collection of Marquis G.-P. Campana, Rome, 1862.

Sarcophagus: *Achilles on Scyros*

2nd century. Attica. *Marble. 168 x 243 cm. Inv. No. A 1026*

The sarcophagus was found in the 1770s on the island of Chios during the war against Turkey. Since the island was known as the birthplace of Homer, the sarcophagus was thought to be the poet's tomb and as such placed in the park of the country residence of Count A. Stroganov, its first owner. The sarcophagus is decorated with a scene from the myth about Achilles, the hero of the Trojan War, which symbolizes the inevitability of the mortal's fate.
From the Stroganovs collection, Leningrad, 1930.

Portrait of Lucius Verus

2nd century. Rome. *Marble. Height 76 cm. Inv. No. A 859*

In this portrait of the young ruler the emptiness of his inner world is manifestly compensated by external effects. His haircut is a 'wonder of the barber's art', and his moustache and beard are elegantly cut. He is depicted wearing a cuirass as a military leader. It is known that his campaign against the mighty Parthian empire in the East nearly ruined the Roman army.
From the Pavlovsk Palace collection, 1924.

Portrait of an unknown woman (Syrian woman)

2nd century. Rome. *Marble. Height 25.5 cm. Inv. No. A 583*

The sculptor managed to reveal the subtlest nuances of the inner world of the woman portrayed: her dreaminess, her slightly bitter smile and melancholic irony. The hair style of the woman from a distant Eastern province (Syria or Judaea) resembles that of the empresses of the 2nd century. Her far from being beautiful appearance bespeaks her rich spirituality characteristic of the educated and refined elite.
Acquired in 1850.

Portrait of Balbinus

3rd century. Rome. *Marble. Height 72.5 cm. Inv. No. A 250*

The mood of disappointment and uncertainty hallmarks portraits from the period of the crisis of the empire. This applies even to the depictions of rulers in the epoch of 'soldier emperors'. Balbinus was one of the rulers chosen by the Senate to guide the young Gordian III, who was proclaimed Caesar by the populace. His rule was short-lived, however, for in a few months he was slain by soldiers.
From the I. Laval collection, St Petersburg, 1852.

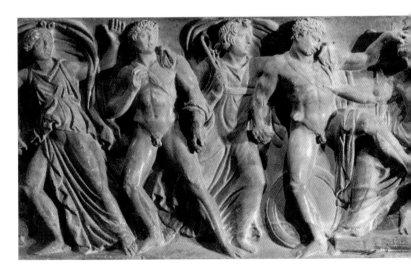

Relief of a sarcophagus:
Orestes Killing Aegisthus
2nd century. Rome. _Marble. 56 x 233 cm._
Inv. No. A 451

It was a custom in Rome to decorate sarcophagi with reliefs on the theme of the untimely death of a mythological hero. Orestes' story was a rather common decorative motif. It might be that the sculptor who created this sarcophagus took as the model an easel picture that has not survived. Orestes and Electra are depicted at the moment of the killing of Aegisthus in revenge for the death of Orestes' father, Agamemnon. Fury, with a whip in her hand, incites Orestes to vengeance. The scene also shows the vengeance of the mother and the purification from this crime by the Judgement of Athena.
From the collection of Palazzo Lezzani, Rome, 1869.

Relief of a sarcophagus: _Phaethon_
2nd century. Rome. _Marble. Height 98 cm._
Inv. No. A 985

This marble plate is a brilliant example of funeral reliefs. The sculptor depicted a scene from the myth about Phaethon, son of Helios. To prove his divine origin doubted by one of Zeus' sons, Phaethon asked his father to let him drive his chariot. When Helios gave him the reins he was unable to control the horses and the runaway sun chariot nearly scorched up the earth. To prevent a universal conflagration, Zeus struck the boy down with his thunderbolt and hurled him into a river.
From the collection of Duke Nicholas of Leuchtenberg, Peterhof, 1929.

Portrait of Antinoüs

2nd century. Rome. *Marble. Height 39.8 cm.*
Inv. No. A 27

In his posthumous portraits Antinoüs
(?–130), a favourite of Emperor Hadrian
(76–138), was usually depicted in the guise
of various gods, including Bacchus.

The youth drowned himself in the Nile in
130, and the inconsolable emperor established the cult of Antinoüs. Altars were
erected in his honour, where Antinoüs was
represented as Osiris, Apollo, Silvanus,
Mercury, and others.
*From the G. Lyde Browne collection,
London, 1787.*

GROUND FLOOR

● BEGINNING
OF THE GROUND-FLOOR
EXHIBITION

▲ ENTRANCE

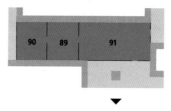

| 90 | 89 | 91 |

▼
EASTERN ENTRANCE HALL

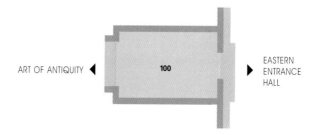

ART OF ANTIQUITY ◄ | 100 | ► EASTERN
ENTRANCE
HALL

▬
ART OF WESTERN ASIA

▦
ART OF ANCIENT EGYPT

ART OF ANCIENT EGYPT AND WESTERN ASIA

The first Egyptian artefacts were brought to Russia in the 18th century: in her collection Catherine II kept several scarab-like charms. However, it was only after Napoleon's Egyptian campaign in the early 19th century that Russia, like other European countries, took a keen interest in Ancient Egypt. The vast collection of Francisco Castiglione, acquired by the Academy of Sciences in 1825, was to form the nucleus of the Hermitage's Egyptian collection. Deserving particular note are the artefacts which found their way to the museum as a result of works carried out by Russian archaeologists in Egypt in 1961–63 under the supervision of Academician Boris Piotrovsky. In addition to the ancient Egyptian exhibits, the art of the Ancient East is represented in the Hermitage by a collection of artefacts from Mesopotamia and Elam, a state which was at one time situated to the east of it.

ART OF ANCIENT EGYPT
(room 100)

Udjanhdjes and his wife

26th century B.C. *Limestone. Height 38 cm.*
Inv. No. ☐ *18107*

In the 3rd millennium B.C. the sculptural
portrait took shape in Egypt for the first
time in the history of world art. This limestone sculptural group depicting Udjanhdjes
and his wife dates from the 4th Dynasty of
the Old Kingdom period (4th–3rd millennium B.C.). The base, in front of the female
figure, carries a hieroglyphic inscription:
The ruler Udjanhdjes, his wife Innefertef.
Udjanhdjes is shown sitting and his wife,
whose figure has unfortunately been partly
lost, is standing beside him embracing his
shoulders. The strict frontal composition
and generalized forms impart to this work
a monumental quality characteristic
of the art of Ancient Egypt.
From the Academy of Sciences Institute
of Books, Documents and Scripts, Leningrad,
1938; formerly in the N. Likhachev collection.

Relief from the Meriraankh tomb

25th century B.C. *Limestone. 135 x 80 cm.*
Inv. No. ☐ *18108*

The limestone slab from the tomb of
Meriraankh, a Sakkara dignitary, executed
in the technique of carved-in relief, is a
fragment of the facing of the entrance
to the tomb. The clear-cut relief contour
makes the portrait look restrained and
solemn as if it were a hieroglyph addressed
to eternity. Each part of the figure is fore-
shortened in such a way as to bring out
its form. While the face of Meriraankh is
depicted in profile, his eyes and shoulders
are shown full-face, the abdomen and
thighs – in a three-quarter turn and the
legs in profile again. This conventional
pose was adopted in Ancient Egypt for
depiction of human beings and, in the
Egyptians' opinion, provided an all-round
notion of the person portrayed.
From the Academy of Sciences Institute
of Books, Documents and Scripts, Leningrad,
1938; formerly in the N. Likhachev collection.

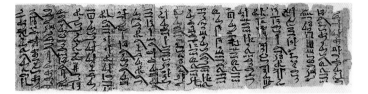

Papyrus with the text of the *Tale of a Shipwrecked Sailor* (fragment)
Ca. 20th century B.C. *Papyrus.*
Length 380 cm, width 11.5 cm.
Inv. No. ☐ *1115*

The text of the tale dates from the Middle Kingdom period and combines fantasy and reality connected with the discoveries of ancient Egyptian seafarers: an Egyptian, who was sent by the Pharaoh to the distant mines, after the shipwreck found himself on an island belonging to a fantastic serpent. Given a favourable treatment and gifts by the gods, the seafarer left the island which disappeared under water. *Provenance unknown.*

Amenemhet III
Ca. 1850–1800 B.C. *Granite. Height 86.5 cm.*
Inv. No. ☐ *729*

The sculpture of King Amenemhet III (*ca.* 1849–1801 B.C.) of the Middle Kingdom period, whose reign was marked by the might and prosperity of the country, is made of black granite. A hieroglyphic inscription on the throne enumerates the titles and names of Amenemhet III. Strictly following the ancient canons, the master, at the same time, brings out the distinctive individual features of the pharaoh's face: his deeply set eyes, protruding cheekbones and closely pressed lips.
Acquired before 1871.

Statue of Maniamon, a grain-counting scribe
15th century B.C. *Limestone. Height 37 cm.*
Inv. No. ☐ *741*

Egyptian nobles used to travel in litters carried by their servants. This may explain the form of statues representing a sitting man with his knees pulled up to his breast. Initially outlined, the body contours under the clothes were later turned into cubes with a protruding head, wrists and feet. The Hermitage statue of a scribe of the New Kingdom period belongs to a group of more realistically rendered bodies.
From the Egyptian Museum of the Academy of Sciences, St Petersburg, 1881.

Figure of a priest

Late 15th century B.C. *Wood. Height 34.5 cm.*
Inv. No. ☐ *737*

Carved from brown-shaded ebony in
a Thebes workshop, the statuette of
a walking priest is one of the masterpieces
in the Hermitage collection. The figure
was evidently created in the reign of
Amenhotep III (ca. 1455–1419 B.C.) as
the appearance of the depicted person
bears a certain portrait likeness with the
powerful king of the 18th-dynasty of
the New Kingdom period.
From the Academy of Sciences,
St Petersburg, 1862; formerly in the
F. Castiglione collection, Milan.

Painted vessel

14th century B.C. *Clay. Height 16.6 cm.*
Inv. No. ☐ *69*

Painted vessels are not typical for Egypt
with its rather low standard of pottery.
The 14th century B.C., however, saw the
appearance of vessels with subject and
ornamental painting, particularly common
during the reign of Amenhotep III, the
most illustrious period in the history of
the New Kingdom which was marked
by the flourishing of arts.
From the Egyptian Museum of the Academy
of Sciences, St Petersburg, 1862 or 1881;
formerly in the F. Castiglione collection,
Milan.

Stele of the royal scribe Ipee

Early 14th century B.C. *Limestone. 95 x 71 cm.*
Inv. No. ☐ *1072*

Ipee, the royal scribe or housekeeper,
appears before Anubis, God of the Dead,
traditionally depicted as a jackal-headed
man. Created in a Memphis workshop, this
work stands out for its rhythmical structure
and colour palette.
From the Egyptian Museum of the Academy
of Sciences, St Petersburg, 1862; formerly
in the A. Montferrand collection,
St Petersburg.

Amenemheb with his wife and mother

14th century B.C. *Granite. Height 91 cm.*
Inv. No. □ 740

Amenemheb, the royal scribe and governor of Thebes, the capital of Egypt in the
New Kingdom period, lived at the time following the religious and political reform
of Akhenaton (Amenhotep IV; 1419–
ca. 1400 B.C.). The best examples of the
new artistic style it brought forth are distinguished by their fine and soft modelling.
These features can bee seen in the modelling of the bodies of Amenemheb, his
wife and mother whereas their faces and
heavy wigs are typical for the dry style
of a later date.
From the collection of Duke Maximilian
of Leuchtenberg, St Petersburg, 1852.

Inner sarcophagus
of the priest Petese

10th century B.C. *Wood, painting.*
Length 204 cm. Inv. No. □ 774

The traditional mummification of human
remains in Ancient Egypt was connected
with the cult of the soul of the dead. All
intestines except for the heart were taken
out of the body during the embalming:
the brain was removed through the nose,
mouth and ears, and the abdomen and
chest organs – through an opening cut in
the stomach. After filling the inner cavities
with myrrh, dry grasses, sawdust or fabric
saturated with aromatic substances, the
opening was sewn up. Then the body was
treated with a natural mixture of common
salt and soda to free it of moisture, aroma-
tized and wrapped in linen fabric for better
preservation. A mummy was placed into
a sarcophagus covered with paintings and
hieroglyphs. The shape of the sarcophagus
for the mummy of the priest Petese exhibited at the Hermitage repeats the form of
the human figure and all its surface is
painted. The black almond-shaped eyes
and arching eyebrows stand out on the
sculpture-like swarthy face.
From the Egyptian Museum of the Academy
of Sciences, St Petersburg, 1881.

ART OF WESTERN ASIA
(rooms 89–91)

Vessel
Late 4th millennium B.C. Elam, Susa. *Clay, painting. Height 23.5 cm. Inv. No. □ 6876*

During the excavations in Susa (or Shushan), the capital of Elam, an ancient state in the southwestern part of the Iranian plateau, the magnificent artefacts of proto- Iranian culture were unearthed. Moulded without the aid of the potter's wheel, this unique vessel is covered with stylized painting including depictions of high-horned goats (in the central frieze of the body), birds (in the upper frieze) and symbolic signs. Such extremely rare artefacts provide a glimpse into ancient cultures on the territory of Western Asia.
From the Institute of Archaeology, Petrograd, 1920s; received by D. Beliayev as a gift from the French archaeological expedition, 1912.

Cylindrical seal with the name of the scribe Kaku and its impression
22nd century B.C. Akkad. *Black steatite. Circumference 3.2 cm. Inv. No. □ 6518*

The Sumerian and Akkad charm seals refer to the earliest artefacts of the artistic glyptics. On the seal, formerly owned by the scribe Kaku, two identical groups are engraved in mirror image: a man-bull fighting a lion, with a figure of a hero offering a libation in-between. The images depicted on the seals were meant to protect the agreements they sealed or sealed-up property from the evil spirits or reverses of fortune. The main subjects were the so-called 'friezes of fighters' illustrating episodes from the tales of the semi-legendary Sumerian ruler Gilgamesh and his companion Enkidu.
Acquired in 1914.

Relief with depiction of King Assurnasirpal escorted by his guardian god

883–859 B.C. Assyria, Calah.
Limestone. 243 x 217 cm. Inv. No. ☐ 3938

In the 1860s the Hermitage acquired stone reliefs from the Assyrian palaces of Kings Assurnasirpal II (9th century B.C.), Tiglath Pileser III and Sargon II (8th century B.C.). The present relief is from the inner apartments of the King's palace in Calah (now Nimrud). It shows Assurnasirpal, the builder of the Assyrian capital, with his victories described in the cuneiform text. The enormous citadel of Calah, which occupied an area of 20 hectares, was surrounded by 15-metre high walls extending over seven and a half kilometres. More than 60 thousand people took part at a time in the feasts held by the King to celebrate his military victories. Similar reliefs were called upon to extoll the majesty of the King and frighten his enemies.
Acquired in 1863.

The Palmyrene tariff

137. Syria. *Marble limestone. 435 x 148 cm.*
Inv. No. ☐ 4187

In the central square of Palmyra (Tadmor), the ancient caravan city on the territory of present-day Syria, a slab of stone with a carved legislative act by the City Council in two languages – Greek and Aramean – was erected in A.D. 130. Evidently, Palmyra was the final station of a wheel-road on the frontier of the Roman Empire. The legislative act was to regulate the duty charges for the transit and local goods.
Acquired in 1904; gift from the Turkish Sultan Abdul-Hamid II to the Russian Ambassador in the Ottoman Empire (1900).

● BEGINNING
OF THE GROUND-FLOOR
EXHIBITION

▲ ENTRANCE

CULTURE AND ART
OF THE CAUCASUS, TRANSCAUCASIA
AND THE GOLDEN HORDE

ART OF THE PEOPLES
OF CENTRAL ASIA

CULTURE
OF THE FOREST-STEPPE
POPULATION; CULTURE
AND ART OF THE SARMATIAN TRIBES;
THE CRIMEA IN THE EARLY
MIDDLE AGES

CULTURE AND ART
OF THE POPULATION OF THE KAMA RIVER
AREA, MORDVA, BALTIC TRIBES
AND LATER NOMADS; CULTURE
OF THE GORODISHCHI IN THE UPPER
REACHES OF THE DNIEPER, VOLGA
AND THE MIDDLE DNIEPER AREA; ANCIENT
FINNS ON THE OKA RIVER; EARLY SLAVS
ON THE SOUTHERN BUG RIVER

CULTURE AND ART
OF THE PALEOLITHIC, NEOLITHIC
AND BRONZE AGE OF EURASIA

SCYTHIAN CULTURE
OF EASTERN EUROPE

CULTURE AND ART
OF SIBERIA AND CENTRAL ASIA
IN THE SCYTHIAN ERA

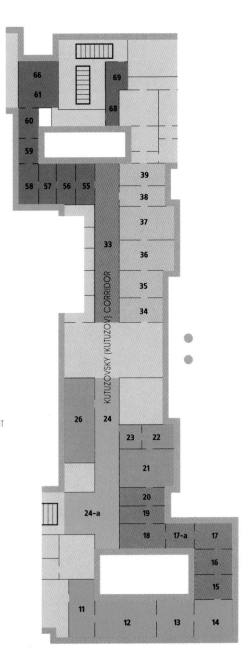

ANCIENT CULTURES OF EASTERN EUROPE, SIBERIA, CENTRAL ASIA, THE CAUCASUS AND TRANSCAUCASIA

The Hermitage exhibition of archaeological artefacts is so rich and varied that it rightly deserves the name of a museum within a museum. The Hermitage collection, which covers a period of more than twenty millennia and comprises over 500,000 items, provides insights into the cultural history of humankind from the Old Stone Age to the Iron Age and the emergence of the first states on the gigantic territory of the former Soviet Union. It includes invaluable paleolithic artefacts, the world's most complete collection of Scythian and Sarmatian antiquities, a large number of finds from the world-famous Pazylyk burial mounds in southern Siberia and the gravesites of ancient Slavs and Vikings, as well as artefacts from the Parthian Kingdom, Chorasmia, Soghdia and the Golden Horde.

ART OF THE NEOLITHIC, ENEOLITHIC AND BRONZE AGE
(rooms 12–14)

Terminal of a staff in the form of a she-elk's head
3rd millennium B.C. Urals. Elk's horn.
Length 19.5 cm. Inv. No. 5546/365

The realistically executed she-elk's head – presumably, the top of a staff – is distinguished by the thoroughly treated contour of the animal's head, which, together with the linear expressiveness in the depiction of eyes and nostrils, has enabled the ancient carver to create a dynamic and severe image.
Unearthed by V. Tolmachev,
the Shipir peat-bog, 1910–14.

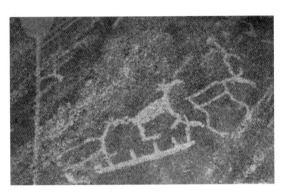

Slab with petroglyphs (fragment)
3rd millennium B.C. North-eastern Europe.
Granite. 308 x 240 cm. Inv. No. 1509/1

1,178 petroglyphs dating from the last quarter of the 4th–3rd millennium B.C. were found on the granite banks and islands of the Onega River. The oldest ones among the sixty-eight depictions on the Hermitage slab are a staff with an elk's head and two solar signs. Separate later depictions and subject scenes with boats, human figures and animals reflect the notions which the ancient inhabitants of the northern Russian plain had about the unity of the world of the living and the dead.
Brought by F. Morozov from the Peri Nos III Cape, Karelia, 1935.

Slab with depiction of a fantastic animal
First half of the 2nd millennium B.C. Southern Siberia. Stone. 115 x 90 cm. Inv. No. 2441/1

The aggressively open jaws of a fantastic animal with a sinewy wolf's body, bear's head and bird's claws reveal two rows of teeth and a sticking-out tongue. The hair covering the animal's body and tail is rendered in transversal and slantwise lines. Initially scratched on the stone, the drawing was then deepened and coated with ochre. The technique of execution along with the subject, relating to the myth about the fantastic animal devouring the sun, is characteristic of the Okunev culture of the Bronze Age.
From the G. Maksimenkov excavations, the Chernovaya VIII gravesite, Krasnoyarsk Region, 1962.

Statuette of a seated woman

Second half of the 4th millennium B.C. Central Asia. *Clay. Length 27 cm. Inv. No. 2844/26*

One of the most vivid examples of the sculpture which took shape during the late Eneolithic Age, this image has typically naturalistic female features brought out by moulding and painting. The head is very schematic, the face features the round eye-holes and the nip of a nose. The figurine has no arms, its shoulders developing into the full bosom. Outlined distinctly in black paint on a red background are the brows, nipples and pubis; the bands and necklace on the neck and bosom; the concentric solar signs on the buttocks and hips; an angular chevron on the left hip. The solar signs must have been intended to enhance the magic power of the figurines. *From the I. Khlopin excavations in the village of Yalangach-depe, southern Turkmenia, 1960.*

Statuette of a seated woman

Late 3rd–early 2nd millennium B.C. Central Asia. *Clay. Height 16 cm. Inv. No. 587/13*

A magnificent example of the Bronze Age sculpture from the south-west of Central Asia, this flat schematic female figure with a thin waist, full hips and the projections of arms, wearing a high cone-like headdress (or coiffure), is coated with light-coloured plaster. Depicted in scratched lines are a hip-belt, a plant sign (?) on the abdomen, and a 'triangle with eye-lashes' on the protrusions of arms and under a braid on the back.
From the V. Mason excavations in the village of Altyn-depe, southern Turkmenia, 1970.

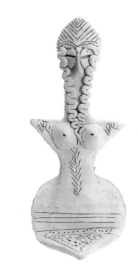

Axe with depictions of dogs and geometric ornament

8th–7th century B.C. Transcaucasia. *Bronze. Length 16.3 cm. Inv. No. 2688/1*

The bronze axes of this type were widely used in western Transcaucasia in the late Bronze Age. They served not only as combat weapons but also as cult items and, probably, attributes of power. The engraved depictions they carried reflected the religious and ideological notions of that period. The Hermitage axe has a straight body, a sharp wedge-like head and a semi-oval, nearly symmetric, blade part adorned with depictions of animals (dogs ?) and geometric figures. There are five animal figures on the axe's facets. The composition also includes circles with rays, presumably, 'suns', around the axe aperture.
Unearthed in Abkhazia, Georgia, 1976.

CULTURE AND ART OF SIBERIA AND CENTRAL ASIA IN THE SCYTHIAN ERA
(rooms 21–23, 26)

Terminals of staffs with an ibex
6th–5th centuries B.C. Central Siberia.
Bronze. Height 18.8 cm and 10 cm.
Inv. Nos. 1121/7, 1124/1

The art of the Tagar tribes reflects their beliefs and notions. It can be included in the circle of the so-called Scythian-Saka animal style, which is typical of the whole span of the Eurasian steppes. Depictions of real and fantastic animals and birds served to decorate arms, clothes, harnesses and labour implements. The purpose of the terminals with figures remains obscure: they might have been the items of a cult.
From the Kunstkammer, St Petersburg, 1859; discovered in the Krasnoyarsk Region, 1730s.

Terminal of a staff shaped like a gryphon holding a stag's head in its bill
5th century B.C. Southern Siberia. *Wood, leather. Height 27 cm. Inv. No. 1684/170*

Dating from the 5th–4th centuries B.C., that is, from the Scythian era, the finds from the Pazyryk burial mounds in the Altai foothills won a world-wide fame. In their perennially frozen ground the mounds have preserved innumerable objects of organic materials, which otherwise are subject to decay. The composition of the terminal conveys in a conventional manner the main theme of ancient Altai art – the fighting of animals. On both sides of the gryphon's neck are the heads of two smaller gryphons, sculpted in low relief. These gryphons are mauling a goose, whose body is also rendered in low relief. It seems that the three-fold repetition of the fighting motif was meant to endow this artefact with a deeper meaning.
From the excavations of the Second Pazyryk burial mound, Altai Region, 1948.

Hearse
5th–4th centuries B.C. Southern Siberia.
Wood, leather. Height 300 cm.
Inv. No. 1687/404

Not a single metal nail was used to make this hearse of birch wood, all its leather joints are fixed by tiny wooden nails. It may have been intended for a funeral cortege. Unearthed in pieces from the northern sector of the grave, the hearse was then put together and restored by the Hermitage experts.
From the excavations of the Fifth Pazyryk burial mound, Altai Regon, 1951.

Felt rug (fragment)
5th–4th centuries B.C. Southern Siberia. *Felt, appliqué. 450 x 650 cm. Inv. No. 1687/94*

The rug, executed in the appliqué technique, features depictions of coloured felt sewn by a twisted sinew thread on the monochrome background. The entire surface of the rug is divided into two friezes framed by three ornamental borders. Each frieze shows a mounted warrior approaching a female deity, seated in a chair, for a benediction to ascend the throne. A similar subject was popular in Western Asian and Scythian art. Initially decorating the walls of dwellings, such rugs were later used in the funeral ceremony.
From the excavations of the Fifth Pazyryk burial mound, Altai Region, 1950.

Swan
5th–4th centuries B.C. Southern Siberia.
Felt. Inv. No. 1687/262

Sewn together from two pieces of white felt, the swan figurine is stuffed with the hair of a deer. The master has truthfully rendered the typical features of the bird: a small delicate head and a long dark-brown bill with a peculiar knob on top. According to the beliefs of the ancient Altai people, the swan bird living on the ground, water and air, personified the three elements of the Universe. The universal motif of the creation of the world by a water bird – a goose, swan or duck – occurs in many prehistoric cosmogonic concepts.
From the excavations of the Fifth Pazyryk burial mound, Altai Region, 1950.

Nap rug (fragment)
5th–4th centuries B.C. Southern Siberia.
Wool. 183 x 200 cm. Inv. No. 1687/93

Executed in the knotting technique, the Pazyryk nap rug is the oldest in the world. Its fine pattern is formed by a multitude of tiny knots numbering up to 3,600 per one square decimetre, which results in a high density and superb quality of the rug. Made in the so-called Turkish technique of knotting, this rug is a rare specimen of the ancient weaving of Central or Western Asia.
From the excavations of the Fifth Pazyryk burial mound, Altai Region, 1950.

SCYTHIAN CULTURE OF EASTERN EUROPE
(rooms 15–20)

Terminal
Late 6th–early 5th century B.C.
Northern Caucasus. *Bronze. Height 26 cm.*
Inv. No. Ky 19091/III

The art of the Scythians, a mighty people of the Iranian language group who lived in the northern Black Sea coast area, the Dnieper Area and the Caucasus in the 7th to 3rd centuries B.C., is represented in the Hermitage by a remarkably rich and varied collection. Despite the abundant archaeological material so far accumulated, the culture and history of the Scythians is still full of enigmas. As the Scythians had no script, information on their beliefs, social and everyday life is usually drawn from the ancient Greek authors, mostly Herodotus (490/480 – ca. 425 B.C.) who must have visited the Scythian lands. The massive terminal shaped like a stylized bird's head with a huge eye and a goat's figure in the centre, was unearthed from the burial mound near the village of Ulskaya, Kuban Region, in 1909. This devotional item is executed in the Scythian animal style of the late archaic period characterized by a wide use of ornamental motifs.
Acquired in 1924.

Amphora (Chertomlyk vase)
4th century B.C. Northern Black Sea coast area. *Silver, gilt. Height 70 cm.*
Inv. No. ДН 1863 1/166

By the 4th century B.C. Scythian art had lost much of its distinctive idiom connected with the nomadic way of life. Objects of luxury that appeared showed a strong influence of antique art. This silver amphora is a typical example of such items. The entire surface of the vessel is covered with depictions in relief. The upper frieze features the scenes of the gryphons mauling the stags, the middle one – an offering of a horse and the lower frieze is made of plant ornaments. On the whole the vessel could be perceived as a derivation of the world tree, being a sort of a cosmogram. The sacrificial motif is basic to the entire system of depictions, including the mauling scenes. Of particular significance is the winged horse's protoma, presumably personifying a deity of the royal Scythians – Thagimasad-Poseidon, the patron of horse breeders. The amphora might have been made on occasion of an important event in a Scythian king's life or his death, connected with the king's cult. At present the vase is on show in Room 260 on the first floor of the Winter Palace.
From the I. Zabelin excavations of a Scythian burial mound near the city of Nikopol', Dnieper Region, 1863.

Vase

Late 4th century. Byzantium. *Silver, gilt, chasing. Height 42.5 cm. Inv. No. 2160/1*

Executed in a style typical of the early Byzantine art of the 4th–5th centuries, which originated from the fusion of old antique trends with 'barbarous' ones coming to Byzantium from the East. The surface of the vase is divided into three friezes, the middle one featuring the scenes of the warriors fighting the Amazons. Every figure is executed in a chased high relief; separate details, the clothes ornamentation and the weapons are marked with dotted and fine engraved lines, some parts highlighted with gilt. The handles are given the form of centaurs, mythical beings to whom Greek legends ascribed a wild temper and a liking for wine.

Acquired in 1814; unearthed from a grave near the village of Concesti, Rumania, 1812.

Situla bucket

Late 4th–first half of the 5th century. Byzantium. *Silver, chasing. Height 22.5 cm. Inv. No. 2160/2*

The central frieze depicts three mythological scenes executed in chased relief. Items of Byzantine origin are frequently uncovered in the graves of the Bosporus inhabitants and the burials of nomadic dignitaries in the steppes of southern Russia dating from the period of Hunnish domination.

Acquired in 1814; unearthed from a grave near the village of Concesti, Rumania, 1812.

Bird-like pendant with a face on its breast

6th–8th centuries. Kama River Region. *Bronze, casting. 4.9 x 7.9 cm. Inv. No. 559/2*

The bird's figure with a wide span of its openwork wings and an anthropomorphic face on its breast is cast in a two-sided mold. The wings have suspension loops. The face was meant to show that the pendant represented a protogenitor man-bird. Such artistic device is typical of the artefacts in the Perm animal style evolved in the Kama River Region in the 1st–early 2nd millennium A.D.

From the Ust-Kishery hoard, Perm Province, 1900.

CULTURE AND ART OF THE CAUCASUS, TRANSCAUCASIA AND THE GOLDEN HORDE
(rooms 55–61, 66, 68, 69)

Helmet of King Sarduri II
8th century B.C. Urartu. *Bronze. Height 20 cm, diameter 23 cm. Inv. No. ☐ 17661*

This Urartu helmet is decorated with relief depictions of the trees of life (on the forehead part) and the winged figures of deities wearing the horned helmets. The four lion-headed serpents framing the composition of the trees of life were to function as the magic protectors of the helmet's owner. The Urartu combat chariots and riders bear a stylistic affinity with similar depictions on the Assyrian reliefs.

From the excavations of the Teishebaini Fortress on Karmir-Blur Hill, Yerevan, 1949.

Figurine of a winged deity
8th century B.C. Urartu. *Bronze, bone, stone, gilt coating (preserved in a few fragments). Height 16 cm. Inv. No.☐ 16002*

After its domination on the Armenian highlands in the 8th–7th centuries B.C., the state of Urartu fell under the onslaught of the Scythians and Medes in the 6th century B.C. Apparently, a decoration for a king's throne, this fantastic Urartu winged figurine was unearthed during the excavations of an Urartu royal residence (the Rusahinili Fortress) on the Toprak-Kale highlands in Turkish Armenia.
From the excavations of the Rusahinili Fortress, Armenia, 1885.

Headdress
8th–9th century. Northern Caucasus. *Silk, leather, canvas, wood. Height 50 cm. Inv. No. K3 4576*

This characteristic peaked headdress was discovered in 1905 in the destroyed grave, probably, of a chieftain of the Adighe-Alan tribes inhabiting the upper reaches of the Bolshaya Laba River. Made of leather, it is covered with Soghdian silk and ornamented by the medallions containing paired jugs. The symbolic character of the subject was, in all probability, related to the celebration of the *nouruz*, the Zoroastrian New Year. Bronze charms of a similar shape have been unearthed in Soghdiana.
From the excavations at the Moshchevaya Balka gravesite, Northern Caucasus, 1935.

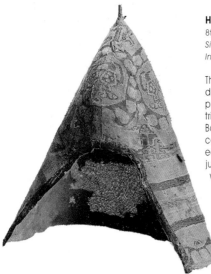

Belt bowl

14th century. Golden Horde. *Silver, gilt.*
Diameter 11.1 cm. Inv. No. Op 38-121

Shaped like a dipper, such Hermitage
bowls were carried by the Golden Horde
nomads on their belts. The depictions of
similar bowls can be seen on Persian
miniatures.
From the N. Veselovsky excavations,
Northern Caucasus; not later than 1894.

Camisole of green silk with *senmurvs*

8th–9th centuries. Northern Caucasus.
Silk. Length 140 cm, width 227 cm.
Inv. No. K 36584

An archaeological find of the clothes
so well preserved is a unique event by
itself. The natural environment, above all,
the dryness of the sandstone terraces of
the Moshchevaya Balka Alpine gravesite,
Northern Caucasus, provided for the
preservation of fabrics, leather and wood-
en items. The camisole is obviously of a
local cut: a tight-fitting top with a clasp on
the trimming and a broad bottom with the
slits for horse-riding. Evidently, this is a costume of a chieftain of the local Adighe-
Alan tribes. It was from the plain fabric that
the locals usually tailored their common
clothes and only the trimming was made
of silk valued on a par with gold. The cover
of this camisole, however, is the most
valuable post-Sasanian silk, which the
Shahinshah of Iran used to wear in his
time. The origin of different silk fabrics
used to tailor the camisole – the Soghdian,
Chinese, Byzantine – was determined by
location of the gravesite on the Silk Road.
The passing caravans paid in fabrics for
the right of using the pass, for guides,
bearers and horses. The superb quality
fabric of the camisole cover is adorned
with a repetitive woven image: the
medallions surrounded by 'pearls' (the
pearl-imitating ornament) contain the
figures traditionally called *senmurvs*.
Depicted with a dog's snout, a bird's
wings and tail, a lion's paws, they
were a benevolent symbol related
to the Shah's power.
From the excavations at the
Moshchevaya Balka gravesite,
Northern Caucasus, 1969.

ART OF THE PEOPLES OF CENTRAL ASIA
(rooms 34–39)

Rhyton
2nd–1st centuries B.C. Parthia. *Ivory.*
Height 41.6 cm. Inv. No. CA 15052

This superb ivory rhyton was made by masters of the Parthian Kingdom, once a mighty state and the main rival of the Romans in the East, spanning the territories from the Mesopotamia to the Indes in the 1st century B.C. It was discovered during the excavations of the ancient city of Nisa (near present-day Ashkhabad), the residence of the Parthian Kings from the 3rd century B.C. to the 3rd century A.D. The rhyton has a mixed decoration: its bell is adorned with a relief frieze featuring heroes from classical mythology, and the other end of it is a figure of a man-bull.
From the Museum of History of the Academy of Sciences of the Turkmen SSR, 1961.

Ossuary shaped like a man's figure
2nd–3rd centuries. Chorasmia. *Clay.*
Height 102 cm. Inv. No. Xp 784

Small receptacles made of terracotta, alabaster or stone for the burial purposes, the ossuaries (from the Latin os, "bone") were widely used in ancient Iran and the neighbouring countries. As the Zoroastrian rules prescribed that the bones of the deceased should be buried cleared of their soft tissues, the bodies were left at special places where, at first, the birds and beasts of prey and, then, the sun and wind reduced the remains to the necessary cleanness. Only after that, the bones were put into the ossuaries and placed into the burial chambers. This ossuary is unique in that the face of the depicted man is endowed with obvious portrait features and rendered in a characteristic manner known as ethnographic realism.
Unearthed in the vicinity of Koi-Krylgan-Kala in the Kyzylkum desert, Uzbek SSR, 1971.

Horsemen (fragment of painting)
7th–8th centuries. Soghdia. *Stucco, painting. 113 x 95 cm. Inv. No. CA 14864*

The unique monuments of Soghdia, a historical area in the territory of Central Asia known from the 1st millennium B.C., brought a worldwide fame to Pendjikent, on the outskirts of which they have been unearthed. The location of Soghdia at the crossroads of the trade routes of the Ancient East laid an imprint on its original culture which shows the influences of Christianity, Buddhism and Manichaeism. The murals uncovered by archaeologists provide evidence that the houses of the rich Soghdians were decorated with a royal luxury. The works of Soghdian artists present scenes from the life of the Soghdian nobility, their hunts and feasts. The *Horsemen* is a detail of a mural on a literary subject.
From the Institute of History of the Academy of Sciences of the Tadjik SSR, 1956.

Hunting on elephant back
(fragment of painting)
7th–8th centuries. Soghdia. *Stucco, painting. 120 x 134 cm. Inv. Nos. CA 14661–14663*

The palace in Varakhsha, another place where the unique monuments of Soghdia have been discovered, was decorated with magnificent wall-paintings. The stylistics of the depictions – in particular, the friezes with animals – attests to the links between the ancient cultures of Central Asia and India.
From the Academy of Sciences of the Uzbek SSR, 1954.

GROUND FLOOR

● BEGINNING
OF THE GROUND-FLOOR
EXHIBITION

▲ ENTRANCE

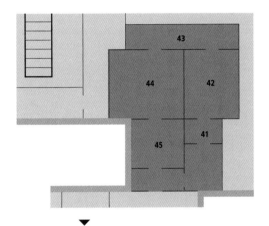

▼
KUTUZOVSKY (KUTUZOV) CORRIDOR

JEWELLERY GALLERY

In Russia, the collecting of gold artefacts of the so-called 'barbarian' cultures of the Eurasian plains began in 1715–18, when, by order of Peter I, 200 ancient gold items, forming what was later known as the Siberian Collection of Peter I, were sent by Prince Mikhail Gagarin from Siberia (Tobolsk) to St Petersburg. Most of these items were bought by Gagarin from the graves' pillagers who had not bothered to record the place of their discovery. A more systematic approach to the ancient treasures was demonstrated at a much later date, when not only their artistic but also their cultural and historical value was recognized. In the mid-19th century, the Siberian Collection of Peter I was transferred from the Kunstkammer to the Hermitage, which subsequently received Scythian and Sarmatian artefacts unearthed from the burial mounds of the steppes on the Black Sea coast. All this has made the Hermitage collection of goldwork one of the most significant in the world. On display in the Jewellery Gallery are also unique Greek gold objects, unearthed from the sites of ancient towns in the northern Black Sea coast area, and Oriental jewellery of more recent times.

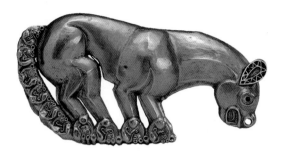

Panther-shaped plaque (Kelermess panther)

Second half, 7th century B.C. Northern Black Sea coast area. *Gold, enamel and garnet. Length 32.6 cm. Inv. No. Ky 1903 2/1*

The famous 'Kelermess panther' is a fine example of the Scythian animal style from the archaic epoch. Some researchers believe that this style originated in Central Asia, others think that it came from the Near East. The plaque may have decorated a shield. The schematic modelling of the predator's body with large sharp planes is a typically Scythian stylistic device that goes back to the technique of wood-carving. Zoomorphic ornamental details are also a typical feature of Scythian art. The paw of every animal terminates in a curled panther, and six similar figures form its tail. The decoration of the eyes and ear with coloured paste and hematite adds palpable accents to the expressive image of the animal. The naturalistic treatment of the jaws and the use of cloisonne enamel show an influence of the artistic traditions of the Ancient East.

From the excavations of the Kelermess burial mound, Kuban, 1905.

Belt buckle

6th century B.C. *Gold. 8 x 5.4 cm. Inv. No. Си 1727 1/15*

The Siberian Collection of Peter I comprises a number of B-shaped gold buckles. Some specialists believe that the depictions on these buckles are based on the ancient myths of nomad tribes (probably, the Huns) once inhabiting Siberia.

From the Kunstkammer (Siberian Collection of Peter I), 1859.

This widely known 'Kostroma deer' is a classical work of Scythian art. The compactness of the silhouette, the ultimately schematic modelling of form with large planes and the ornamental treatment of the he antlers, all are characteristic features of this style. By one theory, this gold figure served as a decoration for a round shield, by another for a quiver. This masterpiece of ancient toreutics was found in the burial mound of a noble warrior, where twenty killed horses were also uncovered. In his accounts of the Scythians, Herodotus mentions some of their bloody rituals, for example, the killing of a king's suite during his funeral and the making of cloaks from the conquered enemies' scalps and bowls from their sculls.

From the excavations of the Kostroma burial mound, Kuban, 1901.

Deer-shaped plaque (Kostroma deer)

Late 7th–early 6th century B.C. Northern Black Sea coast area. *Gold. Length 31.7 cm. Inv. No. 2498.1*

Gorytos
(case for a bow and arrows)
4th century B.C. Chertomlyk burial
mound. *Gold. Length 47 cm.*
Inv. No. ДН 1863 1/435

During the early Hellenistic period, the Scythians inhabiting the
northern Black Sea coast area
experienced a strong influence
of Greek culture. This Scythian
case for a bow and arrows was
found in the famous Chertomlyk
burial mound. The form typical for the
arms of a nomadic warrior combines
with the decor characteristic of Greek art.
The surface of the case is covered with
reliefs depicting scenes from the life
of Achilles, the hero of the Trojan War.
However, the Scythians may have perceived the subject through the prism
of their own mythology.
From the Archaeological Commission, 1865.

Comb with a scene of combat
Late 5th–early 4th century B.C. Northern
Black Sea coast area. *Gold. Height 12.3 cm.*
Inv. No. ДН 1913 1/1

This famous Scythian comb, made by a
Greek goldsmith, is not only an illustrious
example of the jeweller's technique but
also a priceless document giving an idea
of the Scythian costumes and arms. Such
combs were part of a warrior's outfit.
The subject of the decor may have been
borrowed from the Scythian epos known
from works by antique authors.
From the Veselovsky excavations of the
Solokha burial mound, Zaporozhye, 1913.

Vessel with depiction of Scythian warriors

4th century B.C. Northern Black Sea coast area. *Electrum. Height 13 cm. Inv. No. KO 11*

The rich grave of a Scythian king in the Kul-Oba barrow, near Kerch, was discovered by chance by Russian soldiers in 1830. Among the objects unearthed was the now world-famous vase of Greek workmanship with depiction of seven Scythian warriors. The relief decorating the vessel is made by an unknown craftsman in a realistic manner and shows the Scythians in their typical military robes: peaked hats, shirts with belts and tight patterned trousers.
From the excavations of the Kul-Oba barrow, near Kerch, 1831.

Pendant with depiction of the head of Athena Parthenos

400–350 B.C. Northern Black Sea coast area. *Gold, enamel. Height 18 cm. Inv. No. KO 5*

The decorative relief on the disk of the pendant found in the Kul-Oba barrow is above all remarkable for the authentic representation of the head of the non-extant famous statue of Athena created by the great Phidias for the Parthenon. Athena's head is crowned with a tripartite comb (known from Pausinias's *Itinerary of Greece*, 2nd century), shaped like a sphinx between two Pegasus with the symbols of wisdom – an owl and snakes – depicted nearby. The ivy leaves, decorating the edge of the disk, are adorned with green and blue enamels, as are the intricate garland of gold plaits, rosettes and corn-shaped pendants. Garlands of this type are characteristic of the Greek jewellery of the 4th century B.C. The sophisticated ornaments abounding in plant motifs have a symbolic meaning, for women's decorations were not only to reflect their owner's wealth, but also to serve as a means of magic attraction.
From the excavations of the Kul-Oba barrow, near Kerch, 1831.

Grivna (necklace) with depiction of Scythian riders

400–350 B.C. Northern Black Sea coast area. *Gold, enamel. 26.6 x 24 cm. Inv. No. KO 17*

A *grivna*, or necklace, was a sign of power among Scythians. It is a hoop of six intertwined gold rods, at the ends of which two figures of Scythian riders are fastened with the help of bushes decorated with a filigreed ornament and coloured enamels. The subject was most likely chosen by a customer, but in the hands of a Greek jeweller these 'barbarian' elements were harmoniously combined and acquired the brilliance characteristic of the best works of antique jewellery.

From the excavations of the Kul-Oba barrow, near Kerch, 1831.

Earrings

Second half, 4th century B.C. Greece. *Gold. Height 9 cm. Inv. No. Φ 1*

These earrings are undoubtedly the work of an outstanding jeweller. Each of them consists of a disk decorated with a vegetable ornament, a multifigured composition of a quadriga driven by the goddess

Nike, a boat and a garland of gold plaits with corn- and bud-shaped pendants. Each earring weighs about 22 grams. Almost all basic ornamental motifs, characteristic of the works of Greek jewellers of the 4th century B.C., can be seen on these earrings.

From the excavations of a burial mound in Theodosia, 1853.

Burial mask of King Reskuporides

3rd century. Northern Black Sea coast area.
Gold. Height 22.5 cm. Inv. No. P 1

In the 5th–3rd centuries B.C. Panticapeum
(now Kerch) was the capital of the
Kingdom of the Cimmerian Bosporus,
formed on the shores of the Strait of
Kerch from a number of Greek colonies
in the northern Black Sea coast area.
In the 3rd century A.D. the Bosporus lost
its former power and was controlled by
the Roman Empire which experienced
a grave crisis and was on the brink of
disintegration. This funeral mask of a
Bosporian ruler is not merely a mechanical mould of the deceased's face, but
a true work of art full of pathos. When
the burial mound was excavated, it was
named 'the grave of a queen with a
mask' since the mask was originally
identified as belonging to a woman.
From the excavation of the necropolis
in Panticapeum, Kerch, 1837.

Diadem with a Heracleian knot

2nd century B.C. Northern Black Sea
coast area. Gold, garnets and paste.
Diameter 52 cm. Inv. No. Арт 1

The Heracleian knot motif occurred in
Greek pieces of jewellery as early as the
Mycenaean period (3rd–2nd millennia B.C.)
and became especially popular from
the second half of the 4th century B.C.
Symbolically, the Heracleian knot is related
to the theme of marriage: the bride's cloth
tied with this knot was to be untied by her
bethrothed, which was associated with the
starting of a new life. In the centre of the
knot decorating the Hermitage diadem
is a miniature group depicting Eros in the
talons of an eagle – an illustration of the
mythological subject of the kidnapping
of Ganymede by an eagle. The jeweller
added wings to the boy, thus having
turned him into Eros. The Hermitage diadem is a fine example of the so-called
'polychrome style' which flourished in
Greek jewellery during the Hellenic era.
From the excavations of the Artiukhovsky
burial mound, Taman peninsula, 1879.

Diadem

1st century. Northern Black Sea coast area. *Gold, corals, garnets, pearls, glass and amethyst. Length of the circumference 61 cm, height 15 cm. Inv. No. 2213/2*

The diadem is decorated with a sculptural woman's head executed from a variety of quartz and insets of garnet and green glass. It is topped with a frieze of trees and animals. These depictions serve not only as the decor but also reflect the ideas of ancient people about the surrounding world. It is quite probable that the trees symbolize the Tree of Life, and the animals – the sun. The shape of the diadem resembles that of a Greek kalathos, and its decor follows the Greek traditions, while the figures of animals and birds are made in the Sarmatian animal style.

From the Novocherkassky hoard in the Khikhlach burial mound, near Novorossiysk, 1864.

Seal-ring with a monogram

7th century. Byzantium. *Gold. Diameter 2.7 cm (ring), 1.6 cm (seal). Inv. No. 1053*

On 29 May 1912 shepherds from the village of Maloye Pereshchepino (Konstantinovgrad district, Poltava province) found a large number of gold and silver objects in a grave, in sandy dunes. Luckily, most of them were purchased by the Hermitage researchers. The investigation of the location showed that it was the legendary treasure of Khan Kuvrat (d. after 641), the ruler of Great Bulgaria that occupied a vast territory in the Kuban River area and some regions on the Black Sea coast. As is known, Kuvrat was a vassal to the Avarian kagan, but broke with him and entered into an alliance with the Byzantine Emperor Heraclius (610–641) who gave him rich presents and the title of patritian. Among the objects found in the grave were three patrician seal-rings with different monograms which are deciphered as "To Kuvrat the patrician". There is little said about Khan Kuvrat in the Byzantine chronicles. It is known that for some time he lived in Constantinople and adopted Christianity there and that after his death the state disintegrated and part of the Bulgarians went to the Balkans where they founded the state of Bulgaria in ca. 679. The other part of the Bulgarians submitted to the Khazars. The rest of the Bulgarians moved up along the Volga River and founded the Volga Bulgaria, the territory of which coincides with that of present-day Tatarstan. *From the hoard near the village of Maloye Pereshchepino, Poltava province, 1912.*

Bracelet with an inlaid decor

7th century. Byzantium. *Gold inlaid with coloured paste. Diameter 8.3 cm (largest) and 8 cm (smallest). Inv. No. 1930/12*

Following the tradition inherited by the Byzantines from the Romans, such bracelets were used as military rewards or diplomatic gifts. They were among the presents given to Khan Kuvrat by Emperor Heraclius. *From the hoard near the village of Maloye Pereshchepino, Poltava province, 1912.*

Bracelet

17th century. India. Gold, precious stones, enamel. Diameter 11.8 cm. Inv. No. V3 721

Among the jewellery displayed in the Gallery, the relatively small collection of gifts from Nadir-Shah (1688–1747), who ruled Iran from 1736 and was famous for his conquests in India, Central Asia and Transcaucasia, occupies a place apart. The masterpieces of Indian jewellery decorated with splendid enamels, pearls, diamonds, rubies and Colombian emeralds, attest to the fact that Indian masters had no equal in their skill of inlaying objects with precious stones. These unique objects were made for the celebrated Shah Jahan (1592–1666), the mighty ruler of India from the Great Moguls dynasty, whose name is associated with the building of Taj-Mahal. The treasures of the Great Moguls were plundered by Nadir-Shah during his invasion of Delhi in 1739, wherefrom he sent part of the antiquities to Russia as diplomatic gifts. This leg bracelet of the type worn only in India was among those gifts.
From the gifts of Nadir-Shah, 1741.

Jug

*17th century. India. Gold, silver, precious stones and pearls. Height 28.8 cm.
Inv. No. V3 709*

Such slender vessels with a special silver container were intended for rose water. The outer side of the body is inlaid with precious stones, including 1,091 rubies, 322 emeralds, 209 pearls and 20 diamonds.
From the gifts of Nadir-Shah, 1741.

Plate

17th century. India. *Gold, enamel.*
Diameter 19.7 cm. Inv. No. V3 716

The plate is decorated with an ornament
of red carnation which, though being
seemingly simple, is wonderfully refined
and demonstrates the striking skill of Indian
enamellers. The saturated red, transparent
green and opaque white colours of enamel stand out in delicate contrast to
the gold background.
From the gifts of Nadir-Shah, 1741.

Ring for shooting an arrow

Second quarter, 17th century. India. *Gold,*
precious stones. Diameter 4 cm. Inv. No. V3 703

This splendid ring protecting the thumb
while shooting an arrow bears a Persian
inscription on its inner side: *the Second*
Sahibkiran, which made it possible to
determine the name of the ring's owner
as Shah-Jahan (the Second Sahibkiran
is part of his full title).
From the gifts of Nadir-Shah, 1741.

Pitcher in a gold mounting

10th–11th centuries. Egypt. Mount – Turkey,
17th century. *Rock crystal, gold, precious*
stones. Height 16.8 cm. Inv. No. V3 241

The famous articles of rock crystal produced by Egyptian craftsmen were so
highly valued in the Muslim world that
they were later set in gold mountings
decorated with precious stones.
Acquired before 1859.

SECOND FLOOR

BEGINNING
OF THE SECOND-FLOOR
EXHIBITION

ART OF CHINA AND CENTRAL ASIA

▲

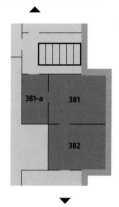

381-a   381

382

▼

ART OF IRAN AND THE NEAR EAST COUNTRIES

In the 4th century, as a result of a grave political crisis, the Roman Empire disintegrated into two parts, Western and Eastern. In 330 Emperor Constantine I transferred the capital of the Roman Empire to the site of the ancient Mégara colony, Byzantium, hence the more familiar historical name of the Eastern Roman Empire – Byzantium – with the capital in Constantinople. The composition of the territories which formed the Empire – the Balkan Peninsula, Asia Minor, Northern Mesopotamia, Syria, Palestine, Egypt and islands of the Mediterranean with their long-established and original cultures – determined the distinctive features of Byzantine art which took shape in close connection with the consolidating Christian ideology. The display of Byzantine artefacts includes magnificent examples of numismatics, decorative and applied arts and a series of remarkable icons.

Paten-dish of Bishop Paternus

491–518. Silver, gold, gilt, paste, stones, chasing. Diameter 61 cm, height of base 1.8 cm. Inv. No. ω 827

Paten-dishes were, as a rule, used for bread in the ritual of the Eucharist. In the centre of this paten-dish, formerly owned by Bishop Paternus, who had a diocese in the town of Tomi (now Constanta, Rumania), are the chrisma, the alpha and omega letters surrounded by a gilded band with a Latin inscription: *Restored from the old by our most venerable Bishop Paternus. Amen.* The rim of the dish features an ornament with depictions of Christian symbols: the baskets calling to mind of the "multiplication of loaves and fishes", the vines and bread symbolizing the ritual of the Eucharist, the doves and peacocks personifying the immortality of the soul. On the bottom of the reverse are four hallmarks dating from the times of Emperor Anastasius (ca. 430–518).

The dotted inscription on the lateral facet indicates the amount of gold and silver used to make the dish.
From the hoard near the village of Maloye Pereshchepino, Poltava province, 1912.

Amphora

First half, 6th century. *Silver, forging, gilt. Height of base 48.5 cm. Inv. No. ω 828*

Moulded from several parts, this typical Greek amphora is coated with a thick layer of gilt. Its body is adorned with three chased friezes, the middle one of acanthus scrolls containing masks, vases and fruit. The set of elements in this frieze calls to mind the mosaics of the Great Palace in Constantinople. The moulded handles of the amphora are shaped in imitation of dolphins' figures. The depiction of dolphins – a symbol of salvation – is in keeping with the Hellenistic and Roman traditions of decorating the vessels intended for grain, oil and wine. The hallmarks and weight seal on the bottom can be dated to either the reign of Emperor Anastasius (491–518) or Justinian I (527–565).
From the hoard near the village of Maloye Pereshchepino, Poltava province, 1912.

Diptych with depiction of circus scenes
5th century. Ivory. 33 x 10.5 cm. Inv. No. *ω* 10

It was in the Byzantium of the early Middle Ages that the art of bone-carving, so popular in Ancient Egypt, China, India and Japan, reached an unprecedented height.

Among the magnificent works by Byzantine bone-carvers housed in the Hermitage collection is this diptych with a 'secular' subject, in which the master presented a dynamic scene of fighting the lions.
From the A. Basilewsky collection, Paris, 1885.

Dish with depiction of a shepherd
Ca. 527–565. Silver. Diameter 23.8 cm; length of base 9 cm. Inv. No. *ω* 277

In the opinion of several scholars, the relief decor of the dish is not simply a depiction of a shepherd but a kind of illustration for a bucolic (pastoral) work. Arisen in the poetry of Ancient Greece and Rome, the bucolic genre was reinterpreted in the Christian era and was often used allegorically to describe Christ's mission as a 'good shepherd'. The bottom of the dish has five hallmarks dating from the times of Emperor Justinian I (482/483–565). Such Imperial control hallmarks are typical for the Byzantine gold- and silverware of the 6th and 7th centuries.
From the Klimovsky hoard, Perm province, 1908.

Forty Martyrs of Sebaste
10th–11th century. *Triptych. Ivory, silver.*
18.5 x 24.2 cm (unfolded). Inv. No. ω 299

Depicted on the centrepiece of the triptych are the forty Christian martyr-warriors who refused to join their comrades in pagan worship and were condemned to an excruciating death. On the wings are the full-length figures of the 'soldier-saints' represented in two rows in pairs: George, Theodore Tiron, Demetrius and Mercury on the left; Eustathius, Eustratius, Theodore Stratilates and Procopius on the right. When folded, the wings form a complete image of a cross with rosettes. The Greek inscriptions indicate the names of the warriors. Near the image of Christ is an inscription: *Forty Saints.* The silver mount and painting of the triptych were executed at a later date.
Acquired in 1928; formerly in the P. Shuvalov collection, St Petersburg.

Molybdovul
11th century. *Lead. Diameter 2.9 cm.*
Inv. No. M 2547

The molybdovuls (from the Greek *molybdos,* "lead" and the Latin *bulla,* "little ball") are the Byzantine two-sided leaden seals. In the Christian era, the inscribed bulls were used as seals and the Christian symbols and saints became the main subjects represented on them. Totalling more than 12 thousand pieces, the Hermitage collection of molybdovuls provides a most valuable source of information on the history and culture of the Byzantine Empire.
This molybdovul with an image of the Archangel Michael carries a Greek inscription saying that it was commissioned by David Vurun, the Armenian patrician and strategus.
From the Russian Archaeological Institute, Constantinople, 1931.

Ὁ ΑΓΙΟΣ ΓΡΗΓΟΡΙΟϹ Ο ΘΟΜΑΤΥΡΓΟϹ

**St Gregory Thaumaturgus
(the Wonderworker)**
12th century. *Tempera on wood. 81 x 53 cm.
Inv. No. ω 14*

The magnificent icon of St Gregory
Thaumaturgus is a characteristic example
of 12th-century Byzantine icon-painting.
*From the State Russian Museum,
Leningrad, 1935.*

SECOND FLOOR

BEGINNING
OF THE SECOND-FLOOR
EXHIBITION

ART OF BYZANTIUM

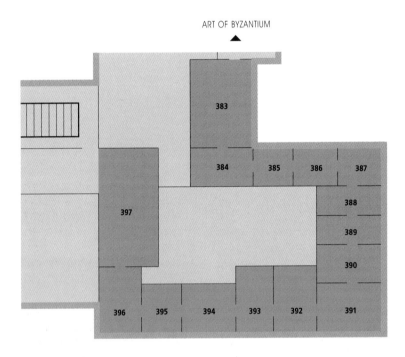

ART OF IRAN AND THE NEAR EAST COUNTRIES

The unique character of this Hermitage collection is determined by the specific geographic location and history of Russia whose destiny has been closely intertwined with the East from time immemorial. According to certain sources, even before the October revolution the museum collection comprised about 10,000 Oriental items (including the artefacts of the Ancient East). Part of the items, transferred to the Hermitage in the mid-19th century, had been gathered in the Kunstkammer throughout the 18th century. Other artefacts found their way to the museum as gifts from various embassies. A prominent place, especially in the collection of artistic arms and armour, is occupied by the trophies of the Russo-Turkish wars. A remarkable growth of the museum collections was connected with the establishment of a special Oriental Department in 1920. The most significant and valuable accretions came from the Museum of the Baron A. Stieglitz School of Technical Design and the State Academy of the History of the Material Culture. In the following decades, the collection continued to expand thanks to purchases and the entry of materials from archaeological expeditions. Although the Hermitage has no separate department of Islamic art, large quantities of artefacts from Islamic countries are kept in its Oriental Department and exhibited in the rooms of the art of the Near East, Middle Asia, the Caucasus and India. Of particular value are the items of Sassanian art and the Khorasan figured bronze of the 11th–13th centuries.

Dish with a scene of Shapur II's lion-hunting

4th century. Iran. *Silver, gilt. Diameter 22.9 cm. Inv. No. S 253*

The Hermitage collection of so-called Sassanian silverware (3rd–7th centuries) is the world's best both in the quantity and quality of its artefacts. The silver dish with a depiction of Shapur II's hunting – the gem of the Hermitage collection – was unearthed by chance in 1927. Such dishes were used during the feasts of Persian kings either as presentation dishes or as gifts for the dignitaries. King Shapur II of the Sassanian dynasty, ruler of Persia (the official name of Iran until 1935) in 309–379, was famous for his military campaigns, following which the vast territories of the Roman Empire were annexed to his domains. The scene of Shapur II fighting the lions shows the beginning and end of the hunt. The King is depicted wearing a high crown, his face is cold and impassionate. Specks of gilt used by the master lend the scene a dynamic quality.

From the hoard found in Vyatka province, 1927.

Dish with depiction of a bird flying a goddess

7th century. Iran. *Silver, gilt. Diameter 22 cm. Inv. No. S 217*

Rich in symbols from the *Avesta*, the motifs of Iranian art were determined by Zoroastrianism professed in Iran until the 7th century. This presentation dish is of the late Sassanian type, its subject stemming from ancient Iranian mythology on which several *Avesta* texts are based. Depicted in a heraldic scheme, the fantastic bird holds in its claws a naked goddess who is offering it a bunch of grapes. The Sassanian master, who might have been familiar with the classical depictions of the love-goddess locked in embrace with Zeus' eagle, offered an analogous version of the Iranian subject.

From the hoard found in Perm province, 1936.

Figure of an eagle

796–797. Master Suleiman. Iraq (?).
Bronze (or brass), silver and copper inlay.
Height 38 cm. Inv. No. ИР 1567

This marvellous figure of an eagle with traces of silver and copper inlays is so far the oldest accurately dated Iranian bronze item from the Islamic era. In all probability, it was used as a vessel for water. The neck bears an Arabic inscription indicating the master's name and date of the vessel's manufacture. Bronze (or brass) items with copper inlay first appeared during the late Sassanian period and persisted into the Umayyad and early Abbasid periods. However, the place of their manufacture remains obscure. The inlay on the eagle's figure suggests that the origin of this artefact should be sought somewhere to the west of Iran, most probably in Iraq, which was the centre of the caliphate in the 8th century.
From the Checheno-Ingush Museum, Grozny, 1939.

Figure of a horse

10th century. Iran. *Bronze (or brass).*
Height 36 cm, length 42 cm. Inv. No. ИР 1984

This figure was originally part of a more complex composition including the figure of a horseman. Richly adorned with the engraved patterns, it was apparently used as a lamp base. Of the Arabic inscriptions cut on the horse's croup (harness belts), only one survived saying: *Allah blesses the owner of this [item].* The form of the letters allows the item to be safely dated to the 10th century.
From the State Academy of the History of the Material Culture, 1925; formerly in the A. Bobrinsky collection, St Petersburg.

Cow-shaped aquamanile

1206. Master Ali ibn Muhammad ibn Abu-l-Qasim an-nakkash. Iran. *Bronze (or brass), silver inlay. 35 x 31.5 x 14 cm. Inv. No. A3 225*

Once lavishly adorned with silver inlay, this famous aquamanile is probably the latest of the fancy vessels known to us. The casting of such a complex composition was obviously considered a difficult task, and the master in his inscription stresses that the entire piece was cast at once. The depicted scene shows a cow patiently nurturing her calf while a predator is mauling her.
From the Antiquariat, Leningrad, 1929; formerly in the B. Khanenko collection.

Incense burner

11th century. Iran. Bronze (or brass), silver and copper inlay. Height 45 cm. Inv. No. ИР 1565

Openwork incense burners of various shapes, such as animal's or bird's figures, were widely used in 11th–12th-century Iran. This one shaped like a feline predator is exuberantly decorated with Arabic inscriptions in the Kufic script. The inscription on the creature's chest: *Ali ibn Muhammad at-Tadji (?)* does not suggest whose name it was – either the owner's or the master's. The style of the handwriting together with the ornament attest that the artefact was manufactured in the 11th century.
From the Main Collection of the Hermitage.

Kettle

1163. Masters Muhammad ibn Abd al-Vahid and Mas'ud ibn Ahmad an-nakkash. Iran, Herat. Bronze, silver and copper inlay. Height 18.5 cm. Inv. No. ИР 2268

The Khorassan bronze experts consider this kettle the most noteworthy item from the 12th–early 13th century as the inscriptions on it indicate not only the names of the customer, owner and two masters but also the date and place of manufacture, which makes it possible to attribute other similar artefacts as well. Besides the Arabic inscriptions, the silver and red copper inlays on the kettle's surface feature frieze-like depictions of hunting scenes, wrestling competitions and feasts. Such water kettles were used for bathing.
From the State Academy of the History of the Material Culture, 1925; formerly in the A. Bobrinsky collection.

Casket

11th century. Southern Italy. *Ivory, wood, carving. 33.6 x 18 x 16 cm. Inv. No. ЕГ 1244*

Similar caskets were produced in various regions of the Mediterranean in the 11th and 12th centuries. The large blank spaces left on the surface of the ivory plaques for hinges and the lock, the manner in which the figures of lions, antelopes, ibices, roosters and fantastic beasts are depicted in the medallions, as well as the arabesque framing and several other features, all prompted the outstanding scholar E. Kühnel to suggest that the casket is an 11th-century Arabic piece manufactured in an Italian or Sicilian workshop where Arab masters worked alongside local ones. Such caskets were probably used as reliquaries.

From the A. Basilewsky collection, Paris, 1885.

Vase: *Polo-Players*

13th century. Iran. *Faience, lustre painting. Height 80 cm. Inv. No. ИР 1595*

The lustre vase with scenes of polo-playing is a unique artefact from the 13th century depicting a favourite recreation of the feudal lords in Iran and the Caucasus and, at a later date, medieval Europe. This monumental vase with the oval body and short narrow neck is decorated with a frieze-like composition: five encircling bands consisting of the frequently repeated patterns of an unimitable beauty. The uppermost frieze on the neck of the vase features a group of musicians and the broadest middle one – the players on horseback holding the polo sticks and servants collecting the balls; all is intertwined with depictions of blossoming plants and animals. The vase is coated with a golden-brown lustre, a special paint with inclusions of metallic salts, which acquired a metallic glimmer after firing.

From the A. Basilewsky collection, Paris, 1885.

Plaquettes
Ca. 1200. Sicily. Ivory, carving. 24.7 x 12.6 cm,
24.6 x 12.7 cm. Inv. Nos. ЕГ 803, 804

The Arab conquests in 6th- to 9th-century
Europe led to the spreading of Islam to
some European territories, particularly,
Sicily, which was conquered by the Egypt
rulers of the Fatimid dynasty in the late

9th century. The Hermitage collection
boasts unique ivory plaquettes made
in Sicily. All vertically oriented patterns on
these rectangular plaquettes are carved
in high relief; the surface is decorated with
animal motifs and intertwined ornaments.
These plaquettes were probably the panels
of a depository.
From the A. Basilewsky collection, Paris, 1885.

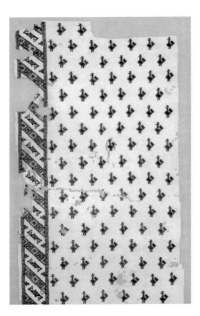

**Fragment of a textile
with rooster patterns**
14th–15th centuries. Egypt. Linen, embroidery.
99 x 56 cm. Inv. No. ЕГ 661

Linen and silk textiles, with printed patterns
and embroidered by means of stencils
or block printing, were in great vogue in
Egypt in the 13th–15th centuries. Most likely
such linen textiles were made for wider circles of the well-to-do population, while
the silk ones were intended for the Sultan's
court. This fragment of a bleached linen
textile is embroidered in black thread, with
the geometricized figures of roosters situated all over the field. The composition of
the embroidery design, ornamentation,
embroidery technique and quality of the
fabric allow to attribute this piece to
the flourishing period of textile production
in Egypt in the 14th and 15th centuries.
Brought from Egypt by V. Bock, 1897.

Lidded box

1st quarter, 14th century. Egypt. *Bronze (or brass), gold and silver inlay, niello. Height 4 cm, diameter 10.5 cm. Inv. No. ЕГ 765 а, б*

The box and lid are adorned with a fine and delicate ornament of lotuses, flying ducks and Arabic inscriptions in the *naskh* and *suls* styles, which are typical of the Mameluke art of that period. The inscriptions extol the Mameluke Sultan Melik an-Nasir Muhammad ibn Qal'un (reigned 1297–1343), hence the dating of the box to the early 14th century. The niello, gold and silver inlays impart a certain picturesqueness to the whole surface. The decor of the box and execution technique attest to a high standard of craftsmanship.
Date of acquisition unknown.

Tray

Mid-13th century. Syria. *Bronze (or brass), silver inlay. Diameter 43.1 cm. Inv. No. CA 14238*

This tray is a superb example of applied art from the era of the Mamelukes, rulers of Egypt and Syria (1250–1517). The output of Damascus, Aleppo (Haleb) and other Syrian art centres won acclaim not only throughout the Muslim World, but also in Europe. Retaining nearly all its decor of silver inlay, the tray bears the images of Christian saints in twelve arches, framed by the Arabic well-wishing inscriptions and ornaments with animal and plant motifs. Similar items, combining Muslim and Christian symbols, are typical of the medieval art of Syria where the Muslims lived side by side with the Christians.
Acquired in 1898.

Horn-shaped cup

13th–14th century. Syria, Damascus. Mount –
Germany, 1551. *Glass, enamel painting, silver,
gilt, repoussé. Inv. No. V3 827*

The horn-shaped glass vessel is adorned
with depictions of Christian saints executed
in colour enamels between the bands of
Arabic inscriptions praising the ruler. Similar
vessels may have been made for the
Crusaders. As early as the mid-14th century
this horn-cup found its way to Europe where
a silver mount with a support of paws clawing a ball was made for it in Augsburg,
Germany, in 1551. The multifigure composition of the Twelve Apostles and other images
on the point of the horn is crowned by the
blessing Christ. The inscription on the middle
frieze says that a Livonian noble Bruno
Drolfagen of Westphalian stock dedicates
this cup to his son Jurgen on his wedding
day in 1551. The newlyweds are depicted on
the peak of the mount. The Drolfagen coats
of arms (two crossed swords and a crescent)
is put between the clawing paws. Regarded
as a confirmation of the marriage agreement, this cup was passed from one person
to another to drink to a happy conjugal
union.
From the Kunstkammer, St Petersburg, 1860.

Lamp
1346–47. Syria or Egypt. *Glass, enamel.*
Height 36.2 cm. Inv. No. EГ 883

Similar lamps served as a sort of lighting device suspended on chains with a candle or oil inside. The lamp is adorned with a heraldic sign and an inscription in Arabic (on the neck and body) saying that it was manufactured for the Mameluke Sultan al-Malike al-Muzarofor Hadji who ruled from 1346 to 1347. A heraldic sign (similar to a coats of arms) was granted to the military and civil dignitaries of the Mameluke state. Initially symbolizing their position and reflecting the sophisticated structure of the military and civil bureaucratic systems, this sort of signs can be seen on all types of items of applied art.
From the A. Basilewsky collection, Paris, 1885.

Dish
Early 16th century. Iran. *Faience.*
Diameter 35.5 cm. Inv. No. VГ 2392

This dish, painted in cobalt of several shades, with the images outlined against a dark background, is an example of the Kubachi pottery. The ornamentation brings out the architectonics of the item, its bottom, walls and rim. The motif of two fishes in a circle on the bottom occurs in a number of artefacts dating from the 16th century. The flower and foliage motif decorating the walls of the dish as well as the shaded arch-like patterns and scrolls painted on the curved rim, are also known from other examples of this pottery. Like many items of Kubachi pottery, this one has a depiction of a twining sprout on the outside walls.
From the Expert-Purchasing Commission of the Hermitage, 1949.

Bottle
17th century. Iran, Kerman. *Faience, painting.*
Height 26.4 cm. Inv. No. VГ 345

The Hermitage takes pride in its collection of fritware of the Timurid (1370–1507) and Safavid (1501–1736) periods, which numbers over 700 items and is probably one of the largest collections of its kind in the world. The period from the 15th to the 17th century witnessed the efflorescence of Persian pottery. One of the main centres of fritware production was Kerman, where this polychrome bottle with the depictions of birds and animals was produced.
From the Museum of the Baron A. Stieglitz School of Technical Design, Leningrad, 1925.

Carpet

Second half, 16th century. Turkey, Ushak.
Wool. 331 x 188 cm. Inv. No. T 19

Original Turkish art began to take shape
in the second half of the 14th century, still
strongly influenced by Byzantium, Iran and
other neighbouring countries. The world-
famous Turkish carpets are represented in
the Hermitage by the output of different
carpet-weaving centres, particularly Ushak.
It is in this city that the carpets, with an
ornament known as *Lotto* in Europe, were
manufactured. The name derives from the
celebrated Venetian artist Lorenzo Lotto
whose models used to sit at a table
covered with a carpet of this pattern.
*From the Museum of the Baron A. Stieglitz
School of Technical Design, Leningrad, 1925.*

Kalamdan

*Ca. 1880. Iran. Papier-mâché, lacquer,
painting. Length 22.5 cm. Inv. No. VΠ 20*

The art of painting on lacquered articles –
the so-called Persian lacquers – was one
of the most widespread artistic handicrafts
in Iran in the 17th to 19th centuries. It may
have been borrowed by the Persian masters from China in the Timurid epoch
(15th century). The most popular
lacquered objects were the covers for
manuscript books and kalamdans, the
pen-boxes for kalams (reed pens), inkpots
and other writing accessories. These exquisite pieces, covered with precious painting
of fine and beautiful patterns, were
famous throughout the world.
*Acquired in 1925; formerly in the C. Fabergé
collection, St Petersburg.*

REZA 'ABBASI
Girl Wearing a Fur Hat
1602–3. Iran. Paper, Indian ink, watercolour, gold. 14.8 x 8.4 cm; sheet 19.3 x 16 cm. Inv. No. VP 705

In the 17th century, during the reign of the Safavid Shahs who made Isfahan the capital of Iran in 1598, the development of Persian art was mainly connected with the Isfahan school. One of its most important artists, probably its founder, was Reza 'Abbasi. The drawing *Girl Wearing a Fur Hat* is the earliest of his known dated works. It is one of the best female images in his output and Iranian art in general, although the depiction of a girl with a high headdress, kneeling on one knee and clasping her hands on the other, was by no means a novelty. Despite the long curls falling on the shoulders, this personage is sometimes considered a youth. Evidently, before us is a visual interpretation of a poetic image. Zinaida Vorozheikina, an authority on Persian literature, wrote: "The subject of the poets' adoration – an idol – is depersonalized. This is partly determined by the very nature of

the Persian language which has no grammatically expressed category of gender."
From the Museum of the Baron A. Stieglitz School of Technical Design, Petrograd, 1924.

MIHR-ALI
Portrait of Fath-Ali-Shah seated
1813–14. Iran. Oil on canvas. 253 x 118 cm. Inv. No. VP 1108

The formal portrait, one of the leading genres with a proclaimatory significance in the art of ancient Persia, regained its former importance in the late 18th century following the enthronization of the Qajar dynasty. The early stage of the reign of Fath-Ali-Shah (1796–1834) was marked by the evolution of the so-called Qajar style characterized by outward splendour and archaism. This portrait shows Fath-Ali-Shah wearing a luxurious formal costume: a huge crown with a plumage of the black heron feathers (a sign of royal dignity) on his head and a red silk robe as lavishly adorned with jewels and pearls as the mace and sword – the attributes of power.
From the Gatchina Palace-Museum, 1932.

SECOND FLOOR

BEGINNING
OF THE SECOND-FLOOR
EXHIBITION

FRENCH PAINTING AND SCULPTURE.
19th–20th CENTURIES; PAINTING
OF WESTERN EUROPE AND AMERICA.
19th–20th CENTURIES

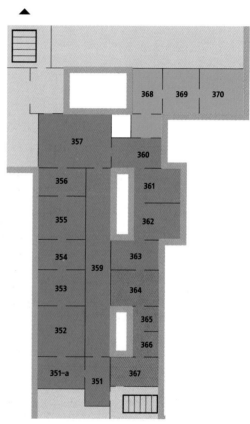

ART OF CHINA

ART OF INDIA

ART OF BYZANTIUM

ART OF TIBET
AND MONGOLIA

HUN CULTURE

ART OF CHINA AND CENTRAL ASIA

By the mid-18th century a considerable knowledge of the art of Western and Southern Asian countries – first of all, India and China – had been accumulated in Russia. The writings of the Russian merchant and explorer Afanasy Nikitin (? –1472) who travelled in Persia and India in 1466–72 – virtually, one of the first Orientalistic works in Rus' – aroused an enormous interest in the Oriental culture which influenced in many respects the Russian art of the 16th and 17th centuries. From the late 17th century items of Chinese porcelain appeared more and more frequently in the household inventories of Russian dignitaries. Their influx to Russia increased dramatically when Peter I began to commission art works and household items through the Dutch East India Company, which maintained a ship traffic with sea ports in the Far East. Following the trade agreement concluded between Russia and China in 1727, the caravans loaded with 'things Chinese' began to arrive directly in Russia. The Russian collections of artefacts of the so-called 'oasis' cultures, which had evolved on the Silk Road, at the sites and cemeteries of ancient nomads in the territory of Mongolia, were supplemented with finds made by such famous travellers and Orientalists as Sergei Oldenburg and Piotr Kozlov. A modest exhibition in rooms 351–370 cannot claim to provide an ample idea of the rich Hermitage collection of the art of the Far East, Central and Southern Asia, but it presents unique archaeological artefacts of the Hun culture, Chinese bronze, enamels, items of bone and lacquer, silk, furniture, Buddhist sculpture and painting.

Lidded *gui* vessel

9th–8th centuries B.C. China.
Bronze. Height 17 cm. Inv. No. ΛM 20 а, б

The ancient Chinese vessels of bronze used as sacrosanct items for sacrifices were placed on the ancestors' altars or in burials as symbols of power and wealth. Several vessels of this kind were found in the individual graves of the Chinese nobles dating from the period of the Western Zhou dynasty (*ca.* 1050–711 B.C.). Intended for food, this vessel is an epigraphic source of the utmost importance. The hieroglyphic inscription on the inside of its bottom is repeated on the lid: *Que of Shi, out of his filial respect for his parents, has made this precious vessel to be granted longevity.* On behalf of Emperor Guangxu it was presented to Nicholas II in connection with his coronation in April 1896 as a sign of respect and recognition of his power as the sovereign of the neighbouring country. Nicholas II kept the vessel in his apartments with his most treasure posessions. *Gift of Emperor Guangxu, 1896.*

Sacrificial *hu* vessel

5th–4th centuries B.C. China. *Bronze. Height 39 cm. Inv. No. ΛM 1201 а, б*

In ancient China the *hu* vessels were used as ritual wine containers for sacrifices. This pear-shaped vessel dates from the period of the Eastern Zhou dynasty (770–256 B.C.). The decor belts in relief include paired depictions of mythical animals and hunting scenes in mirror image. The meaning of the subjects remains obscure. The decor reflects the influence that the Sarmatians, Scythians and other north-western neighbours exerted on Chinese culture in the 5th–4th centuries B.C.
From the Expert-Purchasing Commission of the Hermitage, 1998.

Rug (detail)

1st century B.C. Mongolia, Noin-Ula.
Felt with appliqué work, silk. 73 x 227 cm.
Inv. No. MP 1956

In 1924–25 an archaeological expedition of the Russian Geographic Society headed by Piotr Kozlov conducted excavations of an ancient cemetery in the Noin-Ula Mountains, 100 kilometres from Ulan Bator. It unearthed unique cultural artefacts of the Hunni (later, the Huns), an ancient and, in many respects, mysterious nomadic people whose burials are still found on the Altai foothills. The Hermitage detail of a rug shows a gryphon mauling a deer with alternating depictions of the Tree of Life. The solar symbols in the upper part of the rug (at one time its centre) exemplify the final stage in the development of the 'animal style' in the art of the ancient nomadic tribes of the Eurasian continent. The edge of the rug is trimmed with a Chinese-made silk fabric attesting to the close links between the nomads and the developed countries of the Far East. The fabric's pattern of stylized roosters reflects the well-known myths of ancient China. A rooster was the long-revered symbol of the Sun and played a significant role in the ancient Chinese religion. In most legends

it is mentioned alongside a peach tree. This relationship is evident on the ornament of the Hermitage fabric. Symbolizing the vernal sun, like a rooster, a peach was meant to chase the evil spirits away.
From the Ethnographic Department of the State Russian Museum, Leningrad, 1934.

Western merchant

7th century (?). Western China, Xinjang, Kuchar oasis. *Clay, painting. Height 43 cm.*
Inv. No. Ky 260

According to the Chinese, the 'west' included all the lands to the west of China – Soghdiana, Iran, Byzantium and the Caucasus. A merchant was not only the principal character on the Silk Road which connected the 'west' and China, but also the main donor to the Buddhist monasteries and temples emerging in the oases and by the wells along the caravan routes. From the Chinese master's point of view, the 'western' appearance of the merchant and his characteristic costume were not a curiosity either in the capital of the Chinese Empire or, even less so, in the oases where the trade flourished and representatives of all nations and civilizations met.
From the Ethnographic Department of the State Russian Museum, Leningrad, 1932.

Head of a bodhisattva

8th century. Central China, Dunhuang,
Mogao cave temples. *Clay. Height 37 cm.*
Inv. No. ДХ 15

Bodhisattvas are the enlightened beings
second to Buddhas in significance, whose
role is to help and save all the living creatures on the earth. The cult of bodhisattvas
was popular in Buddhism beginning from
the 4th–5th centuries. The Mogao complex
of cave temples (366), from which this
clay head of a bodhisattva originates,
was enlarged and adorned up until the
14th century. The head of a bodhisattva is
dated to the flourishing period of Buddhist
art in Central Asia and China.
*From the Museum of Anthropology
and Ethnography, Leningrad, 1931.*

Bodhisattva Avalokiteshvara

*956. Central China, Dunhuang, Mogao cave
temples. Canvas, paint. 142 x 65.5 cm.
Inv. No. ДХ 68*

The merciful and compassionate
Avalokiteshvara (Guanyin in Chinese),
is the most popular bodhisattva in the
Buddhist world, reincarnated in Dalai
Lama XIV and all his predecessors. The
word *bodhisattva* is translated as "he
who hearkens unto the noises of the world".
Here Avalokiteshvara is depicted with
eleven faces and six hands, that is, in his
esoteric form. According to tradition, after
looking at the human misery, the head of
the bodhisattva broke into many parts,
hence his multi-faced image. The
Amitabha Buddha gathered and piled the
parts in a pyramid and crowned it with his
own head. In the lower part of the icon are
the people who commissioned the icon –
members of one family – and their names
are written on the cartouches. In the centre is the prayer with which the head of the
family addresses Avalokiteshvara to allow his
deceased parents be happily reincarnated
in the Pure Land of Amitabha Buddha.
*From the Museum of Anthropology
and Ethnography, Leningrad, 1934.*

Two-headed Buddha

13th–14th centuries. Mongolia, Khara-Khoto.
Clay, painting. Height 62 cm. Inv. No. X 2296

The clay sculpture of two-headed Buddha belongs to the culture of Tanguts, the people who established the state of Western Hsia in the late 10th century. The Tangut state was laid waste by the armies of Chinghis Khan in 1227, but the city of Khara-Khoto ('black city' in Mongolian) survived until the late 14th century. The majority of Tangut artefacts were discovered in a *suburgan* (the Mongolian for *stupa*, an architectural memorial on a grave) during the excavations of 1907–9, which were conducted by the expedition headed by Piotr Kozlov (1863–1935), a scientist and associate of the famous traveller Nikolai Przhevalsky. The iconography of two-headed Buddha is based on a legend: when two poor men commissioned an image of Buddha from an artist, He, merciful and kind, divided His body and head in two, so that each man could have his own image.

From the Ethnographic Department of the State Russian Museum, Leningrad, 1931.

Eleven-faced and eight-handed Avalokiteshvara

12th–13th centuries. Mongolia, Khara-Khoto.
Cotton, painting. 132 x 94 cm. Inv. No. X 2355

The Khara-Khoto artefacts – the sculptures and miraculously survived icons on canvas and silk – have turned the Hermitage collection into a world-famous treasury of Buddhist art. Avalokiteshvara is shown sitting on a throne of lotuses surrounded by the Guardians of Light and other deities. The back of the throne is flanked by the vividly painted faces of two monks. The icon is remarkable for its combination of the Tibetan and Chinese styles.

From the Ethnographic Department of the State Russian Museum, Leningrad, 1931.

Round dish with two birds and peony flowers

Second half, 14th century. China. Carved red and ochre-coloured lacquer. Diameter 31 cm, depth 3 cm. Inv. No. ΛΗ 488

This dish is the earliest red lacquer carving (produced from the juice of lacquer wood Rhus Vernisiflua) in the Hermitage collection. By its stylistic and artistic features it can be dated to the second half of the 14th century, the early Ming dynasty (1368–1644). The lacquerware masterpieces of that period remain unsurpassed. Each layer of lacquer is meticulously polished, so that the material looks semi-transparent. To the left of the low round base of the dish is a six-character Xuande mark (1426–35), carved and inlaid with gold. However, under the mark one can see traces of an earlier scratched inscription. This might be the name of one of the most celebrated lacquer carvers – either Zhang Cheng or Yang Mao, active in the second half of the 14th century. The purpose of such dishes, totalling about twenty-five pieces worldwide, is not quite clear. The depictions of birds warrant the conjecture that the dishes were Imperial gifts granted to civil servants of high rank.
Acquired in 1955.

Bowl with five dragons in the clouds

Second half, 18th century. Imperial Workshops. China. Carved jade. Height 17 cm, diameter 31 cm. Inv. No. ΛΟ 153

The most valuable stone in China, jade was used for ritual purposes in ancient times and for decoration at a later date. This bowl, made for the Emperor's study in the palace during the reign of Qianlong (1736–95), served as a table decoration, but could also be used as a brush-pot. The bowl carries benevolent symbols: the five-toed dragons symbolized the emperor, the pearl-playing dragons – wishes coming true. There are several similar bowls worldwide, dating from the second half of the 18th century. By their form and ornament, these artefacts derive from an enormous wine-bowl carved in 1265 by order of Emperor Khubilai (1215–1294), grandson of Chinghis Khan, and placed in the Guanghan Palace on an island at Lake Beihai. During the change of dynasties in the 14th century, the bowl disappeared from the palace to be discovered in 1745 in a Taoist temple where it was used for storing vegetables. Qianlong built a special building for the bowl on the territory of the Round Fort at Lake Beihai, where it has been kept to this day. This remarkable discovery prompted the emperor to commission several similar, although smaller, bowls.
From the Ethnographic Department of the State Russian Museum, Leningrad, 1931.

Ice box

18th century. China. *Brass, cloisonné enamel, gilt. Height 47 cm. Inv. No. ΛM 499*

The outer and inner walls of the box with Qianlong mark from the Yuanmingyuan Summer Palace are adorned with turquoise and multicoloured enamels and its decor – the 'one hundred flowers' – symbolizes prosperity and well-being. In the reign of Alexander III it was used as a flower box in the Anichkov Palace.
From the State Museum Reserve, 1928.

Basin with depictions of lotuses

First quarter, 18th century. Jingdezhen Imperial Workshops. Central China. *Porcelain, painting in the famille verte palette, gilt. Height 31.2 cm. Inv. No. ΛK 658*

The 17th–early 18th century was the heyday of Chinese porcelain. From as early as the 16th century its manufacture was centred in Jingdezhen city (Jiangxi province, Central China), where the Crown Workshops catering mostly for the Imperial Court functioned alongside private workshops whose products, intended for domestic market and export, were, by the end of the Ming Dynasty (1368–1644), not inferior in technology to those made at the Crown Workshops. In the reign of Emperor Kangxi (1662–1722) it was the Jingdezhen Workshops that evolved the so-called *famille verte* porcelain (the term originates from Europe), in which the five-colour painting is dominated by the green palette. Perfect and beautiful, often traditional, forms, skillfully heightened with painting, are typical for this ware. The subjects include a wide variety of themes with prevailing depictions of flowers and birds.
From the Museum of the Baron A. Stieglitz School of Technical Design, Leningrad, 1926.

Dragon

17th–early 18th centuries. China. *Coral. Length 15 cm. Inv. No. ΛO 714*

The dragon in China was a symbol of springtime and the East, it ruled water and rain, being an Imperial symbol at the same time. It is not known how this figurine was brought to Russia, but it found its way to the Hermitage not later than the second half of the 18th century. The entry D No. 237 in the 1789 inventory of "various precious items brought from the entresol to the Hermitage of Her Imperial Majesty" says: "Crocodile of red coral". Red-shaded corals were highly rated in China, and their use was strictly regulated at the Imperial Court. In the reign of the Qing dynasty (1644–1911) only members of the Imperial family were allowed to wear the necklaces and decorations made of red corals; the coral rosaries were used exclusively by hierarchs of the Buddhist (Lamaist) clergy.
From the Main Collection of the Hermitage.

WINTER PALACE OF PETER I

MILLIONNAYA STREET

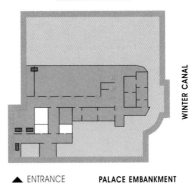

WINTER CANAL

▲ ENTRANCE   PALACE EMBANKMENT

MENSHIKOV PALACE

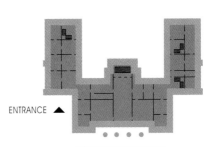

ENTRANCE ▲

● ● ● ●

UNIVERSITY EMBANKMENT

EXHIBITIONS IN THE GENERAL STAFF BUILDING

MOIKA RIVER EMBANKMENT

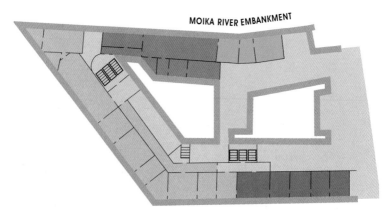

▲ ENTRANCE

PAINTINGS BY BONNARD AND DENIS

WORKS IN THE EMPIRE STYLE

EXHIBITION OF PORCELAIN

MEMORIAL ROOMS OF CHANCELLORS

PALACE SQUARE

WINTER PALACE OF PETER I
MENSHIKOV PALACE
EXHIBITIONS IN THE GENERAL STAFF BUILDING

The exhibitions of the State Hermitage housed in its branches – the Hermitage Theatre, the Menshikov Palace and the General Staff building (in the rooms of the former Ministry of Foreign Affairs and the Ministry of Finance) – are truly unique in their artistic merit. The reconstructed interiors of the Winter Palace of Peter I (now the Hermitage Theatre) and the Menshikov Palace attest to the grandeur of the Petrine reforms. The General Staff building has a magnificent display of works in the Empire style and canvases by eminent French artists. Assembled by the Russian manufacturers, patrons of art and collectors Sergei Shchukin and Ivan Morozov, these canvases demonstrate the best achievements of French monumental and decorative painting in the early 20th century.

WINTER PALACE OF PETER I

1716–27. Architects G. Mattarnovy,
N.-F. Härbel, D. Trezzini, B. C. Rastrelli (?)

The most luxurious palace in the St Petersburg of the Petrine era, the Winter Palace of Peter I was designed by the architect Georg Mattarnovy and built approximately in 1716–20. It was expanded by Domenico Trezzini in the early 1720s. The architectural aspect of the palace is well known from documentary descriptions and paintings. It was on the first floor of this palace that Peter had his office where he worked, made drawings and died on 28 January 1725. Earlier on this site stood the wooden Smaller Winter Mansion of Peter I (1708–11) and the Wedding Palace (1711–12), whose name derives from the wedding ceremony of Peter I and Martha Skavronskaya (the future Catherine I). A recent restoration in the Hermitage Theatre, which was built on the site of the so-called 'third' palace of Peter I, has accidentally revealed that its brickwork was left intact to form part of the theatre construction. Following the research, archaeological and restoration works on the reconstruction of this unique relic of the Petrine era, the visitors can already see a magnificent gallery decorated with marble sculpture and a balustrade separating it from the inner yard paved in yellow Dutch bricks as well as the private rooms of Peter I (so-called 'smaller chambers') with a display of his marvellously preserved possessions (the turning lathes, tools, costumes) and paintings from his collection. It is known that in the Winter Palace there were a great hall, the private apartments of the members of the Imperial family, a dining-room, a greenhouse, a chapel and other premises.

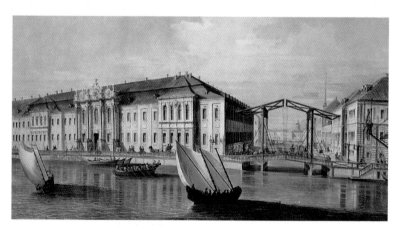

**UNKNOWN VENETIAN ARTIST
OF THE 18th CENTURY
View of the Winter Palace of Peter I**
*1750s–early 1760s. After the drawing
by M. Makhaev. Oil on canvas. 71 x 120 cm.
Inv. No. ЭРЖ 2591*

A valuable historical document, this painting gives an idea of the architecture of the Palace Embankment in the Petrine era. On the left is the building of the third expanded (or the fourth) Winter Palace of Peter I.
From the Main Collection of the Hermitage.

BARTOLOMEO CARLO RASTRELLI
1675–1744
Effigy of Peter I (The Wax Person)
1725. St Petersburg. *Wood, wax. Full-size height 204 cm. Inv. Nos. ЭРТ 8556–8572*

The life-size wax effigy of Peter I was made by order of Catherine I immediately after Peter's death on 28 January 1725 to preserve the authentic appearance of the great Emperor for posterity. The face and open parts of the body were reproduced from the plaster casts taken after his death and the wig from Peter's own hair. The effigy wears the dress coat formerly owned by the Emperor.
From the State Ethnographical Museum, Leningrad, 1941.

Ceremonial carriage of Peter I
After 1723. Russia, St Petersburg.
Masters G. Belin, J. Michel, N. Pineau.
Wood, gilt, fabric, leather, metal.
150 x 160 x 350 cm. Inv. No. РМб 630

The highlight of the main courtyard of Peter I's Winter Palace is a rare example of the garden promenade carriages from the first quarter of the 18th century. It was made by the carver Nicolas Pineau, planer Jean Michel and turner G. Belin – all French masters who worked in St Petersburg. The back and elbow-rests of the armchair have the metal insets painted by the artist Louis Caravaque. Such carriages, which Peter I saw during his stay in Paris in 1717, were intended for the unhurried ceremonial promenades of the sovereigns along the paths of regular parks rather than for fast driving. The Russian Emperor wished that the gardens of his countryside residence at Peterhof be not inferior to those of the French king at Versailles, and his drives be as pompous. It was for such drives that the garden carriage was commissioned from the French masters.
From the State Ethnographical Museum, Leningrad, 1941.

MENSHIKOV PALACE

1710–27. Architects G. M. Fontana,
G. Schädel, D. Trezzini, B.C. Rastrelli,
G. Mattarnovy, J.-B. Leblond

The palace of Prince Alexander Danilovich Menshikov (1673–1729), the closest associate of Peter I, used to be the venue of political, cultural and society life in St Petersburg in the first quarter of the 18th century. The construction and exterior of this first masonry palace in the young city represent an original blend of Western European and traditional Russian architecture. Turned into a branch of the State Hermitage, the palace houses an exhibition entitled *Russian Culture of the First Third of the 18th century*. It includes the architecture of the building proper, its interior decoration as well as paintings, engravings, sculptures and rare Russian and foreign-made items of applied art, illustrative of that period. The presentation of works of different origin reflects the state of affairs during the Petrine era when Russia established wide-ranging trade relations with Western Europe.

Main Staircase

The spacious anteroom with two rows of columns and the stately two-flight staircase of oak wood in the central part of the palace have retained their original appearance. As high as the building itself, the staircase is illuminated by twenty-one windows arranged in two tiers. Architecturally the staircase is designed as an inner 'Italian' courtyard with its walls painted in imitation of marble and adorned with the arches resting on pilasters and columns. The entrance to the anteroom and the state apartments on the first floor features a tripartite triumphal arch with the columns distinguished by their stone-carved capitals. The panels between the windows of the first and second floors were decorated with paintings of the elements, and the windowsills – with tiled shafts whose blue plant ornament was a unique feature in early Petersburg architecture. The banisters of the first-floor staircase have retained the intertwined monograms of Peter I and Alexander Menshikov. The statue of the Sun-god Apollo (its Roman torso dates from the 2nd century B.C.) is one of the seven Italian and classical sculptures decorating the large anteroom of the palace.

Antebedroom

Called the antebedroom in Menshikov's *Daily Journal*, this antechamber served as a reception room for the Governor's immediate assistants. The room has retained the original finishing of its ceiling and walls in white and blue ceramic tiles, mostly with paintings on pastoral subjects which are combined with extensive stucco ornament, carved paneling and mosaic parquetry. The furniture and other decorative items of the late 17th and early 18th centuries conform to the purpose of the antebedroom: a carved Italian commode, a rare English standing clock provided with a music device; a Dutch inlaid walnut cabinet and faience vases on the commode. The room walls are hung with portraits of Prince Menshikov, his wife and daughters – Maria and Alexandra – by unknown Russian artists active in the 1720s.

Menshikov's Walnut Study

From the five windows of this small corner room Menshikov could observe not only the Neva River, the Admiralty and the Winter Palace but also the Peter and Paul Fortress and the Galley Shipyard. The natural walnut finish of the walls, very unusual and rare at that time, distinguished this room from the other premises of the palace, hence the name 'Walnut Room' it was given in 1720. It served both as a state study and a room for especially secret affairs. As the vogue for such rooms spread to Russia from France, the wooden finish, the painted plafond on the ceiling and the furnishing including the fireplace – a new heating device for Russia – all bore an European imprint. According to the common practice of the period, Menshikov not only gathered and demonstrated all kinds of curiosities and objets d'arts here, but also would quite often play chess, a very popular game in Russia in the first quarter of the 18th century. Among the items displayed in the study is a unique amber chess set of early 18th-century Prussian make.

EXHIBITIONS IN THE GENERAL STAFF BUILDING

The building of the General Staff was erected in 1827 by Carlo Rossi (1775/77–1849), the outstanding exponent of the Russian Empire style. He was born in Naples and lived with his mother and stepfather in St Petersburg from the 1780s. Brought up in the family of the famous architect Vincenzo Brenna, Rossi was trained in the Florence Academy in 1802–04. Upon his return to Russia he did much work for the Imperial Porcelain Factory and Glassworks, designed park constructions in Pavlovsk and built a magnificent palace 'in the Italian style' on Yelaghin Island. The young architect, however, dreamed of excelling the monumental ensembles of French Classicism. The Russian victory in the Patriotic War of 1812 proved to be the right occasion for creating a grandiose ensemble of Palace Square. In 1819 Alexander I entrusted Rossi with developing a project for the reorganization of space in front of the Winter Palace. A year later, the project for "constructing a regular square in front of the Winter Palace" was submitted to the Emperor. By the autumn of 1827 a majestic building rose opposite to the Winter Palace, enclosing the confines of the newly formed square within a vast area from Nevsky Prospekt to the bend of the Moika River. The façades of amazingly noble classical forms extended for more than five hundred metres. The alternating snow-white colonnades, the gilded balustrades of balconies and the strict and refined contours of the window openings were integrated into the spatial framework of the square. Striving to create a strictly symmetrical form, the architect eventually arrived at a strikingly harmonious solution in which the major role was assigned to the smooth curve of the façade line as if bent under the pressure of the square space. The two parts of the colossal construction are linked together by a triumphal arch crowned with a monumental chariot of Glory – a symbol of Russia's triumph in the 1812 War. According to Rossi's project, the left wing of the General Staff was to house the departments of the Ministry of Foreign Affairs and the Ministry of Finance. In order to meet the requirements of these important government bodies the architect planned the interior layout of this part of the building. The second floor of the eastern wing of the General Staff building houses an exhibition of artworks from the Empire period. Created after Carlo Rossi's plans in the 1820s, the well-preserved interiors of the Eastern wing show the Russian Empire style at its best. The exhibition provides a unique possibility to trace not only the development of the Empire style as the continuation of French Neo-classicism during the First Empire period, but also the mutual influence and differences of the European and Russian national schools. On display are paintings, graphics and sculptures, items of decorative and applied arts of very high standards. An exhibition of paintings entitled *Pierre Bonnard and Maurice Denis. The Decorative Ensembles in the Hermitage Collection* is to be seen next door. The monumental panels, commissioned from the French artists by Ivan Morozov in 1907 and 1910 to decorate the Concert Hall and the Main Staircase of his mansion in Prechistenka Street in Moscow, are the outstanding examples of decorative painting of the Art Nouveax period.

Items from the Egyptian Service

1806–8. Painting after designs by D. V. Denon.
The Sèvres Porcelain Manufactory. France.
Porcelain, overglaze painting, gilt.
Inv. Nos. 14851–14857

The Egyptian Service was presented by
Napoleon to the Russian Tsar Alexander I
when they met in Erfurt in 1808. The idea
to create the service was conceived by
Dominique Vivant Denon, Director of the
Louvre, who accompanied Napoleon in
his Egyptian campaign. The subjects on
the items were taken from the collection
Travels in Lower and Upper Egypt, published in 1802. An inscription on the bottom of each item specifies the subject.
The Hermitage houses only ten pieces from
this enormous service. The larger part of it
is in the Ceramics Museum of the Kuskovo
Estate in Moscow.
From the Main Collection of the Winter Palace.

Furniture items from the sets manufactured for the Winter and Anichkov Palaces in St Petersburg

1817–18. Workshop of I. Baumann after
designs by C. Rossi. St Petersburg.
Wood, carving, painting, gilt, silk.
123 x 250 x 75 cm (settee), 91 x 64 x 53 cm
(armchairs), 93 x 53 x 45 cm (chairs).
Inv. Nos. РМБ 605, 611, 755–775

This room is the reconstruction of an early
19th-century salon. Especially prized at
that period were the furniture sets made
after designs by Carlo Rossi and Andrei
Voronikhin, as well as French furniture
pieces from the Jacob Brothers workshop,
made after drawings by Charles Percier
and Pierre Fontaine. In general, Rossi's
interiors were notable for their painted
ceilings, pilaster-articulated doorframes
and lavish gilded details. Quite often,
a prominent place in the decoration was
assigned to fabrics. The furniture upholstery
was either selected in unison with the
general colour scheme or, on the contrary,
the items became part of a sophisticated
play of contrasts.
From the Main Collection of the Winter Palace.

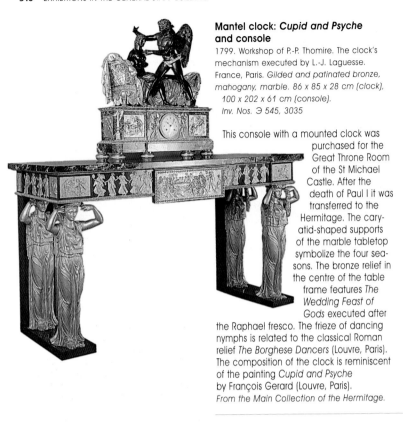

Mantel clock: *Cupid and Psyche* and console

1799. Workshop of P.-P. Thomire. The clock's mechanism executed by L.-J. Laguesse. France, Paris. *Gilded and patinated bronze, mahogany, marble. 86 x 85 x 28 cm (clock), 100 x 202 x 61 cm (console). Inv. Nos. Э 545, 3035*

This console with a mounted clock was purchased for the Great Throne Room of the St Michael Castle. After the death of Paul I it was transferred to the Hermitage. The caryatid-shaped supports of the marble tabletop symbolize the four seasons. The bronze relief in the centre of the table frame features *The Wedding Feast of Gods* executed after the Raphael fresco. The frieze of dancing nymphs is related to the classical Roman relief *The Borghese Dancers* (Louvre, Paris). The composition of the clock is reminiscent of the painting *Cupid and Psyche* by François Gerard (Louvre, Paris). *From the Main Collection of the Hermitage.*

Toilet table

Ca. 1817. Workshop of M.-G. Biennais. France, Paris. Amboine and ebony wood, gilded bronze, glass. 190 x 119 x 73 cm. Inv. No. Э 7593

The toilet table with a cheval glass (also known as the horse dressing glass or psyché) was created in the Paris workshop of Martin-Guillaume Biennais. There is an extant drawing for this table, executed by the architect and decorator Charles Percier together with Pierre Fontaine, who became the founder of the Empire style. The table was made for the wedding of Grand Duke Nikolai Pavlovich, which took place in 1817. *From the countryside palace in Ropsha; formerly in the Anichkov Palace, St Petersburg.*

Pieces from the furniture set executed for the Count Alexei Bobrinsky's palace in St Petersburg
Ca. 1822. After drawings by Andrei Mikhailov the 2nd (?). Russia. Wood, carving, gilt, silk. 130 x 214 x 80 cm (settee), 97 x 60 x 50 cm (armchairs), 87 x 55 x 45 cm (chairs). Inv. Nos. РМ6 501/1–23

In his building practice the architect Andrei Mikhailov the 2nd (1773–1849) frequently turned to the decoration of interiors. The furniture pieces executed after his designs have an elegant silhouette and an elaborate carved decor. The set on display is upholstered in the original Lyons silk.
From the A. Bobrinsky Mansion, St Petersburg.

Armchair with swan figures
Early 19th century. France (?). Wood, paint, gilt, carving. Upholstery renovated. 82 x 55 x 56 cm. Inv. No. Э 114

This armchair is part of a set including settees, armchairs, tables and gueridons (wall tables with two legs). All pieces are decorated with swan's figures. The set shows the influence of the armchair design by Charles Percier and Pierre Fontaine for the boudoir of Empress Joséphine in the Saint-Cloud Palace. The four armchairs from this set, made by Jacob Desmaltes, are in the Palace at Fontainebleau.
From the Main Collection of the Hermitage.

Dress with satin-stitched embroidery and reversible scarf

Dress: late 1810s. St Petersburg. *Cotton fabric, satin-stitched embroidery. Length 113 cm. Inv. No. Эрт 19551.*
Scarf: second quarter, 19th century. Workshop of D. Kolokoltsov. Russia, Saratov province, Village of Alexandrovka. *Fluffy thread, weaving. 236 x 56 cm. Inv. No. Эрт 7065*

Among the new ideals which took shape in Europe after the 1789 French bourgeois revolution was that of female beauty. The classically beautiful forms and curves of the body, not to be corrected by means of a costume, became a customary object of adoration. At that time the noble women of France, and, in their wake, of all Europe, were striving to look like classical statues and their toilets often echoed the rhythm of the draperies of ancient dresses. The low-necked decollete dresses with a high waist came into vogue, to be complemented with all sorts of shawls and scarves. Particularly noted and distinguished in Russia for their fine craftsmanship were the shawls made by serf woman weavers on the estates of D. Kolokoltsov and N. Merlina. These were manufactured from the fluff of Tibetan goats and saigas in a sophisticated technique of double-sided weaving with the right and wrong sides being absolutely the same unlike the Eastern and Western samples, which always had the wrong side.
From the Expert-Purchasing Commission of the Hermitage.

Jacket and a cloak from the smaller coronation costume of Eugène de Beauharnais, viceroy of Italy

First quarter, 19th century. France. *Silk, gold and silver threads, spangles, foil, embroidery. Length 105.5 cm (jacket), 114 cm (cloak). Inv. Nos. T 15455, 15456*

The jacket and cloak of green silk are parts of the smaller coronation costume of Eugène de Beauharnais made for the ceremony of his inauguration as viceroy of Italy. Prepared by Count Ségur, the former Ambassador of Louis XVI to the court of Catherine the Great, it took place in Milan Cathedral on 26 May 1805. Embroidered with gold threads in satin stitch, the laurel and oak twigs alternate in a clear-cut rhythm to build up a dense border on the front and back sides of the jacket, on the sleeves, cuffs and stand-up collar. A similar border adorns the green cloak. The rosettes, embroidered in silver threads and scattered all over the cloak's field, are shot with a cold glimmer. The stars of the Order of the Legion of Honour and the Order of the Iron Crown, instituted by Napoleon, were perceived as details of decor rather than signs of distinction. Costumes and embroidery patterns for them were created by the court artists Jean-Baptiste Isabey, Charles Percier and Pierre Fontaine.
From the Arsenal in Tsarskoye Selo, 1885.

Costume of a knight of the Order of the Holy Spirit for the consecration ceremony

First quarter, 19th century. France. *Velvet, silk, silver brocade, gilded silver threads, spangles, metal laid-on plates, foil, laminated wire thread, fringe, embroidery. Length 306 cm (mantle), 56 cm (camisole back), 70 cm (culottes). Inv. Nos. T 15462, 15439, 15440*

The French Catholic Order of the Holy Spirit was instituted by King Henri III in 1578 to consolidate the Catholic faith and royal power during the period of discord and the Wars of Religion. Only noblemen (initially not exceeding one hundred persons) from the most distinguished families, with a record of the highest titles' holders in at least three generations, could join the Order. They took an oath to the monarch, swore allegiance to the Catholic Church and were given a special costume. Each of its colours had a symbolic meaning. The green meant "honour, love and gallantry", the orange stood for the sun and gold. In the course of centuries the cut of mantle changed along with the pattern of embroidered border. Reinstated by King Louis XVIII after his accession to the throne in 1815, the Order existed until 1830. Louis XVIII hurried to acknowledge the Russian emperor Alexander I's services in the restoration of the French monarchy. The solemn ceremony of consecration took place in the Tuileries Palace on 25 August 1815. On that day several more foreigners became the knights of the French Order – Emperor Franz I of Austria, King Frederick II of Prussia and the English Duke of Wellington. Alexander I, however, was more greatly honoured than the allies. Besides himself, his brothers also became the knights of the Order.
From the Arsenal in Tsarskoye Selo.

MAURICE DENIS
1870–1943
Martha and Maria
1896. Oil on canvas. 77 x 116 cm.
Inv. No. 9124

In 1890 a number of artists, including Maurice Denis, Paul Serusier, Edouard Vuillard, Pierre Bonnard and Xavier Roussel, united around the group Nabis (prophets in Hebrew) in their Symbolist opposition to the naturalistic attitude of the Impressionists. The name of the group reflected the profound religiosity of its leader and theoretician, Denis. The painting *Martha and Maria* illustrates a subject from the Gospels (Luke 10; 38–42), which had a special meaning for the artist inasmuch as Martha was the name of his wife. In spite of their similar facial features in the picture, Martha and Maria seem to oppose each other like darkness and light, like two hypostases of human essence. Numerous details of the painting can be interpreted in the context of the Symbolists' world outlook. For them, a house meant a receptacle of wisdom while a house or a fenced garden also embodied the female essence. Martha is carrying a dish with grapes and apples – symbols of Christ and Original Sin. The well is a source of pure faith.
From the State Museum of Modern
Western Art, Moscow, 1948; formerly
in the S. Shchukin collection, Moscow.

MAURICE DENIS
1870–1943
First panel from the series
The Story of Psyche: The Flying Cupid
Is Struck by the Beauty of Psyche
1908–9. Oil on canvas. 394 x 269.5 cm.
Inv. No. 9666

After his visit to Italy where Denis was greatly impressed by the Italian frescoes of the Early Renaissance, he paid more attention to the material world: in his works the light and air perspective became traditional and the forms well delineated. It was during this period that he painted *The Story of Psyche* series, including eleven panels and two borders commissioned by Ivan Morozov to decorate the concert hall of his Moscow mansion. The subjects of the series, based on the story by the Roman writer Apuleius, were selected – "due to their idyllic, mysterious character" by Denis himself, who was also inspired by Raphael's frescoes at the Villa Farnesina in Italy, which he strove to excel.
From the State Museum of Modern
Western Art, Moscow, 1948; formerly
in the I. Morozov collection, Moscow.

PIERRE BONNARD
1867–1947
The Mediterranean
1910. Triptych. Oil on canvas. 407 x 152 cm (central panel), 407 x 149 cm (side panels). Inv. Nos. 9663–9665

Pierre Bonnard is considered the greatest colourist of modern art. In 1890 he shared a studio with Denis and Vuillard at Montmartre. He illustrated works by the Symbolist poet Verlaine and made designs for tapestries and stage sets. In 1910 the success that *The Story of Psyche* series had in Moscow, prompted Ivan Morozov to commission from Bonnard a triptych for the decoration of the main staircase of his mansion. A year earlier, in 1909, Bonnard, drawn to landscape painting, visited Saint-Tropez and discovered for himself the South of France. The magically attractive Mediterranean landscape, which he selected for the triptych, became a masterpiece of decorative and landscape painting.
From the State Museum of Modern Western Art, Moscow, 1948; formerly in the I. Morozov collection, Moscow.

PIERRE BONNARD
1867–1947
Morning in Paris
1911. Oil on canvas. 76.5 x 122 cm. Inv. No. 9107

This canvas, though part of a suite of paintings from Parisian life commissioned from Bonnard by Ivan Morozov, is a work of art in its own right. The Hermitage houses a companion painting, *Evening in Paris*, which is characterized by a similar treatment of the foreground. Bonnard was attracted by the idea of creating numerous compositions, which would convey a multitude of impressions and reflect a long process of observations.
From the State Museum of Modern Western Art, Moscow, 1948; formerly in the I. Morozov collection, Moscow.

INDEX

The State Hermitage
Guide

Plans and schemes by Sergei Leonov
Proofreader Irina Stukalina
Technical coordination by Tatyana Kustova

Slavia
20, Moika River Embankment, Box 8
191186 St Petersburg, Russia

PRE-PRINTING PREPARATION BY GOLAND, ST PETERSBURG

PRINTED IN ITALY